To Emmy

I hope you

Enjoy reading about

UCLA Basketball History

Best Wishes

Larry Farmer
UCLA '73

ROLE OF A LIFETIME

Larry Farmer and the UCLA Bruins

by Larry Farmer

with Tracy Dodds

Foreword by Bill Walton · Afterword by Jamaal Wilkes

SANTA
MONICA
PRESS

Published by:

Santa Monica Press LLC
P.O. Box 850
Solana Beach, CA 92075
1-800-784-9553
www.santamonicapress.com
books@santamonicapress.com

SANTA
MONICA
PRESS

Printed in China

Santa Monica Press books are available at special quantity discounts when purchased in bulk by corporations, organizations, or groups. Please call our Special Sales department at 1-800-784-9553.

ISBN-13 978-1-59580-115-9

Publisher's Cataloging-in-Publication data

Names: Farmer, Larry, author. | Dodds, Tracy, author. | Walton, Bill, 1952-, foreword author. | Wilkes, Jamaal, 1953-, afterword author.
Title: Role of a lifetime : Larry Farmer and the UCLA Bruins / by Larry Farmer; with Tracy Dodds; foreword by Bill Walton; afterword by Jamaal Wilkes.
Description: Solana Beach, CA: Santa Monica Press, 2023.
Identifiers: ISBN: 978-1-59580-115-9 (print) | 978-1-59580-774-8 (ebook)
Subjects: LCSH Farmer, Larry. | Basketball coaches--United States--Biography. | UCLA Bruins (Basketball team)--History. | University of California, Los Angeles--Basketball--History. | BISAC BIOGRAPHY & AUTOBIOGRAPHY / Sports | SPORTS & RECREATION / Basketball | SPORTS & RECREATION / Coaching / Basketball
Classification: LCC GV884.F37 F37 2023 | DDC 796.32/3/092--dc23

Cover and interior design and production by Future Studio

Contents

This book is dedicated to Clarice and Larry Farmer Sr.

Thank you for loving me and giving me
the courage to believe that anything is possible.

Like my father, I share my full name, and a strong resemblance, to my grandfather. Sharing the same name can intensify the weight of assumptions and expectations. Conversely, it can open various doors fostering immediate and meaningful connections. My father's legacy, detailed in this biography, has and will continue to serve as a fount of inspiration. I could not have asked for a better role model and steward of our shared name. To quote the magnificent Maya Angelou, "People will forget what you said, people will forget what you did, but people will never forget how you made them feel." This rings true for all those I have met who interacted with my father throughout his career. Each person kind enough to share their memories described my father as a great player/coach and an even better person. My character has been molded by the traits my father exemplifies. What I admire most about him are his perseverance, humility, dedication and respect. I have seen him uphold these core principles every day of my life. I am truly blessed and honored to be named after my grandfather. I already have a better jump shot, but if I am able to become half the man my father is, I know I will be a great father, teacher, and role model for future generations.

— **Larry C. Farmer, III (Tre)**
Bachelor of Science in biochemistry from Denison University;
MBA from Boston College's
Carroll Graduate School of Management

Little did you know when you signed a letter of intent with UCLA 49 years ago how much it would change your life. From being a player with an 89–1 record, playing for one of the best coaches ever, you ultimately became the head coach yourself at the age of 30. You have given your all to one of the most prestigious universities. Today you were inducted into the UCLA Athletics Hall of Fame, to have your name remembered forever in history. I am overwhelmed with emotion. I am so incredibly proud. I'm not sure anything I write will ever truly express how I feel in this moment. I love the dirt you walk on Papa Farm.

— **Kendall Farmer**
Bachelor of Science in biochemistry/molecular biology
from Wittenberg University; Master of Medical Science from
Wake Forest School of Medicine (Physician Associate)

From The Darkness—Comes the Light
by Bill Walton

January 18, 1968. The Astrodome. UCLA and Houston. It was—to this day—the biggest and most important college basketball game ever played. In a quiet family home in Denver, Colorado, a young Larry Farmer gathered with his loving parents in the basement of their modest home in a neighborhood in the urban core of their mile-high city. Larry witnessed, on their black-and-white TV, the Houston Cougars with Elvin Hayes, Don Chaney, and Coach Guy Lewis beat the UCLA Bruins with Kareem, Mike Warren, Lucious Allen, Lynn Shackleford, and Coach John Wooden. That day, Larry Farmer fell in love with the losing team. The rest is history. That story is brilliantly told in *Role of a Lifetime*. Larry's joyous, purpose-driven journey has taken him around the world. His most improbable life is one of dreams, choices, sacrifice, discipline, honor, and being part of special teams. Teams whose records and marks still stand and impact our lives today as he has come to help define the tradition, heritage, culture, foundation, and future of the wonderful world of college basketball. The focus of the close-knit Farmer family, crowded into a one-bedroom apartment in the early days, was love, hope, and opportunity—all leading to the dream of a better tomorrow through education.

Larry, as the middle child, was late to come to basketball and sports. He first picked up a basketball when he was in the 7th grade. His first real game—with refs—didn't come until he was in the 9th grade. And that was in a junior high school gym class. He quickly fell in love. Larry was part of an early school-busing program in the mid-1960s. He rode that bus every day, for 30 minutes each way, to and from an all-white junior high school. His basketball dreams were starting to take shape as he chose Elgin Baylor as his hero and role model. When it was time for high school, Larry chose Manual High School, the dominant basketball power in the city of Denver. Larry was not an early star, and he knew he was taking a huge risk. But Larry believed in himself when no one else did. Larry sat the bench on the sophomore team at Manual. He began his junior season on the junior varsity squad but was soon moved up to the varsity. And then—The Game. In the Astrodome. The Game that changed everything for everyone. Shortly after The Game, Larry was moved permanently into the varsity's starting lineup. As a senior at Manual, Larry again played a significant role. A guidance counselor there encouraged Larry to blindly send an 8 mm game film and his transcript to UCLA—who was most definitely unaware of this young dreamer trying to launch his life from high in the Colorado Rockies. It wasn't until after his last high school season and career ended that he even heard back. Denny Crum was the one who called. He had played at UCLA for Coach Wooden, and then became the second assistant basketball coach in school history. Denny was responsible for UCLA's future. He put the teams together. Denny Crum never saw Larry Farmer play in person. Coach Crum did invite Larry to come to UCLA for a visit. It was on that trip that the Bruins offered Larry that coveted scholarship. Larry arrived in Westwood in the fall of 1969. Kareem had just graduated. UCLA had won five of the previous six NCAA basketball championships.

Now the team leaders were Sidney Wicks and Curtis Rowe. They made Larry Farmer carry their bags. With the NCAA rules of the day, Larry was limited to only three years of varsity basketball. Over the four years that Larry was at UCLA, the Bruins won four NCAA titles. While on the varsity, Larry's teams had a cumulative record of 89–1. Larry Farmer is the single winningest player in the history of men's college basketball. Larry Farmer is one of only 14 people to have ever won three NCAA Men's Basketball Championships. Everyone on that list went to UCLA. As a sophomore, in the 1971 Regional Final, playing behind and in support of Sidney and

Curtis, Larry—in for most of the second half against Long Beach State and Coach Jerry Tarkanian—made a spectacular game-saving block from behind that enabled UCLA to win one of the few Bruin games of the day that was ever up for grabs. I had the privilege of playing with Larry Farmer for his final two years at UCLA. Larry started every one of the 60 games. We did not lose a one. We established records and standards of excellence and perfection that still reign supreme today. Larry was a critical component of our team. He was part of the defensive front line—along with Henry Bibby and Larry Hollyfield—of our full-court zone press. He was dazzling in the open court on the fast break. In our structured set offense, Larry played the right wing.

Greg Lee—the key to the team—had the ball out front. Greg always had to deal with Henry, Jamaal Wilkes, and me wanting the ball every time. As our superb and supreme team had our way with whomever and whatever came our way, the other teams tried everything to slow us down. Greg was under direct and specific orders to get the ball to me and Jamaal—every time. Failing to do so would lead to his immediate benching—forever. One night, during a game at Pauley Pavilion, the opponents tried denying the wing-entry pass from Greg to either Henry or Larry. With quick recognition and eye contact, Jamaal moved up his right-side lane, and Larry flashed backdoor. Greg arched a perfect direct-line lob pass up at the upper-right corner of the square on the glass backboard. Larry, gliding effortlessly to the rim, grabbed the ball with two hands, and seamlessly and gracefully laid the ball in, per the rules of the day, which prohibited dunking. We all stopped momentarily. We had never done that before. We had never seen it done before. The next time down the floor, the exact same thing happened. With the exact same result. As Larry was basking in the glory of the historical moment and his perceived future, on the way back up the court for defense, I ran right by Greg, probably hitting him with a forearm shiver, while explaining in no uncertain terms that that new play, the reverse back-cut lob, had my name written all over it. The rest is history. Larry is a better than perfect teammate. He is an even finer human being and friend. He is a pillar of humanity, excellence, accomplishment, and determination. When you're part of something truly special, there is an eternal bond. We all have that, to this day, and presumably forevermore. When Larry's brief NBA and European experience were not as he imagined it, he immediately started a coaching career at UCLA. His coaching ultimately spanned 44 years and took him everywhere—and beyond. Forever the teacher, he also did a bit of broadcasting.

As great as it was to play ball with Larry, to be his teammate and travel the land as part of what is generally recognized as the greatest college basketball team of all time, it's even better to be his friend. Larry is a happy, proud, loyal, and grateful man. He learned from the best. He was part of the best. He became the best. *Role of a Lifetime* is the story of what it means to be the best. And what it takes to get there. Enjoy the ride. And learn to love your role.

CHAPTER 1

The Game of the Century

It was Saturday afternoon, January 20, 1968, and I was in the basement of our home in Denver, counting the minutes until the Game of the Century would be on TV. UCLA, ranked No. 1 in the country, was about to play the University of Houston, ranked No. 2, before a crowd of 52,693 in the Astrodome. It was the first time a regular season college basketball game was shown on nationwide TV in prime time. My usual seat on the couch was not close enough for me, so I sat on the ottoman in front of my mom's chair, inches from the 32-inch black-and-white screen.

It was unusual for me to claim rights to our only television. I had established a routine of watching the NBA Game of the Week on Sundays after church, but most of the time I had to watch whatever someone else had chosen. Every now and then my dad would come down to watch a little bit of a basketball game with me. If he did, he would be reading the Sunday edition of the *Rocky Mountain News*, glancing up only occasionally.

But I had been building up the importance of this game for days. I had purchased every basketball magazine I could find at the start of the season, and on every cover was the name UCLA with a picture of Lew Alcindor (later Kareem Abdul-Jabbar), who was called the best college player in America. I had brought a couple magazines from my bedroom to show my mom and dad, so not only was Dad in his chair for tipoff, but I had even piqued Mom's interest and she was in her chair to see what I was so excited about.

Coach Al Oviatt, my coach at Manual High School, had suggested that we watch this game to get a look at big-time college basketball. I was in my junior year, and I had just been moved up from the junior varsity. It wasn't a promotion I was seeking because I was finally starting to get some playing time with the JV team, whereas the year before I barely got off the bench. But Coach Oviatt said the move was for the good of the varsity and they weren't moving me up just to sit on the bench. I would do everything this coach asked of me.

As the game started, the announcer, Dick Enberg, talked about an injury to Lew Alcindor's eye. He had been hit in practice and hadn't played all week, but he would play now despite the injury. The more Enberg talked about it, the more Alcindor appeared to be not only extraordinarily gifted, but also courageous and dedicated to his team.

It was hard to believe that at 7-foot-2 Alcindor was so quick and graceful. The 7-foot centers in the NBA were big, slow, physical players. Alcindor was agile! There was a style and grace to the way all the Bruins played. Their two starting guards, Mike Warren and Lucius Allen, were quick and played a fast-paced game. They could both score. The Bruins played as a team on both offense and defense.

The game went down to the wire, and Houston's Elvin Hayes had the game of a lifetime. "The Big E" scored 39 points, including two free throws with 28 seconds left in the game to put Houston up by two, and they won 71–69. I felt like I was on the losing team and I was not happy when the Houston fans rushed the court and carried him off the floor.

Alcindor had scored 15 points, making just four of 18 shots, which meant he was not at his best, nor was the rest of the team.

At that very moment I decided I wanted to wear those four letters on my chest: UCLA. I wanted to play for UCLA in a game like the one I had just witnessed. I turned to my mother and father and announced: "That's where I'm going to college. I'm going to UCLA!"

Neither Mom nor Dad said a word at first. At least they didn't laugh. They both just smiled awkwardly and looked at me. There were a lot of things my dad could have said to me, the first, maybe, being, "You might want to make your high school team's starting lineup before you pack." Or maybe something closer to reality but still encouraging, like, "You better pray to be offered a scholarship by a local school or any school, period!" But that was not my father's way. Finally, he said, "You are really going to have to work hard if you want to play for a school like that!"

There's a moment in everyone's life that determines one's path, even if it doesn't make any sense at the time. Ralph Waldo Emerson wrote, "The only person you are destined to become is the person you decide to be." I was 16 years old, watching a basketball game on TV, when that moment came for me. My heart belonged to the Bruins.

I was so blessedly naïve that I was oblivious to the odds. As far as I was concerned, my journey to Westwood had just begun!

If it was going to take hard work to make it happen, I was ready for hard work. I would give everything I had to make Manual High School's starting lineup before my junior season ended. I would be on the half-court outside Harrington Elementary School every minute I wasn't in the high school gym.

It was also going to take the help of my coaches, my parents, my school principal, and my guidance counselor along with perfect timing, a growth spurt, and more than a little luck. I prepared myself as best I could, and when the stars fell into alignment for me, I was ready. I believed, and it came to pass.

- UCLA gave me a full scholarship, making me a Bruin at the height of the dynasty built by the legendary Coach John Wooden.
- In those days, all first-year players were on the freshman team. At the end of the 1969–1970 season, I was given the award for the outstanding freshman of the year. Others to be named MVP of their UCLA freshman teams were Lew Alcindor, Bill Walton, Marques Johnson, Henry Bibby, Mike Warren, and Gail Goodrich.
- I made the UCLA team as a sophomore. In my three years, we lost only one single game. I'm the only player to have a record of 89–1 for Coach Wooden. (Kareem was 88–2.)

My junior and senior seasons we had a perfect record, 60–0.

- We won three National Collegiate Athletic Association titles.
- I was drafted by the Cleveland Cavaliers but did not make the team. When I was cut, Coach Bill Fitch told me that Coach Wooden was holding open the graduate assistant spot on his coaching staff for me.
- I served as an assistant for the first three coaches who succeeded Coach Wooden—Gene Bartow, Gary Cunningham, and Larry Brown.
- In the spring of 1982, when I was 30 years old, I was named head coach of the UCLA basketball team.
- That made me UCLA's first black head coach in any sport.

CHAPTER 2

Manual High School Thunderbolts

I might have given up on basketball altogether had it not been for a few words of encouragement from Coach Julie Yearling after my last game for the sophomore team, and Coach Yearling probably wouldn't have given me the gift of those words had it not been for three straight baskets I made in the final minutes of the final game.

I had been the 12th man on the sophomore team all year, sitting at the end of the bench hoping there would be enough scrub time to get in the game. But for the final game I was the eighth man—only because four sophomores went to the junior varsity to replace the JV players who went to the varsity when the roster was expanded for the state tournament.

So, for the final game, I got in with about two minutes to play. Manual was safely in the lead. The first time I got the ball, I was open. I was so nervous that I just aimed the ball toward the basket and I pushed it. It went in. I'm amazed the ball didn't just drop out of my hands and hit the floor. But it went in. It must have been divine intervention!

The next time down the court, I was open again. On this one, I felt like I had a little bit of control. I got a little more juice on it. And that one went in!

We go back on defense and I'm bursting with excitement! I've just made two baskets in a row! The next time I was open, I actually felt like I shot that one. Swish! I'm three-for-three and the game ends. Six points was both my season high and career high.

We go back to Manual and all the guys are in the locker room talking and laughing. That's when Mr. Yearling, the sophomore coach, came over to me and said something like, "You've improved quite a bit. You played well today. If you work really hard and come back next year, there's a chance that you might make the junior varsity." Not the varsity. The junior varsity.

That little bit of encouragement made me feel like maybe I had a chance. I had been thinking about how hard it would be to make the JV team. I would be competing against all the players who were ahead of me on the sophomore team as well as older players who didn't make the varsity. His words gave me the push I needed not to quit.

He started to walk away, but he turned back to give me a bit of advice. He said, "You know what you might want to do from now on is take your socks out of your locker and wash them."

Those suckers were so dirty they were standing up by themselves. I'm sure the coaches followed the smell and opened the locker to see whose socks were that bad.

I hadn't taken my dirty socks home all season because my parents didn't know I was playing basketball. I didn't want them coming to games to watch me sit on the bench. I could get away with that because the sophomore practices were right after school. The games were right after school, too. If they ever asked where I had been, I could always say I had some ROTC duty, maybe at the range shooting or drill team or color guard. But I didn't have a P.E. class so there was no way to explain dirty gym socks.

(During my junior year at UCLA we won the Bruin Classic Christmas tournament and we all received watches. As soon as I got back to Denver, I gave Mr. Yearling that watch and thanked him for encouraging me.)

I became dedicated to basketball in the summer of 1967. I would get up and do whatever Mom had me doing around the house and shoot baskets in the backyard in the morning. In the afternoon, I'd go to Harrington Elementary School, where there was an outdoor court and usually 10 to 15 guys for the games. On Sunday it would be after the church-going folks got home. My mother, Clarice, had me in church before I was out there shooting hoops.

Mom and Dad supported my serious summer routine, which

meant Dad and I went fishing less frequently. We used to go fishing on Saturdays every summer. We'd get up before sunrise and drive two hours to Sterling. Dad would cook breakfast on his Coleman stove, and we'd fish for bass, blue gill, and crappie. Mom insisted that we always eat Sunday dinner together, but during the week, my family would eat while I was at Harrington. When I got home, Mom would have my plate, with the aluminum foil over it, sitting on the back of the stove. I'd eat alone, then clean and fold the foil to be used the next night.

One weekday morning I was at Harrington shooting. I had never dunked to that point. I had stopped trying because there were other things I needed to work on. That day I thought, I'm all alone out here, why not try? I took two dribbles and went up and YOW! A two-handed dunk! I couldn't believe I did it. I was like, "Oh, sh*t! I did it!" But there was nobody there to see it.

So I ran about a block to the home of my basketball buddy, Louie Armstrong, still carrying my basketball. I told him that I had just dunked! Louie was equally excited. We both ran back to Harrington, where I did it again. BOOM! Louie asked if I could reverse dunk? I said, "I don't know!" We both laughed. I went up and reversed. WHAM! That worked, too!

My dunk shot made its public debut that very day. I dunked in front of all the guys while we were warming up. I acted like it was no big deal, but it was! It was that year, 1967, the NCAA made the dunk illegal. Some were calling it the Lew Alcindor Rule. High school rules changed at the same time, so the first season I was finally able to dunk I wasn't allowed to do it!

I went into my junior year at Manual High School with great anticipation. Late that fall I was at school feeling pretty good about myself when up came one of the starters on my sophomore team. I didn't play behind him, I played behind the guy who played behind him, so I was three-deep on this depth chart—and he asked if I was going to try out for the JV team. I thought he was asking in a friendly way, so I said, "Yeah, I'm really excited about it." He rolled his eyes and smirked and walked away. Funny how clearly you remember moments like that.

I should not have been surprised at his reaction to my plan to try out. No one from Manual had seen me play during the summer of my first dunk because we had moved out of Manual's district years earlier. We weren't in the same neighborhood games.

Manual High School was a basketball power. I knew as early as the ninth grade that my best chance of going to college on a basketball scholarship would be at Manual. My parents had to petition for me to go to there because we had moved into the East High School district.

At tryouts I could tell I was going to make the JV team. It wasn't long before I was in the JV starting lineup. I had shared that news with my parents and they, of course, started coming to the games.

A few days after one really good JV game I was called over the school intercom to report to the gym to see Mr. Oviatt.

Al Oviatt had been the varsity coach at Manual for 20 years. He was white, taught social studies, and had coached many great teams and many gifted black players. More than 40 years later his undefeated 1966 state championship Manual team was named by the Colorado High School Activities Association the state's best team ever.

Mr. Oviatt told me I was moving up to the varsity. I didn't want to move up and go back to sitting on the bench. He could see I was not happy, so he gave me this lecture on what's best for the team. He told me I would have to earn my minutes, but they weren't moving me up to sit on the bench.

I came off the bench for one or two games.

My first few minutes of my first varsity game, I was only in long enough to foul some guy, and then I was rotated back out. I sat down next to a teammate who was a senior. He told me I just got my name in the newspaper. What? I didn't do anything. He told me that if you take a shot or get a rebound or get a foul, your name goes in the box score. That will be in the paper tomorrow morning. I got back in the game and I didn't know how many points or how many rebounds I had that would also be in the box score. But I knew my name would be in the paper.

I had never seen my name in the newspaper. I couldn't sleep that night. When the kid rode by on his bike and threw the *Rocky Mountain News* on the porch at 5:30 A.M. or whatever, I was sitting there waiting for it. I opened it up and there it was: Frmr. In order to get the names to fit on the line, they take out the vowels. I didn't know that. I was awake all night waiting for Frmr.

In the next game I came off the bench and had some unbelievable stats. That box score had me down for 14 points and 22 rebounds. Years later I saw that clipping in the scrapbook my mother kept and I was like, "Damn!" The reason I had so many rebounds was that I was so nervous I kept missing my initial shot, but would get the offensive rebound and shoot again, no matter how many times it took to score a basket. My shooting percentage was awful, but my rebound total was impressive. I was cleaning up on those missed shots. That's what they call a garbage man!

Shortly after that, I was a starter on the varsity.

Playing for Manual High School meant playing Denver Public League games in the Denver Auditorium Arena, an iconic old stone building downtown. Every game held there was an event. It was built at the turn of the century and was the site of the National Democratic Convention in 1908. The Denver Rockets of the American Basketball Association and later the Denver Nuggets of the National Basketball Association played there. For our league games all 6,841 seats would be filled.

Every team in our league had a strong following and brought a pep squad, band, and cheerleaders as well as hundreds of fans. It got pretty crazy. Throughout my junior year we played league games at the Auditorium Arena. That changed after the assassination of the Rev. Dr. Martin Luther King April 4, 1968.

Our country had been experiencing social unrest for several years, starting with demonstrations in the South over the Civil Rights Act of 1964. The riots in the Watts neighborhood of Los Angeles occurred in 1965. There were race riots in Newark and Detroit in 1967. In the days after Dr. King was killed, there were marches and demonstrations in every major city.

There had never been any really ugly incidents at our games downtown. However, the league decided before the 1968–69 season that it might not be a good idea to have these groups of black people and groups of white people converging downtown at the same time, so our biggest games were moved to neutral sites. The crowds were much smaller with only two teams involved.

It lost the majestic feel. But winning is never disappointing and we were winning.

By the end of my junior season, as Manual was winning another city title and playing in the state tournament, I had established myself as a solid starter. I made honorable mention on the All-City team.

I was finally on the radar. I was even getting my whole name in the newspaper.

With athletic success comes a bit of social standing also. I had never been one of the cool kids who went to parties on the weekends. So when I was handed a really nice invitation to a party on the upcoming Saturday night I was excited. I would be out of my element, but I wanted to go. The invitation said the party started at 10 P.M. but there was nothing filled in for when the party would end. When I asked my dad if I could go and, of course, use his car, he asked me, "What time do you think you should be in?" We had never discussed a curfew because I hadn't been going out. So I said, "The invitation doesn't say when it ends, so I guess whenever I feel like coming home."

Apparently, that wasn't the right response. Dad told me my curfew was midnight. That doesn't mean leave the party at midnight, it means have his car back here at midnight. I reminded him that the party didn't even start until 10 P.M. and he suggested I'd better get there right at 10 P.M.

I may not have been cool but at least I knew I didn't want to be the first one there and the first to leave, just when the party was getting good. I was so ticked off I decided not to go at all.

That evening I got on my 10-speed bike and rode over to

Harrington. I got there at about 10 P.M. and there was nobody else on the court. I was out there shooting under this one big light. It gets to be midnight. I keep shooting. I have an attitude now. I'm not going to be home at midnight and that's intentional.

Dad, who trusts me, has gone to bed at his usual time. But now it's 12:30 A.M. and I'm not home. My mom wakes him up and says, "Larry, I think Junior went to that party." Now my dad is really hot. He's not happy that my mom woke him up, but he's really not happy with the possibility that I have not been truthful about where I was going. Not to mention that it's after midnight.

I'm still shooting baskets under the big glaring light. I can't see anything but pitch black beyond the perimeter of the playground. But I think I see movement by a tree just outside the Harrington playground. I see a silhouette of someone walking, hiding behind a tree, walking a little closer, hiding behind another tree. I'm thinking that if this person gets too close I'm on my bike and I'm out of there. When the silhouette gets to about 30 or 40 yards away, I can tell it's my dad. So I start dunking the ball and putting on a show and the next time I glance over, he's gone. Mom and Dad told me years later, he had gone back home and told my mom, "As long as he's playing basketball, we don't have to worry about him, or the time he comes home."

That year, I got my first two letters from colleges showing an early interest in recruiting me. They were the standard letters, congratulating me on a good season, telling me they'd come to see me play the following year, hoping I'd have a great summer. The first letters were from the University of Colorado and the University of Denver (from Coach Stan Albeck, who would go on to coach several NBA teams).

I was summoned to the office of my counselor, Mrs. Beverly Biffle. Letters from colleges went first to your counselor. Mrs. Biffle had experience helping Manual High athletes handle recruiting. Her first order of business during that meeting my junior year was making sure I got signed up to take some test called the SAT.

The summer before my senior year I got my first job. It was

working for the Shell Oil company. I had to learn how to read oil production charts, and then draw a graph showing how much oil was coming out and how much water was being pumped in to produce output. Having a job meant there was no shooting in the morning, which put more pressure on me to shoot after work. I played in the evening games at Harrington and shot some more before going home.

Harrington had become *the* place to play on the weekends in East Denver. Players were coming from all over the city. I heard one guy walking up ask, "Which one is Farmer?" The better I got the more people came to play. I was no longer standing on the sideline hoping to be picked to play.

When school started the first thing that kicked into high gear for me was ROTC. As a senior I was promoted to lieutenant colonel and became battalion commander, making me the highest-ranking ROTC student at my high school. Plan B, if I had not received a college basketball scholarship, was to join the service. I was always proud to wear my uniform and lead the battalion in parades. I wore my uniform the day I went to the courthouse to register for the draft. I'm sure ROTC was the reason the Air Force Academy recruited me to play basketball there.

Basketball offered some new challenges my senior year. When Coach Al Oviatt had been forced out at the end of the previous season, Coach Ed Calloway took over. Coach Calloway had been a standout basketball and football player at Manual. He was a terrific football coach who had the reputation of being tough on his players. We had 10 seniors on our team and all 10 of us were recruited to play college basketball.

We opened the season winning games and running up scores. We may have gotten a little overconfident because we lost in a Christmas tournament in Colorado Springs to West High School 69–57. In our third league game we avenged our loss to West 90–76.

The last game of the regular league season was against our rival, East. East's star player was Greg Lovato, who lived in my neighborhood and was a regular player at Harrington. Their center was another friend, David Goens. We both attended Jordan Chapel AME Church.

We beat East 80–67 and for the fourth year in a row were Denver Public League champions. We were 8–0.

We advanced into the state quarterfinals ranked No. 1 and favored to win the state championship. We beat La Junta High School 102–82 then beat Palmer 104–85. Those two scoring outputs set and then broke the state tournament scoring records. This was done with no shot clock and no 3-point shot.

In the title game we played South. They had finished seventh in the DPL with a 3–5 record. From the start of the championship game South played a delay game, holding the ball and milking the game clock. We were soon frustrated, both with the way the game was being played and with each other. We wound up losing 69–53. It was just our second loss of the year, and a heartbreaking way for my high school basketball career to come to an end.

When the season ended, recruiting switched into high gear. I made first team All-City, All-Metropolitan, and All-State as chosen by both *The Rocky Mountain News* and the *Denver Post*.

I received a lot of letters and regional interest. Manual High School had a tradition of outstanding basketball players, so I had an experienced team of advisers at school. My parents, like most parents, were new to the recruiting game. I didn't know much about it myself. Coach Calloway met with my parents about coming up with a strategy. Mrs. Biffle had set her strategy in motion earlier, having me send transcripts and game film to schools I would like to attend. The correspondence was getting some response.

Getting recruited in those days was a lot of fun. The rules were different back then. As a matter fact there are many rules in place now because of how loose the recruiting rules were in the late '60s and early '70s. For example, a college coach would come to my high school and talk to Coach Calloway and our principal, Mr. Ward. Those conversations were usually about my character and getting the basketball coach and the principal's opinion of what kind of person I was. Coach Calloway would get me out of class so I could go down to his office and meet with that college coach. We might leave school and go to lunch. Or we might make arrangements for the college coach to pick me up that evening and take me to dinner. I was loving getting out of class and eating free meals at nice restaurants once, twice, sometimes three times a week. College coaches can't do that today, with the impromptu lunches and dinners.

At that point I wasn't saying no to anybody. I was open to speaking with any coach that wanted to recruit me. It was usually during one of these lunches or dinners that a scholarship was mentioned directly to me (or offered if they were serious) and I was also given a chance to make an official visit to their campus.

Official visits were paid for by the university, including transportation, food, and housing. Official visits are now limited to five. We were allowed to take as many recruiting trips as we could fit in. I actually took a trip to Hutchinson, Kansas, to watch the National Junior College Athletic Association tournament. It was the first trip I was offered, and I had never flown on an airplane. No one thought that trip was a good idea except me.

On one visit I was told I could live in my own apartment. When I asked how I would get to campus, the head coach told me that one of their boosters owned a Buick dealership. He asked if I had noticed some of their players driving Buicks. I had. He said that would be arranged for me.

I believed I needed to leave home to go to college, but I made an official visit to the University of Colorado, and I really liked the head coach, Sox Walseth. There were lots more visits to come.

I was really excited to hear from Drake University. They had made it to the Final Four that year. When they called, I agreed to an official visit. I would fly to Des Moines the following weekend.

On Monday of that week, I was summoned to the office of our principal, Mr. Ward. When I got there Mr. Ward and Coach Calloway were both waiting for me. I sat down and Mr. Ward said that they had just received a call from UCLA. I could barely contain my excitement! They both seemed happy for me but they were also protective. I heard comments like "They can get anybody they want" and "We don't want you to get lost in the shuffle." What they said made sense. But it was UCLA! I was told UCLA would call me later at home. When school ended, I sprinted home!

Early that evening I got a call from Denny Crum, an assistant coach at UCLA. He said he had watched the film I sent and he liked what he saw. Then he asked me if I thought I was good enough to play at UCLA. Without hesitation I said, "Yes, I am." He said they had one scholarship left, and they needed a forward. Coach Crum then asked if I could visit that weekend. I told him I was visiting Drake but I would love to come the following weekend. He asked if I was going to take any more visits and I told him no. I had not yet decided that, but it felt like the appropriate thing to say. He told me to plan to visit UCLA the following weekend.

I went to Drake University and had a great visit. When I arrived, they showed me the arena and the team locker room and then took me to the film room. They played about 10 minutes of their NCAA semifinal game. They had played UCLA in a very competitive game but had lost by three points. It was the closest game the Bruins won in Kareem's senior year. I must have smiled while watching the film, because Assistant Coach Gus Guydon asked if UCLA was recruiting me. I said yes, and after another minute or two the film was turned off.

I got a chance to play Saturday morning with some of Drake's players. There were three other recruits visiting at the same time—two other big guys and one guard. The plan for that Saturday was for us to play, eat lunch, and take a campus tour. We would go back to the hotel and rest before meeting some Drake players who would host us for the night. We would go out for pizza.

I had played basketball on most of my recruiting trips. Recruits weren't required to play but I enjoyed the competition and always wanted to see what I might be up against. At Drake I played really well. I was the leading scorer in all the games we played. One of the other recruits was a 6-foot-9 center and I blocked several of his shots.

I was back at the hotel when I got a call from Coach Guydon,

THANK YOU, MRS. BIFFLE

I have only one person to thank for the phone call from UCLA that changed my life. Thank you, Mrs. Beverly Biffle.

Mrs. Biffle, my counselor at Manual, let me know early in my senior year that she was not satisfied with the scope of my college search. I was taking a passive approach, she said, by waiting to be contacted by schools wanting me to play basketball. She said I was a terrific student and shouldn't limit my choices. She wanted me to be more proactive. I was amazed when she showed me an envelope addressed to me from Brown University. Mrs. Biffle had contacted the Ivy League school on my behalf, and Brown was responding. She was showing me how to aim high.

Then she told me I had one week to give her a list of 20 schools I would like to attend. Schools might make my list because of location or academics or athletics, or simply because I thought it would be cool to go there. I didn't know where to begin, until I realized that my dream schools were the top basketball programs. Working from the rankings in my preseason magazines, I soon had a list which, of course, included UCLA, Houston, Kentucky, and Drake. I cross-referenced the rankings with research on where the schools were and what kind of academics were offered. I even typed the list to show how seriously I took the assignment.

Mrs. Biffle then gave me another assignment. I was to compose letters to those schools, one to the admissions office and one to the basketball office. I would attach a copy of my transcript with each letter. (I wrote the letters, but she improved them.) In 1968, coaches were not sent well-edited highlight packages like they are today. They would get an entire game on 8 mm film, to be played on a reel-to-reel projector. My coach provided the game film, my father paid to have it copied and did the mailing. It was a wise investment.

By the time the letters were typed, transcripts copied, and game film duplicated, our season was over. Ending with a loss in the state championship game was one of the biggest disappointments of my life. I had no way of knowing that one of the packages being posted would give me my biggest break.

who told me they wanted me to go out to dinner with head coach Maury John and his wife. At dinner, I was offered a scholarship. I would have accepted if my other top option had been any other school but UCLA.

CHAPTER 3

Meeting Coach Wooden

My visit to UCLA started Friday evening, and I left straight from school. As the plane descended into Los Angeles, I was amazed at how large the city was. It seemed endless, stretching on and on to the end of the horizon. It was one thing to know that Los Angeles was a major city; actually being there was something else.

I was met at the gate by assistant coaches Gary Cunningham and Denny Crum who drove us to a really nice steakhouse in Santa Monica called The Bat Rack. It was filled with sports memorabilia and pictures of the "who's who" of Southern California professional sports. When we left the restaurant, it was dark, and the lights of Los Angeles seemed brighter than anything I had ever seen. They drove me past UCLA and through Beverly Hills. They said we were on Sunset Boulevard. As a kid I had watched the TV show *77 Sunset Strip* and when we drove past Dino's, the restaurant where the outside scenes were shot, I thought I was going to burst with excitement.

The coaches pointed out one famous landmark after another. It felt unreal to be seeing sights in person that I recognized from TV and movies. When we passed the Whiskey A Go Go, I pictured the black light poster that immortalized Jimi Hendrix playing there. When we got to Hollywood and Grauman's Chinese Theatre's Walk of Fame, I admit to feeling awed, seeing the names of the stars embedded in the sidewalk.

The other high school recruit who was visiting that weekend was a point guard from Tallahassee, Florida, named Tommy Curtis. Tommy was six feet tall and had big hands, big feet, and was bowlegged. He had a flamboyant personality. I'd never seen him play but he told me early in the visit that he was a *Parade* magazine All-American. He was also the Player of the Year in the state of Florida. This kid was good and he knew it!

At the end of the evening, we headed for the Bel-Air Sands Hotel, which was majestically set on a slight ridge, adorned by magnificent palm trees. As I walked into the hotel lobby I reached out and touched a huge leaf of the first palm tree I had ever seen. The coaches told us that the team stayed at this hotel on nights before home games. The team also had breakfast and pregame meals at this hotel. I was really impressed by that. I had not heard that on any of my other recruiting trips.

Saturday after breakfast we drove to Disneyland. As a kid, I had watched *The Mickey Mouse Club* religiously. I had a crush on Annette Funicello. We spent the day there. That evening we went to the Anaheim Theater, where we had front row seats to watch Ray Charles in concert!

It was widely reported that Kareem Abdul-Jabbar had chosen UCLA, in part, because of its academic reputation. He also felt comfortable about the success that other African American athletes had at UCLA. Jackie Robinson and Arthur Ashe had blossomed at UCLA. Also, Dr. Ralph Bunche, who was a Nobel Prize winner, was a UCLA graduate and had a building on campus named after him. He had played basketball for UCLA. My reasons for wanting to go to UCLA were far less cerebral. I was totally enamored of its basketball program and, now, the beauty and excitement of the city that surrounded it.

Tommy and I were split up on Sunday. I walked around campus with Gary Cunningham while Tommy met with Coach Wooden. The UCLA campus was beautiful and it was huge. To the north of campus was the city of Bel Air. Just to the east was Beverly Hills. On the south side of campus was the city of Westwood, which was packed with restaurants, clothing stores, and more than a dozen movie theaters. UCLA's rival, the University of Southern California, did not have the same kind of surroundings. USC coaches have been known to take their recruits to Westwood.

The weekend was over and my bag was in the car when it was finally my turn to meet Coach Wooden. I'll never forget what it was like walking into his office for the first time. I could feel my heart pounding. The office was understated and not fancy at all. The first thing I noticed was a large square working table that had 8 × 10 black-and-white pictures of championship teams placed under the glass tabletop. There were windows on the right side of his office with a view of the south side of campus. The wall on the left displayed rows of framed *Sports Illustrated* covers featuring UCLA players and teams. Only *Sports Illustrated*; only covers; only UCLA. It was jaw dropping! There were trophies on a couple of end tables, which I later learned were conference championship trophies. The trophy case in the student union was full, so the newer trophies were in Coach Wooden's office awaiting a permanent home.

While I took all this in, Coach Wooden got up from his chair and walked around his desk to greet me. I had seen this revered coach on TV and in pictures and I recognized the gray hair and black horn-rimmed glasses. In person he seemed shorter than I had imagined but he had a very big presence.

Coach Wooden met me with a firm handshake. His greeting was warm, and I started to relax a bit. He was soft-spoken yet his voice had a firm and confident tone. As he went back around his desk to sit down, I sat in one of the two chairs in front of the desk. When we were both settled, he offered me some jellybeans from the jar on his desk. I remember smiling and saying no thank you. But that made me relax even more. There is nothing intimidating about jellybeans.

I'd been on many recruiting trips. It was always at these meetings with the head coach (at the end of the visit) that you were hit with pressure to make a decision. The head coach was the closer. The assistants had done all the groundwork, and when I finally sat down with the head coach, I was going to get the big sales pitch! The head coach would make it seem urgent that I make a commitment. I had been instructed by Coach Calloway to say that I would make a decision when I had taken all of my visits, and then, only after I discussed it with my mom and dad.

With Coach Wooden there was no such pressure. He put me entirely at ease with what seemed to be an everyday conversation. He asked me about my parents, what they did for a living. We talked about academics. He knew I was a good student and he encouraged me to continue to be a good student. At times he recited poetry. We talked briefly about church. At no time during the conversation did he talk to me about my basketball ability. He brought the conversation to a close by asking me if I had any questions. I said no, but that was not true. I really was desperate to ask if he would ever let me play if I came to UCLA.

When I left his office, I realized that I had not heard a formal offer of a scholarship. I was starting to wonder if maybe they had changed their minds about me. A very short while later the assistant coaches made the offer.

In retrospect I understand the importance of the time I spent with Coach Wooden. It was less than hour. It may have felt like a friendly chat but he was getting to know me, assessing my character, and learning about my background. He was considering what I would be like to work with over the next four years and how I would affect the chemistry of his team.

Now, after my years of recruiting as an assistant coach and as a head coach, I know Crum and Cunningham needed nothing more than a nod to proceed. They had spent time with my game film and the whole staff would have discussed how I might be used on the court before they ever made the first phone call. They had seen my transcripts. They had vetted me with my high school coach and principal. Coach Wooden was simply signing off on a decision that was already made. Still, if I had thrown up any red flags, Coach Wooden certainly could have nixed the deal.

On the ride to the airport, I was asked how long it would take me to make a decision. I told them as soon as I talked to my mom and dad I would call. But they knew and I knew that it was over. I was beaming and there was nothing that was going to change that.

My parents picked me up at Stapleton International Airport

and we didn't need any longer than the 10 minutes it took to drive to our house in East Denver to make the decision final. I called Coach Crum the next day. Gary Cunningham flew to Denver for my signing, which took place in Mr. Ward's office at Manual High School. It was no longer just a rumor that I was being recruited by UCLA.

It was official. I was going to be a UCLA Bruin!

CHAPTER 4

The Brubabes

My plan was to work in Colorado for most of the summer, then fly to Southern California in time to get a job on campus and get acclimated to both UCLA and living on my own. It also would allow me to play basketball against top competition, including UCLA players.

What I needed to work on more than anything else was my confidence. I had told the coaches that I was good enough to play at UCLA, but I would have to prove it to them and, more importantly, to myself. It was widely known that I was a last-minute recruit and that the scholarship I was offered was available only because Bruce Clark turned it down to go to USC. I had to prove that UCLA had, in fact, ended up with a great deal!

There was another recruit coming to campus early, a talented guard from Oakland named Marvin Vitatoe. Marvin accompanied Coach Cunningham to pick me up at LAX looking like a well-dressed hippie wearing a beautiful floral shirt, flashy bell-bottom pants, and bare feet. Coach Cunningham told us we would be working on the campus grounds with the outdoor maintenance guys. We'd share a room at one of the fraternity houses.

About a week into it, Marvin and I developed our daily routine, punching in on time, working hard until lunch, then sneaking off to shoot in the Men's Gym. The groundskeepers would let us cut corners as long as we gave them at least some real help. It was important to punch out on time, too, because if you left early, the foreman let the coaches know.

The most important part of the day was evening, when games were played in the Men's Gym.

Competition there was off the charts! If you played, you had better bring your A game because the competition was fierce. You also had to know the guys running the games—UCLA star forwards Sidney Wicks and Curtis Rowe. There were often really good players who didn't know Sidney and Curtis who sat and watched.

PICKUP GAMES

Until I got to Los Angeles, I thought the pickup games in Denver were incredible. Not only were some of the top players from around the city playing at Harrington now, but Coach Calloway took Saturdays to a different level when he started leaving the back door to the Manual High School gym unlocked. The Denver public schools didn't allow open gyms once school ended, so all summer basketball had been played on outdoor half-courts using rubber basketballs. The half-court game is quicker with no real offensive or defensive transition and no fast break. Games were usually 3-on-3 or 4-on-4 because 10 players made it much too crowded. Playing indoors on a wooden floor with a leather ball surely would better prepare me for my move to L.A.

On Saturdays at Manual, there would be players from the University of Colorado, Denver University, and Colorado State University as well as other top high school players. Pros from the Denver Rockets' ABA team also showed up, including Spencer Haywood who had just left college early to go pro.

Kids playing in high school summer leagues in Southern California could play from 20 to 30 games with their high school teams. As long as their head coach wasn't coaching the team, they could compete in different tournaments or leagues. Even pickup basketball in Southern California was an indoor game, full-court or half-court.

When I started playing in the Men's Gym at UCLA, it was against current UCLA players and former UCLA players now on NBA rosters, as well as other NBA players who were in L.A. for the offseason. There were current Lakers and players from crosstown rival USC.

This was Saturday basketball at Manual High School on steroids!

Marvin and I remained roommates when school started. Our room in Sproul Hall overlooked the main entrance so we had a good view of all the pretty Southern California girls moving in. I was never so excited for school to start!

Each of us had been required to sit down with Coach Cunningham to plan our schedules. I was a "special action" admission because my English score on the SAT did not meet UCLA's requirement, which meant I had to take Subject A, a remedial English class. Marvin and Tommy were also in Subject A. Cunningham told me while I was writing this book that he, too, took Subject A. He now has a PhD.

Years later, when I was the head coach, "special action" status was going to become an issue.

As the start of practice approached, we'd have about 18 UCLA scholarship players in our nightly games, and we moved the games to Pauley Pavilion when the annual resurfacing of the court was finished. We still had a lot of time to play before practice began in the middle of October.

What made it different when we were in Pauley was Coach Wooden, Coach Crum, and Coach Cunningham would stop by to watch. I noticed guys playing smarter. In the strictest sense, it was illegal for coaches to be in Pauley, but I figured it was less illegal because they sat way up at the top among the NCAA Championship banners. If we played for two hours, the coaches might watch for 30 minutes.

I was 10 minutes early for my first team meeting, and I was one of the last to arrive.

Coach Wooden gave us two handouts, which he read to us, line by line. The first listed his expectations for UCLA players off the court. These had to do with going to class, being a good citizen, and not taking public political stands. In those days we were in the midst of the war in Vietnam and the civil rights movement, which included issues of racial inequality and injustice. Coach told us we could have our own political views, but he didn't want our views to reflect on the team. We weren't there to play politics, we were there to go to school and play basketball.

The second handout listed his expectations about practice. Everything from being on time to the length of our hair. We would run, not walk, from one drill to the next. We would not "nag" or "razz" a teammate.

Then he stepped away from the podium and sat down in a chair. From where I was in the back, I had to stand up to see what he was doing. He took off one of his shoes, took off his sock, and then began to show these All-Americans and national champions how to correctly put the sock back on (with no wrinkles) and lace up the shoe (tight).

Now that Coach Wooden is a legend and this story is so familiar to so many, it's not so surprising. But that day I was stunned as I watched in disbelief. The veterans were showing no reaction, but all of the freshmen were looking at each other like, "You've got to be kidding me!"

Coach Wooden often said, "Little things make big things happen."

Picture Day was always October 14, the day before practice started. It was also Coach Wooden's birthday, so it was an annual thing for the secretaries to bring out a birthday cake. The players would gather around and he'd cut the cake, with the media there in force. The players posed for pictures individually and in staged action shots while Coach talked with the media. If you showed up on Picture Day and your hair wasn't the right length or the beard or mustache or mutton chop sideburns weren't gone, you were not in the pictures.

In those days we had six weeks of practice before the first game. With players that good and competition that serious, you can imagine how tough practices were.

Freshmen practiced at the same time as the varsity, but a huge curtain was lowered from the top of Pauley Pavilion to separate the courts. We had one full court with two baskets on the west end of the arena, while the varsity had the rest, including six baskets and two full courts.

Coach Cunningham told us our first scrimmage, against Compton Junior College, would be very competitive. They had not lost a game in the last couple seasons. We were scrimmaging them as a courtesy to Larry Hollyfield, who had been recruited by UCLA but had to go to junior college for a year before joining us. These guys got off the bus in full uniform, including warmups and berets. Although you don't keep score in a scrimmage, that team came in ready to light us up.

It was in that game I learned that even though I was playing forward, when we played a team with a big, powerful center, I would draw the defensive assignment. I weighed about 185 pounds, so I was going to get pushed around at times. I also learned that Hollyfield was very tough and very talented.

The freshman team played its home games at Pauley Pavilion, before the varsity games. I was pretty excited going into my first game on that court, but I wasn't prepared for what happened when the horn sounded at 5 p.m. during our warmups. The student section held 4,000 or 5,000 fans. They were good seats, right at center court. It was first come, first served. The students were lined up outside, waiting for the doors to open. For big games, they would start to line up the day before the game. When the horn sounded at 5 p.m. and the doors were opened, it was like the running of the bulls. The students would come thundering in, run down those steep concrete steps and sprint for the best seats. So we had really good crowds for our freshman games.

Our game was in the second half, with nothing particularly exciting happening, when all of a sudden, the place starts going nuts. Looking around, I see why. The varsity guys are walking in through the tunnel.

They would usually file into Pauley Pavilion around the beginning of the second half of our game and walk right in front of the student section on their way to the locker room. The crowd would be in a frenzy the entire time.

To me, the most important freshman games were the back-to-back games against USC at the end of the season. We had 10 players on the freshman team, including four scholarship players. I went into the last two games as the leading scorer and the leading rebounder. This was my chance to prove who was the better player, me or USC forward Bruce Clark.

The UCLA freshmen (Brubabes) beat the USC freshmen (Trobabes) both times. In the two games, I had a combined 53 points compared to Clark's 27 points. The second game, the season finale at USC, was probably my best game of the season. I put back an offensive rebound with seven seconds to play to send the game into overtime. I had 34 points and 22 rebounds. When I was inducted into the UCLA Athletic Hall of Fame in 2018 I used a minute of my acceptance speech to thank Bruce Clark for going to USC.

His decision to turn down the scholarship that went to me had to be timed just right. It was one of many events that I consider divine intervention to get me to UCLA. If Mrs. Biffle had pushed me to get my film to the UCLA coaches earlier, when they thought they had high school All-American forward Bruce Clark and no more scholarships, I might have been overlooked, but when the UCLA staff took their first look at me, they had just lost Clark to USC and the scholarship had become available. UCLA had been recruiting Clark all year and thought they had him.

My freshman season could not have ended any better. The varsity was going on to the NCAA tournament. I was going home to Denver for spring break. I watched UCLA win the NCAA title that year on the same black-and-white TV in the basement that I was watching when I felt destined to play for UCLA. Jacksonville gave UCLA a real challenge.

Jacksonville had Artis Gilmore and Pembrook Burrows, and they were both seven feet tall. Coach Wooden had Sidney fronting Artis because our center, Steve Patterson, was only 6-foot-9 and Sidney was quicker and more athletic. Well, they kept throwing the ball over the top and Gilmore kept catching it and putting it in.

That was the game UCLA trailed at halftime.

I have since been filled in on what happened at halftime. Sidney said, "Coach, you have to let me play behind Artis. I can do it."

Coach Wooden, always the motivator, said to Sidney, "You can't guard him that way." And Sidney insisted, "Yes, I can." That was all Coach Wooden needed to hear.

Coach had Sidney behind Artis to start the second half.

Artis got his first three or four shots blocked or changed and it turned the game around. It got to the point that Artis would look to see where Sidney was before he shot the ball.

People thought Coach was very inflexible, but that was not true. He was inflexible on some things, but when it came to listening to his players, especially during games, he would listen and that would work to his advantage.

UCLA won its sixth straight NCAA title.

Of course, the postseason awards dinner was packed.

The freshmen were sitting at tables on the floor in front of the podium, which held the varsity players and their dates as well as the coaches and administrators. The evening started out great for me. I was given the only freshman honor, the Seymore Armand Award for the outstanding freshman. Walking up to claim that trophy and shake Coach Wooden's hand proved I was good enough to play at UCLA.

After varsity awards, it was time for senior speeches. John Vallely, the team captain and the second-leading scorer, behind only Sidney Wicks, gave a nice, traditional speech.

When Bill Seibert got up, he said he couldn't agree that it was a great thing to play for UCLA because, he said, "For me, it was an unhappy experience." He talked about double standards and unequal treatment between the stars and the reserves. It was reported in the *Los Angeles Times* the next day that people in the banquet room of the Beverly Hilton Hotel were "squirming in their seats" and "toward the end of it there were some catcalls and boos from the audience." In the days after the event, I was told that his father yelled, "Sit down!" and that his mother was crying. Seibert walked off to scattered applause. But the varsity guys, up there on the podium, were clapping. I did not clap because Coach Wooden could clearly see the freshman tables.

When Coach Wooden got back to the microphone, he acknowledged Bill for having the courage to say what he said. Coach said he disagreed with most of it, but he had always taught his players to speak their minds. Coach cleaned it all up and the banquet was over.

Monday, Coach called every returning varsity player, individually, to his office. He told each one—including Sidney Wicks and Curtis Rowe and Steve Patterson and Henry Bibby—that if they felt the same way Bill Seibert felt, they were free to leave the team.

The players called a team meeting to assure Coach that they were with him and nobody wanted to leave. As a freshman, I wasn't involved, but we all knew it was serious. The next year the basketball dinner was combined with the alumni dinner at the Dorothy Chandler Pavilion. And there were no senior speeches.

After that, Coach Wooden had no more awards banquets.

CHAPTER 5

Learning from Super Sidney

It's amazing how much more I heard and learned from the annual team meeting the second time around. The script was the same every year, but as a sophomore I had different concerns. What stuck out to me was Coach saying, "I play eight players until the game is won or lost." That meant the starting five, and one substitute at each of the three positions. "Won or lost" meant ahead or behind by 20 points.

The other thing that stuck with me was when Coach said, "The slate has been wiped clean, and you will be evaluated based on what you do now, not how you played last year." I realized that no one would beat out Sidney Wicks, Curtis Rowe, or Steve Patterson, the returning frontline starters, but it did mean that if I practiced better than the upperclassmen ahead of me, I would play.

Sidney and Curtis were the two best forwards in the country, so I was determined to use every practice to learn from them and improve my game. My competition for making the 12-man varsity roster and getting playing time would come from returning varsity players senior John Ecker and junior Jon Chapman. Also in the mix were Jay Helman, a talented shooting forward who was one of the other three scholarship players on my freshman team, and Larry Hollyfield, the versatile left-handed scorer from Compton. I was facing serious competition, but it was like that every year at UCLA.

On October 14 the media showed up at Pauley Pavilion in force. And why wouldn't they? We were defending national champions and the preseason pick as the No. 1 team in the nation. It was easy to see who the stars were. Steve Patterson, the starting center, had a nice crowd of media around him, as did returning guard Henry Bibby.

Around Wicks and Rowe reporters were pressing in three and four deep. We were all in our game uniforms. I was No. 54. I would have preferred my high school number, but Bibby wore No. 45.

The next day was my first day of practice with the varsity. The culture at UCLA could not have been more clear. As a freshman we had done the same drills, but these guys went harder and jumped higher. We moved with precision and discipline. We had a drill called "rebound pass-out." After a couple of precise passes and cuts, the rebounder would toss the ball off the backboard underhanded, move quickly into rebound position, jump, and snatch the ball into

THE UN-DUNK

When Picture Day ended and the varsity players left the floor, Marvin Vitatoe and I were still on the main floor of Pauley Pavilion shooting on a side basket.

The TV game lights were being turned off, a sure sign that the people running the building wanted to get us out. At that moment Coach Wooden walked out of the coaches' locker room and headed toward the nearby stairs. It was his superstition to always make your last shot before leaving the court, so I made mine. We had new nets on each rim. My shot stuck in the bottom of the net. That happens until nets get broken in.

I was just about to step underneath the basket and punch the ball out when Marvin, who was standing just beyond the top of the key, said, "Wait, I'll get it." He came gliding in, not sprinting but almost casually measuring his steps so he could take off at the right spot. Coach Wooden slowed to watch. Marvin took off and put both of his arms down through the top of the rim, inside the net. He literally pulled the ball out of the net and back up through the rim. I had never seen anything like that, and judging by the look on Coach Wooden's face, neither had he! Marvin's head was clearly rim level and both elbows were inside the rim so his hands could reach through the basket and down to where the ball was. I asked him "What was that?" He laughed and said, "The UN-DUNK!"

his chest with two hands. I knew the drill. The older players went first. I was impressed that each of them (especially the frontline players) would rebound the ball well above the rim. Everybody put his maximum effort into rebounding the ball at the height of his leap. It was a learned behavior and everyone did it. Even practicing shooting without a ball was at game speed. This was how UCLA practiced. Coach Wooden demanded it and the effort was contagious.

For the next three weeks it would be controlled warfare. Coach Wooden's practices were meticulous. He carried a 3 × 5 index card with the schedule on it. Two and a half hours every day. The coaches met every day from 10 A.M. until noon to plan practice. Everything was timed to the minute. There was no frivolity or goofing around. The first time I heard Coach say "frivolity" I didn't know what it meant, but I learned quickly. Also, there were no water breaks. If we had an activity at one end of the floor and Coach blew the whistle and said move to the other end, everyone jogged. Nobody walked. Drills came one after the other, some half-court and some full-court. Strenuous drills were followed by ones less strenuous. All drills were "game-like" to teach fundamentals while maximizing effort. The last hour of practice was for scrimmaging, which was used for evaluation as well as conditioning.

We had a lot of student managers keeping stats. Stats were kept for each day's scrimmage and became part of the cumulative stats. The stats were posted on the equipment room door. Every day when you came to pick up your fresh practice clothes, the stats were right there for you to eyeball. They were kept by position (guards, forwards, and centers). And they were kept overall, 1–15. So on any given day I could look at the stat sheet and see how I compared to everybody on the team, or just the guys I was competing against. Practice stats were as complete as official game stats. Shots taken, shots missed, offensive and defensive rebounds, assists, and turnovers. Posting those stats daily made it impossible for you not to know how well you were doing. Hard to go in and ask one of the assistant coaches how you were doing in practice when your statistics were posted.

The coaches mixed up the teams every day. Not only did it keep the games competitive, but it also kept the teams even, for the most part. Coach would gradually start to add our offense to the scrimmages. Usually in the third week, the time we scrimmaged got cut back, and Coach would blow the whistle and stop the action to make corrections. As he felt we were getting in better condition, more emphasis would be placed on teamwork and fundamentals.

We never practiced on the weekends with the exception of one Saturday when we would practice for about an hour. It was a shortened version of what we would regularly do. This practice was held in conjunction with Coach Wooden's annual coaches' clinic. UCLA was winning national championships every year, and coaches from all over the country (high school and junior college coaches) would come to hear Coach lecture. There might be two or three guest speakers to teach some aspect of the game. The lectures would be in the morning. The coaches would eat lunch and come over to Pauley Pavilion to watch us practice. That one Saturday's practice was very different. Coach Wooden would be on the microphone, explaining to the 300 or more coaches what we were doing and why we were doing it.

By the fourth week the guys who had earned starting positions were playing together more. The final event before the season began was the intrasquad game, which had always been the freshmen against the varsity until Kareem's freshman team beat a varsity team ranked No. 1 in the country! Since then only varsity players participated, on teams that were divided somewhat equally. Not only did the game draw 12,000 fans, but it was also televised in Southern California. Before the start of the game, the players would gather at half-court and raise the championship banner from the year before. Little did I know at that time that I would be a part of that banner ceremony every year!

By that time, it was clear who would make up our 12-man roster. The players that weren't in that first 12 could redshirt. Tommy Curtis, Marvin Vitatoe, and Jay Helman, all from my freshman team, would redshirt. Larry Hollyfield and I were the only two sophomores who made the varsity team.

The first two games of our 1970–71 season were at home against Baylor and Rice. On Friday, we beat Baylor 108–77. After the game we went back to the Bel-Air Sands Hotel, and the next morning, after team breakfast, we were free until our 3 P.M. pregame meal.

We ate the same meal every game day throughout my three years with the varsity. It was a steak, baked potato, and green beans with Melba toast and four pats of butter. There was also honey on the table. I learned to mix two pats of butter with the honey and spread it over the Melba toast. The other two pats of butter went on my baked potato. We drank water; no ice. Never milk. Ducky Drake, our famous trainer, believed it took dairy products too long to digest and that could make us sluggish on the court.

As I started to eat that day I didn't notice anything different. We were allowed to talk during the meal, we just didn't talk loudly or laugh. Our game preparation actually started during the meal. About 10 minutes into our pregame meal, in walk Sidney and Curtis. They had never been late for anything before, so I assumed that whatever they had been doing had been approved. When they came in they said nothing to the coaches, they just sat down and started to eat. I looked at Coach Wooden and his expression never changed. I continued to mind my own business, which was eating.

None of the coaches had food on their table because they always ate after the team ate.

We got to the arena while the freshman game was going on, and this was a really good freshman team! Bill Walton, Keith Wilkes (later Jamaal), Greg Lee, Vince Carson, and Gary Franklin were the headliners. Still, when we walked past the students, they went wild! It was as cool as I thought it would be. We had a dress code, but this was our opportunity to express our individuality and sense of style.

The routine before the game was to get dressed and then sit quietly waiting for Coach Wooden and Coach Crum to come in and talk about our opponent. It wasn't Coach's philosophy to talk about our opponent during the week. After he finished going over their tendencies, we would go out to warm up. At the 11-minute mark on the clock, the teams would be instructed to go back to the locker room before the national anthem. The NCAA did not want players making political statements or protesting during the anthem. After all, with the civil rights movement in full swing and our troops still in Vietnam and Cambodia, there was a lot to protest.

Once back in the locker room Coach would come in and give us the matchups. The matchups were written on the chalkboard next to the shower. That's what had happened before the Baylor game.

This time when I looked at the board, instead of seeing Sidney's name across from the guy he would be guarding, I saw John Ecker's name. On the next line, instead of seeing Curtis Rowe's name, I saw my name! Coach was not going to start those two because they were late for pregame meal. I was shocked. I was about to start my first game for UCLA!

Ten minutes into the game, the crowd erupted. Sidney and Curtis had gotten up to come in. Ten minutes late; 10 minutes they sat and watched. UCLA won this game 124-78. Sidney used his less than 30 minutes to get 29 points and 18 rebounds. Curtis contributed 27 points and 13 rebounds. Coach Wooden called their play "inspired."

No one was late for another pregame meal.

Several weeks into the season, we were ranked No. 1 in the country with a record of 13–0 (4–0 in the Pac-8) and preparing to play at Loyola of Chicago and Notre Dame. That week in practice, for the first time, Coach Wooden addressed an opponent by name, specifically Notre Dame. During our controlled scrimmages, he had the second-string run a few plays that Notre Dame ran. Hollyfield was to be Austin Carr, a preseason All-American who at the end of the year would share the College Player of the Year award with Sidney.

Coach Wooden told Hollyfield to shoot whenever he got the ball, which was music to Larry's ears.

We flew to Chicago and beat Loyola 87–62, then bused to South Bend, Indiana. This game was huge and would be nationally televised. If I got in the game, everybody back in Denver would see me play for UCLA for the first time. In the first 13 games sometimes I would come off the bench as the third forward, other times John Ecker would go in first.

The game was an absolute barnburner. Austin Carr scored 46 points and essentially won the game by himself. Late in the game Coach decided that it was out of reach, so he cleared the bench. I went in with Hollyfield for the first time. I could just never seem to get the ball. Hollyfield was still thinking he was Austin Carr and doing all the shooting. We lost the game 89–82. It was our first loss of the year.

We went to the locker room and sat quietly waiting for Coach to come in. Hollyfield had never lost a game, all through high school and junior college, and was crying. I was also fighting back tears. Not only had I not taken a shot, but I also hadn't even gotten a rebound. I'm sure that Coach thought my tears had to do with losing. But it was me being selfish and upset. Only once in my college career did I ever hear Coach Wooden speak after a loss. After all, my record was 89–1. This was the one.

Coach walked in and said: "We got licked. They played better than we did. So I don't want to hear or see any bellyaching. Those of you who are asked to talk to the media, I want you to be positive and say only good things about Notre Dame and how well they played. Now get showered, get dressed and let's get out of here." That was it. The two words "licked" and "bellyaching" will forever stay in my memory.

There was a rumor that quickly spread among UCLA followers that Coach Wooden didn't do anything to intentionally lose the Notre Dame game, but he didn't do anything to win it late in the second half either. The theory was that somehow, the team needed to lose in order for Coach Wooden to regain full control of the team's mindset. To get knocked down a peg and lose our No. 1 ranking. That could not have been further from the truth. When you played basketball at UCLA and you were winning, the media focus and fan attention was unrelenting. Everything we did was closely watched, monitored, and scrutinized. More preparation had gone into the Notre Dame game than any game we would play all year. All of that preparation had completely gone against the grain of the way Coach Wooden had prepared us for every game before Notre Dame, and every game subsequent to it. I believe when Coach Wooden emptied his bench, some took that as a sign of accepting the loss for teaching purposes. Since UCLA had rarely lost a game, people just weren't used to seeing what coaches do when they believe that winning is no longer a possibility. A coach clears his bench to give deserving players an opportunity to play. That rumor got back to us, but we knew it was not true.

As we got back into league play, we continued to improve, and Coach never stopped preaching fundamentals and team play. Coach always said, "Repetition is the key to success." The better we got, the more critical he got. Practice was truly Coach Wooden's classroom.

Some of the most amazing plays every year at UCLA happened during practice. One play my sophomore year—one that I would rank in my all-time top 10—happened when Coach Wooden deviated slightly from the usual routine.

During a defensive segment of practice, he brought Bill Walton over from the freshman side.

Bill was a 6-foot-11 freshman, an unbelievable talent, and he was having a sensational freshman year. He was quick, agile, and moved with the grace of a much smaller man. He was doing things on the court that the UCLA faithful were comparing to Kareem.

Coach brought Walton over for our 2-on-1 fast-break drill. A lot of emphasis was placed on the two men on offense keeping the correct spacing and the player with the ball attacking to get the lone defender to commit. If the defender didn't attack the ball handler, he would attempt a layup. If the defender committed to the man with the ball, he'd pass to his teammate who would attempt a layup. Simple in its description but practiced over and over.

The fast break would always end with a layup. The dunk was not legal at the time and it was not allowed in our practices. Ever.

Sidney Wicks was not pleased to see Coach Wooden walk to the far end of the court with Bill.

Coach Crum and Coach Cunningham got the rest of us

organized at the other end of the floor.

The drill started with two rebounders on either side of the basket, and two other players farther out on the floor. A coach would take a shot, rebounders would go hard to get the ball, the outlet pass would go to the perimeter player on the rebounder's side of the floor, and the fast break was underway.

Bill was an amazing shot blocker and after several fast breaks, nobody had scored on the Big Redhead!

Coach was giving his extraordinarily talented freshman his undivided attention. Sidney said to Curtis, "Oh, I got this!" The stage was set.

Sidney told Henry Bibby to position himself in line so they could go together in the last pair.

When it was their turn, the shot went up, the ball was rebounded, and the outlet pass went to Bibby.

He and Sidney took off, crossed half-court, and it seemed like Henry was committed to taking the shot himself. Bill was on the balls of his feet, arms wide, pointing one index finger at the ball and one index finger at Sidney. Henry waited until the last possible split second and passed the ball to Sidney, who was trailing slightly on the other side. Bill turned and had a great angle to either block Sidney's shot or make him miss.

Bill jumped. Sidney jumped and seemed to keep going up! He reached the peak of his jump, cocked the ball, and slam dunked it so fast that Bill had no time to react. It was like Sidney was trying to rip the basket down. BOOM! The play was over in an instant! Sidney had pulled a fast one on Bill, who had no reason to expect a dunk. Two of the greatest players in UCLA basketball history had met at the top of the mountain and Sidney brought down the house.

Coach Wooden blew his whistle so loud I thought the pea would fly out of it. He immediately started yelling at Sidney. Even from our end of the floor, we could tell that Bill's face was as red as his hair! Curtis Rowe fell to the floor and rolled over on his back laughing. The rest of us collectively went "oooohhhh" but said nothing. The drill was over. Coach sent Bill back to the freshman side.

Sidney and Curtis were always the instigators. When I was a freshman, before classes started, it was Sidney and Curtis who came pounding on my door on a Saturday morning to take me and my roommate, Marvin Vitatoe, to Disneyland. They were amused to find us "freshman knuckleheads" watching *The Adventures of Rocky and Bullwinkle*. They started calling Marvin "Rocky" and me "Bullwinkle." My nickname stuck and eventually became "Moose."

At the start of my sophomore season Sidney and Curtis told me and Larry Hollyfield that it was tradition for sophomores to carry the seniors' bags on road trips. We complained but carried them anyway.

On one of those road trips Sidney and Curtis were walking through the airport and spotted me in a phone booth. Those old phone booths had a door for privacy, but I couldn't close the door. I could stuff one leg into a corner of the booth, but the other leg had to stick out. They saw me. Sidney demanded to know who I was talking to. I said it was my mother, but he didn't believe me. He leaned into the booth, took the phone, and said, "Who is this?" Then he said, "Mrs. Farmer, this is Sidney Wicks. I want you to know that you don't have to worry about your son. We are taking good care of him." Sidney passed the phone to Curtis, who concurred.

Playing against our archival, USC, my sophomore year was truly unbelievable. They were led by Paul Westphal, a junior who later would be a first-round NBA draft choice. They were undefeated and had been ranked in the top 10 all season. USC had a record of 16–0 when we beat them 64–60 at the L.A. Sports Arena. We played them again at the end of the season at Pauley Pavilion and beat them again. Thanks to us, USC finished with a record of 24–2. They were second to us in the conference, which meant they did not make it to the NCAA tournament, because in those days, only 25 teams made the tournament field.

UCLA finished 14–0 in Pac-8 play to win the league title for the fifth year in a row. Larry Hollyfield was not allowed to play in the tournament because of an NCAA rule regarding junior college transfers. We started the NCAA tournament in Salt Lake City, beating BYU 91–73. Next up was Long Beach State, led by Hall of Fame Coach Jerry Tarkanian.

Coach Tarkanian played a zone defense and a very deliberate slowdown offense. He had recruited great players and we knew this game was going to be difficult. Long Beach State featured sophomore Ed Ratleff, a 6-foot-6 scoring point guard who was a terrific shooter and could play with his back to the basket inside. Ratleff, along with George Trapp and Chuck Terry, did the bulk of the scoring. Long Beach State could hurt you with a fast break, but they liked to play their deliberate half-court style. Their three best players were very good at playing one-on-one and exploiting matchups. On the defensive end they played a 2-3 zone, which further slowed the tempo of the game.

I played a lot in that game because I could match up with either a forward or a guard defensively.

Starter Kenny Booker was in foul trouble, and although he was a guard, I was able to substitute in for him and play against Long Beach State's zone defense. I stayed in most of the second half because Long Beach State's style had us playing defense for long stretches. I knew Coach Wooden was leaving me out there during crunch time for my defense.

The score was 55–55 with just over 3½ minutes left to go in the game. Long Beach State was running their offense to get a high percentage shot, because whoever scored next would have a decided advantage. In this slow-paced game there would be only a few possessions remaining. I had been defending guard Dwight Taylor but switched to another man because of the action they were running. They made more moves and Curtis yelled for me to switch again. I switched, but I was late.

My man, sensing I was out of position, cut toward the ball, which had been passed from the top of the key to the opposite wing. That wing immediately passed my man the ball, and he had a two-step advantage on me as he turned toward the basket. For a split second I almost didn't chase the play. My man was about to score and put Long Beach State ahead in a game that could be decided by a single basket. That thought flashed through my mind and something told me to try to catch up with him. If he had taken just one dribble and two steps and laid it up, he'd have scored. Instead, he took one dribble and came to a two-foot jump stop. That allowed me to make up the distance and I was able to block his shot from behind. Sidney picked up the loose ball before it went out of bounds. The teams exchanged missed shots—we missed first, then Long Beach State missed. I snatched the rebound, passed the ball to Bibby, and Coach Wooden called a timeout.

Now that we had the ball we could dictate when the last shot would be taken. Coach Wooden wanted to pull Long Beach State out of that zone defense and was prepared to hold the ball for the remainder of the game clock. If we took the last shot and missed, at worst we would go into overtime. Sidney brought the ball up the court and dribbled it for a while. I remember him passing the ball back-and-forth with Henry Bibby. Occasionally the ball would go to Steve Patterson at the free throw line, but then immediately back out to either Sidney or Henry. At one point Henry stood out near half-court with the ball tucked under his arm, just standing there letting the clock run down.

Finally, Long Beach State extended their defense and tried to make a steal when Sidney had the ball. They fouled him with 25 seconds left to go in the game. Super Sid made both free throws and we led 57–55. Long Beach State came down the floor and missed their next shot. Sidney got the rebound and was immediately fouled, this time with just 12 seconds left ago. He again made both free throws, making the score 59–55. Long Beach State managed to hit a meaningless short shot as time expired to make the final score 59–57.

We were headed to the Final Four.

I had come so close to bearing the burden of a loss. Instead, I made a play that helped us win. If I had given up on that play it might have been Long Beach State heading to the Astrodome for the Final Four. Under the weight of that realization, I went to the bench and sat down while the team celebrated. Bibby came over and slapped me five. Denny Crum walked over and said he was proud of me. I was still sitting there, emotionally exhausted, when Coach Wooden came over and said good job.

Many years later when I was working as a broadcaster for ESPN I had a game at Fresno State, where Tarkanian was then coaching. I walked into the media room to congratulate Coach Tark when he was at the podium. He stopped midsentence and said, "You see that guy right there? Larry Farmer. He cost me an NCAA championship." He smiled. I smiled back.

Imagine how excited I was to be playing in the Astrodome, knowing that my parents would be watching on TV at home just as we had watched together when UCLA had played Houston in the Astrodome just three years earlier. And playing against Kansas was going to bring about a reunion for me, because Mark Williams from South High School was a sophomore at KU. Mark and I were friendly, but I hadn't forgotten that loss to South in the 1969 high school state championship game.

Late in the game, when UCLA had a comfortable lead, Coach Wooden subbed me in, and Mark and I played the final three minutes against each other. Mark had two points, and I had two rebounds. The final score was UCLA 68, KU 60, but it wasn't that close! We shook hands after the game. Mark Williams might be a state champion, but I had a chance to be a national champion.

The final game against Villanova was like hand-to-hand combat. Their best player was Howard Porter, a 6-foot-8 forward who was later found to have signed two contracts with agents during his senior year. The NCAA ruled him ineligible and Villanova's name on the Final Four bracket got an asterisk put by it. Steve Patterson, our starting center, had the game of his life and scored 29 points. Henry Bibby shot well and had 17 points. I cheered like crazy, and was truly ready to play, but I never got in the game. Coach Wooden used only seven players in the game. Only Henry and Steve scored in double figures. The game was that strange! But we won 68–62 and I was finally on a championship team!

I was one of the last guys to get back in the locker room. I was ready to start jumping up and down and doing whatever UCLA players did when they won a championship. This was UCLA's seventh championship, and its fifth in a row. But when I went in, the seniors were just sitting there smiling and looking more relieved than happy. Starters Steve Patterson, Kenny Booker, Sidney Wicks, and Curtis Rowe had played their last college games. Coach Wooden came in and congratulated us.

There was more celebrating at the hotel where the UCLA alumni and fans were headquartered. It was a tradition that the team would go to the hotel to have some food and celebrate with the boosters.

As I was walking through the lobby, I happened upon UCLA and NBA basketball great Willie Naulls, who had also become a highly successful businessman. We had met several times at basketball alumni functions. Willie came over and shook my hand and told me that he was proud of me. Willie told the well-dressed man who was with him that I was going to be the next great forward at UCLA. I extended my hand. The man shook my hand and said, "My name is Sam Gilbert."

CHAPTER 6

Three Great Men: My Father, My Coach, My Friend

In the movie *A Bronx Tale*, the mob boss Sonny tells his young protégé that if you're lucky, you meet three great women in your life. You meet them, fall in love, and are changed forever because of the experience. For me, it was three great men; three mentors who at different stages of my life and in very different roles loved me, looked out for me, and showed me the way.

My father raised me with the values and work ethic I needed to get a basketball scholarship. My coach made me the best basketball player I could be, made sure I earned my degree, and assured my coaching career. My "godfather" taught me how to navigate the real world.

I needed all three.

My father, Larry Sr., was a proud but humble man. He worked hard for everything he had. He grew up working in a lumberyard and working on my grandfather's farm in Arkansas. He was an amateur boxer but his love for that sport was superseded by the need to help his parents support his siblings. He enlisted in the Army Air Force and sent home most of what he earned. He achieved the rank of Staff Sergeant and was known for a mix of toughness and sensitivity.

Larry Sr. was 6-foot-2, handsome, strong, and ran a strict household. It was not a democracy. There was never any talking back or arguing. My brothers and I had little to say about anything! Mom did, and would from time to time speak on our behalf, but we could only follow the rules. I operated at my absolute best living that disciplined life. By simply watching the way he lived his life, I learned to be responsible, courageous, and aware of the needs of others. He sacrificed everything for his family.

My dad always worked two jobs. At first, while working as an apprentice electrician and going to night school, he worked in the evenings as a waiter and a bartender at the Denver Country Club. When he became a full-time electrician, he continued to work two or three nights a week. At times, Mom and Dad would work private parties together with Mom cooking and Dad tending bar. They always worked on holidays, especially Thanksgiving and Christmas. They worked for the family that employed my mom full time (as a domestic) for many years. It wasn't until I was a freshman at UCLA, home on Christmas break, that my parents were able to open gifts with us and not have to run off to serve dinner and drinks to another family. It was watching how hard my father worked that convinced me I needed to get a college degree.

Knowing how hard he worked also made me appreciate what it meant for him to spring for $15 Chuck Taylor Converse shoes when he thought the $8 PF Flyers and Pro Keds he had been providing me were sufficient. I told him Chuck Taylors would help me play better! From the beginning he made sure I took care of my school-work because he was determined that I would go to college. He was always saving so that he could help pay for college. On the chance that I might get a basketball scholarship, he invested what he could on that front.

One crucial lesson he taught me was not to underestimate myself. It was a lesson I watched him learn the hard way. When the lead electrician and supervisor in his office retired, he recommended Larry Sr. as his replacement. After a few days of agonizing consideration my father turned down the promotion because he did not feel ready. It was a decision that I watched him regret. I vowed that before I ever turned down an opportunity, I would accept the challenge, do my best, and operate on faith. If I screwed it up, it wouldn't be for lack of trying! Larry Sr. always found a way to encourage me. There were those who laughed when I signed my letter of intent to go to UCLA, saying that I would never play there. My dad's belief in me helped me believe in myself. I loved and idolized my dad.

Coach John Wooden saw something in me, though I wasn't one of his elite players. He had superstars, future NBA stars, on his team every year. What he saw was my potential and he coached me into the player he needed to help pull all that talent together. He offered me the scholarship that changed my life, hoping that I would develop into a player that could help his team. He took a chance that I would be the power forward he needed. It could have gone either way, but I was determined that he would not regret signing me.

From the day I arrived on the UCLA campus, I was his student. I heeded his maxims and learned the fundamentals—the lessons of life and of basketball. During the entire four-year process he was hard on me. He was a disciplinarian, just as my father had been. I was one of only two sophomores to make the 12-man roster. I earned playing time and was given a lot of defensive responsibility by demonstrating, at all times, my willingness not only to work hard, but also to do exactly what he asked me to do. That is, I was coachable.

I thought that when my senior season was over, he would no longer have any influence over my career. I was very wrong about that! I know that the year Coach Wooden retired, he encouraged Gene Bartow to hire me as a full-time assistant coach despite my lack of experience. I know he gave me his blessing before the chancellor, Charles Young, and the athletic director, Bob Fischer, decided to name me the head coach at UCLA, at age 30.

Every step I took at UCLA, Coach Wooden was there to point me in the right direction and clear a pathway for me. Coach Wooden's impact on my life went well beyond my playing days and planted itself in my coaching. More importantly, it influenced me as a father as well. My son Larry III (Tre) and my daughter Kendall would hear me say those maxims to them before athletic competitions in high school. I would send them in text messages while Tre was playing college basketball and Kendall was playing college volleyball. As elementary school students they could recite: "It's amazing what can be accomplished when no one is concerned over who gets the credit."

It was long after I had joined the real world that I realized how much he had actually prepared me for life. I loved and respected Coach Wooden.

Sam Gilbert, also known as "Papa Sam" or "Papa G," was like my Godfather! He was to me what neither my father nor my coach could be. He was my friend. Larry Sr. and I had a father/son relationship and Coach Wooden and I had a teacher/student relationship. Those relationships come with established limits. But Sam wasn't restricted by such parameters or protocols. My father and my coach had accepted certain responsibilities. Sam, on the other hand, had a choice. He didn't have to look out for me, but he chose to do that anyway.

The public image of Sam is that of a source of money and gifts for UCLA players, but that image is distorted. The first thing Sam ever "gave" me was the opportunity to work all summer on a drywall crew. I believe it was the elbow grease I put into that job that led to his respect for me and, eventually, our unique friendship. Through his friends and business alliances he could get things done by simply picking up a phone and calling in a favor. Along with his influence, his generosity, and his love for UCLA basketball, came a lot of speculation and rumor. In fact, he was just meaning to be helpful.

Papa Sam was street-wise and was able to relate to me and most of the young student athletes at UCLA with more of a clear understanding of the times. I could talk to Sam about anything except religion. Sam was an atheist. Shortly after we started to become close, we decided that we would never discuss religion again, and we didn't. I also couldn't go to him and complain about UCLA or Coach Wooden. I tried that one time and he stopped me midsentence saying that if I had issues with basketball, playing time, or coaching, I needed to man up and talk to the coach himself. Sam never badmouthed Coach Wooden, ever.

Sam taught me how to be shrewd and tackle issues head on. When I needed a place to live or a job, Sam would advise me on what to wear and what to say during my conversation or interview. It forced me out of my comfort zone and made me work on my own behalf. Sure, he could have done it for me, but he wanted me to learn to do it for myself. Sam exposed me to deal making, gaining an advantage but not taking advantage. Sam negotiated my professional contracts, took me to political events and introduced me to important people. Sam and I once had lunch with Los Angeles Mayor Tom Bradley. He introduced me to NBA owners and Hollywood actors. He was generous and extraordinarily giving to both me and my family. It was his generosity that was often talked about and maligned, especially when it came to UCLA and any of its basketball players. That was a very small part of our relationship, and an even smaller part of who he was. I loved and valued Sam Gilbert.

CHAPTER 7

"Goodness, Gracious, Sakes Alive!"

Coach Wooden played such an important part in my life and became so very dear to me it's hard to explain why, for years, I didn't feel close to him. My relationship with him was good from the beginning, but not clearly defined. I knew that he liked me and respected my playing ability, but that was pretty much it.

We did not have a lot of personal interaction off the court. As a player I rarely went into his office just to visit. It wasn't because I didn't think I was welcome. Coach would tell us at the beginning of every season that his office door was always open. I had known since my recruiting visit that I could have talked to Coach about whatever was on my mind. I just didn't. Some of my teammates were in his office all the time. Bill Walton, for one, would routinely go in and talk.

Had I gone to see Coach Wooden as a sophomore, it would have been about playing time. Wicks and Rowe showed me every day in practice why I had to wait my turn. The next two seasons, it would have been about getting more shots. I did want to shoot more, but I always assumed he knew that. So why tell him? The only thing that that would change was, possibly, his opinion of me.

But even then, I was closer to Coach Wooden than I realized. Our relationship grew over the years.

I respected him when I played for him, but like most players, I didn't always like him when I wasn't getting my way. I would sometimes pout, but when Coach called my name I would go in and give him everything I had. Coach Wooden did not miss much, and I'm sure he was aware of my immature attempts to show my displeasure. But everyone playing ahead of me was clearly better. I know that now and deep down I knew it then. I think Coach ignored my behavior because I was never disrespectful to him. Plus, I worked hard in practice and did everything he asked me to do. As long as I kept my sulking to a minimum, he could wait for me to grow out of it.

He was a brilliant coach who knew how to handle each player as an individual. He knew how to push my buttons. I played hard every day, and I wanted to hear Coach say, "Good job, Larry." He would say it to other players, but he rarely said it to me. All that did was make me play harder. Coach figured that out. The more he appeared not to notice my effort, the harder I worked for his approval. He motivated each of his players in the way that was most effective.

His genius as a coach was recognizing that we were all different, and he knew what made each of us tick. That was how he managed to get so many talented, smart, complicated individuals to work hard and play as a team—to all pull in the same direction at the same time. It's a lot harder than it looks.

When Coach made me team captain, he was saying so much more to me than just, "Good job." He was telling me that he trusted me as a person and as a leader. Coach Wooden kept a year-by-year list of his team captains, written in his hand on lined paper. It was a position he did not choose lightly. And he chose me.

I appreciated the honor at the time, but it means even more to me now to see that Coach Wooden wrote my name on the same list where he wrote Lew Alcindor, Lynn Shackleford, Mike Warren, Willie Naulls, Keith Erickson, Gail Goodrich, Bill Walton, Sidney Wicks, Dave Meyers, and Steve Patterson.

I always thought Coach underestimated me, but for me to think that tells me it was me who was underestimating him. He knew me, my basketball skills, and my personal strengths very well. One of my strengths was being able to handle the supporting role he was asking me to play. It is difficult for a kid of 18 or 19 to set his ego aside, even when he knows he is surrounded by extraordinarily gifted athletes.

I was talented enough to think selfishly but smart enough not to act or play that way. Not if I wanted to play for Coach Wooden.

But I also wanted to play in the NBA.

My senior year, I needed Coach to say positive things about me publicly. I thought anything that he might say to tout my development as a college player with professional potential would work in my favor. When you win as much as UCLA was winning and you play alongside great players, you are sure to be seen by pro scouts. I thought I needed a little push across the finish line to get drafted high enough to get a good contract offer up front. I wanted him to point out all the little things I did to help the team win. When he finally did make those statements, it was too late to influence the draft, but not too late to let me know how much he appreciated my importance to his team.

In March of 1985, Maylee Wang, my dear friend who was close to Coach and his wife, urged me to stop by St. Vincent Hospital to see Mrs. Wooden, who was very ill. When I arrived, Coach was there with Reverend Donn Moomaw, a former UCLA football player who was pastor of Bel Air Presbyterian Church. I didn't want to intrude, but I certainly wanted to let Coach and Mrs. Wooden know that I was praying for her, and I wanted to support Coach. I was not there long before Rev. Moomaw asked us to join hands and stand around Mrs. Wooden as he led us in prayer. I closed my eyes and pictured her well and happy in the stands, waiting for Coach to share a brief look with her, as he did before the start of every game. I thought of the cross he always had in the palm of his hand under that rolled up program he carried on the court. It was heartbreaking to see my coach now, so sad and so vulnerable. In that moment, I felt like his friend.

Nell Wooden, his wife of more than 50 years, would pass away about a week later.

My last conversation with Coach Wooden was very special to me, even though nothing special was said. It was in May of 2010. I called Tony Spino on his cell phone to ask how Coach was doing. Tony and I had been friends since our days as UCLA students. Tony became an athletic trainer at UCLA, and as Coach Wooden's health declined and his need for assistance increased, UCLA kept Tony on payroll knowing that a lot of his time would be spent caring for Coach Wooden. For the last three years, Tony essentially lived at Coach Wooden's condo. When I called that day Tony was just getting Coach in the car after a visit to his doctor. I was concerned that I was interrupting, but Tony said, "No, no, hold on, here's Coach." The familiar voice said: "Hi Larry! How you doin', Fella?" Typical Coach Wooden. I called to see how he was and the first thing he did was ask how I was. It wasn't a long conversation, nothing profound, but I was relieved to hear his speech so clear, to sense his high spirits and to know he was happy to speak with me. As the call was coming to an end, I told Coach that I loved him.

Later that day I spoke to Tony again. He said he had put Coach on the phone, despite the awkward timing, because he was having a good day. There had been days when his once razor-sharp memory was clouded by his 99 years of life. I don't know how many times since his death I have thanked Tony Spino for giving me the opportunity to talk to Coach one last time. John Wooden passed away June 4, 2010.

CHAPTER 8

Sam Gilbert: "Papa G" to Me

Just a few months after I met him in Houston, I went to Sam Gilbert's office in Encino to ask for a favor. I had decided to stay in Los Angeles for the summer and needed a good job. My roommate, Marvin Vitatoe, needed a job, too, and he was the one with a car so we went together.

Mr. Gilbert's office was on the top floor, the 12th floor, of an office building he owned on Ventura Boulevard. His office was impressive, but not ostentatious. It was spacious and the chairs and couches were beautiful leather, and the artwork was rugged and unique. He sat in a high-backed leather chair behind a desk that was big and stacked with neatly organized paperwork.

The office seemed appropriate for a man with power and wealth who had work to do. The work did not stop because we were visiting. He would pause to answer his secretary and to take calls, then pick up our conversation just where he had left it.

The most impressive feature was the large window that he used to point out nearby properties. Mr. Gilbert was in the construction business. His company built office buildings and managed them, renting the space within them to various businesses, which explains why he had connections in sports, politics, and even Hollywood.

On the credenza behind his desk he had multiple copies of Mario Puzo's *The Godfather*, which had been published two years earlier, with the movie version currently in production. Sam explained that each book was a gift from a different person. Apparently several people thought he fit the profile. Our relationship began when we talked that day in his office. He told me to stop calling him Mr. Gilbert and call him Sam. He did not seem to be at all rushed and seemed interested in what we had to say. And, then, in typical Sam fashion, he asked, "How can I help you?" We told him we both needed summer jobs. He asked what kind of jobs. Marvin told him he would like to work in a men's store. Sam told him that could be easily done. I told him that I wanted to make as much money as I could, and Sam asked me if I meant I was willing to do real work and work hard.

He called me later to tell me I would be a laborer on a drywall crew. I would earn a terrific salary and be required to "bust my ass" every day. I had no idea how heavy and cumbersome drywall was. That summer job was the hardest job I had in my entire life. I punched in at 7 A.M. and started lifting 4′ × 8′ drywall sheets. We had to lift the sheets and place them on a dolly, then wheel them into the caged elevator to be delivered to the designated floor. It was an open-air elevator and I could see through the openings in the cage and look straight down. I do not like heights so I was always uncomfortable.

The men I worked with were career construction workers. They worked hard and expected me to do the same. We wore gloves, hardhats, and steel-toed boots. Even though we followed all safety protocols, one of the construction workers fell to his death at this site. This was serious work.

When Sam phoned his contact to check on me, he was pleased to hear that I was, in fact, a hard worker. I was aware that my performance would, if even in a small way, reflect on Sam. I didn't want to embarrass him or disappoint him. I showed up every day on time and gave the crew an honest day's work. That was the first step in earning Sam's respect.

I was feeling like I was really on my own, saving money for the upcoming school year and helping my parents out with my monthly car note. But my father said as long as I was doing well in school, he would find a way to make that payment each month. He wanted me focused on school and basketball.

About a month into the summer, Sam invited me to breakfast at his home in Pacific Palisades. I drove up early one Sunday morning to their beautiful home where I met his wife, Rose, who was as welcoming as Sam. Rose was an Advanced Placement English teacher at Palisades High School. It was just the three of us that morning. Sam cooked what he called "Jewish soul food." The dish had eggs, chopped up salami, peppers, and onions, served with lots of sausage, a variety of toasted bagels, lox, and cream cheese, and washed down with freshly-squeezed orange juice. Breakfast was much better than anything Marvin and I could have cooked in our two-bedroom apartment in Van Nuys.

After breakfast, Rose and I cleared the table while Sam washed the dishes. When the kitchen was clean he took me on a tour of his home. Sam's study was amazing. The walls were filled with framed pictures of UCLA basketball superstars, all signed with personal messages to him. As I walked from picture to picture reading the messages, Sam told me stories about them. Sam told me he had negotiated a contract for each of these players for an autographed photo.

He had negotiated Kareem's first contract, as well as contracts for Lucius Allen, Sidney Wicks, Curtis Rowe, and Steve Patterson. Eventually he would handle contracts for me in addition to giving me all sorts of advice about how to handle negotiations.

Sam sat at his desk with the chair turned around so he could face me, and I sat across the room on a beautiful leather couch with my back to the "Wall of Fame." We talked about many things. My family, school, my future goals. We were still getting to know each other. Toward the end of the conversation, I told Sam that although Marvin and I were living together for the summer, we weren't sure Coach would allow us to once again be roommates. I told Sam that I did not want to live in the dorm as a junior. I took a deep breath and asked Sam if he knew of anyone who might be willing to rent me an apartment.

This was the second time we had spent time together and this was the second thing I was asking him to do for me. I wanted his help, but I didn't want him to think that every time he saw me I was going to be asking for a favor. Sam was the only person outside of the UCLA coaching staff that I had asked for help of any kind. The question came out awkwardly. After thinking about it for a moment Sam said he would look into it and get back to me. He said he had a few ideas.

He then suggested that we go outside because he needed to wash his car. I didn't think he was serious. This rich guy was going to go outside and wash his own car? Are you kidding me? So back toward the kitchen we went, to the back of the house. He opened his garage door and there were two beautiful Mercedes-Benz cars parked side by side. His four-door S-Class on the right with the license plate PAPA G and Rose's two-door Coupe on the left with the license plate MAMA G.

He backed his car out into the driveway, filled two buckets with water and soap, dropped a sponge in each, and handed me a bucket. We washed his car, dried the sides of the car with a chamois, and the windows with newspaper. He then told me to get in and we drove up the hill through his neighborhood, turned around, and drove back at a slightly higher speed to get it completely dry. Then we washed my car.

This was his Sunday routine. Throughout my friendship with Sam we would repeat that sequence many times. Some of our best conversations were held in his driveway washing cars. I wasn't the only one who was invited to his home, and I wasn't the only one to wash cars with him. But I didn't talk to other players about their relationships with Sam. Each of us had a unique relationship with him.

Some of his friendships with UCLA players lasted until the day he died, like mine, Willie Naulls', and Lucius Allen's. It was Lucius who gave Sam the name Papa Sam or Papa G. I learned this one day when I was at Sam's house and Lucius came to visit. It was the first time I met Lucius, whose first season in the NBA was my freshman season at UCLA. Lucius explained that as a child he had called his grandfather Papa and he had the same feelings for Sam. I could see that Sam liked the name, so I started calling him Papa Sam.

Some players graduated and moved on. Others, like Marques Johnson and Jamaal Wilkes, parted with hard feelings. I knew both

Marques and Jamaal well, but I didn't know that their feelings for Sam had fallen apart until I read it in the newspaper years later.

Sam was different things to different people. He was a unique figure. He certainly was much more than the shady money source he was made out to be during the controversy over NCAA violations that surfaced just before my first year as head coach.

Making a call to a friend to help secure my summer construction job is a perfect example of the kind of help he gave me, as well as others before me and after me. It is important to note that I had completed two basketball seasons at UCLA before I met him. I had not even heard of him until well into my freshman year. From other players I learned that Sam Gilbert had been a friend to players going back to 1967 when he reached out to Lucius and Kareem. He was described to me as a successful businessman who knew a lot of people in Los Angeles. He enjoyed being helpful.

I came to understand that he was not overly concerned nor intimidated with the letter of the law when it came to NCAA rules, which he considered outdated and sometimes racist. He liked to point out that he was a private citizen, not even a UCLA alum, and he did not have to justify what he did for his friends. Sam joked about the NCAA and their ironfisted rule over amateur athletics, saying it was called "amateur athletics" because it was run by amateurs who were often out of touch with today's reality. However, he always did things carefully, because despite his disdain for some of the more archaic NCAA rules, his aim was to help, and not to put the university or the basketball program in any jeopardy.

Recent NCAA legislation and a Supreme Court ruling have acknowledged the gap between what student-athletes are allowed and what they need. Sam would be pleased. I never heard or saw anything regarding gifts of cash or cars to entice high school basketball players to come to UCLA. Recruits were not introduced, told about, nor promised meetings with Mr. Gilbert while being recruited. That's a significant distinction to make, especially when NCAA investigators or journalists are trying to nail down proof of illegal "incentives."

While being recruited by other programs and certainly while recruiting against other programs, I was well aware that some schools were offering incentives beyond "books, fees, and tuition." I know that when I was there, UCLA was never involved in those bidding wars.

Sam Gilbert was named in accusations the NCAA presented to UCLA administrators in 1980 so that each item could be addressed. Most of the accusations could be explained away. Eight held up and led to sanctions against UCLA in 1981. Not all eight involved Sam, and none were during Coach Wooden's tenure. The issue that involved Sam was his role in helping players' families get good deals on used cars. That was fair. NCAA rules were quite clear about not allowing athletes special favors.

What I found unfair was the way Sam was vilified during the investigations. I was offended that the *Los Angeles Times* made it seem that anyone connected to the UCLA basketball program was somehow tainted for calling him a friend.

He was my friend and I never denied it. Not to the NCAA, UCLA, or the media. When Papa Sam passed away in 1987 Rose asked me to deliver a eulogy. It gave me an opportunity to publicly acknowledge him and to thank him while saying goodbye. He was a tough man, but I knew him as a kind and good man.

CHAPTER 9

Real Job, Real Home, Real Progress

The summer of 1971, between my sophomore and junior years, was a coming of age in my young life. Instead of going home to Denver I was staying in Los Angeles, sharing an apartment with Marvin Vitatoe, driving the car my parents were helping me with, and working a very real job in construction. I was no longer an out-of-state student. Los Angeles would be my home for the next 12 years. By any measure, the summer of '71 could not be considered a summer break.

In addition to wrestling heavy sheets of drywall every weekday from 7 A.M. to 4 P.M., I was taking a night class at Santa Monica City College that would count toward graduation at UCLA. I chose a class in communications, which I made use of throughout my coaching career and into my broadcast assignments.

The instructor was Bobby Dye, who was also the head basketball coach at SMCC. When Coach Dye learned that I was shooting on an outdoor court between my job and my class, he started opening the gym for me. I was always prepared to play outdoors or indoors. I kept in my car both a rubber basketball for outdoor courts and a leather one for indoor courts.

Coach Dye was nice about the gym, but he was tough on me when it came to speeches. He would purposely get me up to speak in front of the class more than I wanted. I was nervous at first, but I got better.

After class I would drive from Santa Monica to UCLA to play in the evening at the Men's Gym. When I did not have class I would leave work and drive to an outdoor court in Culver City to shoot until it was time to head to UCLA. It made for some very long days.

A few days after I had asked Sam about a place to live during the school year, he called to say there was a possibility that I could live in a guest house. First, I asked him, "What's a guest house?" He explained it was a small house behind a main house, not unusual in Southern California. I'd never heard of anything like that in Denver. My mother worked for wealthy people and none of them had additional little houses. Sam said it was a long shot because the owners had let only one other person live there, and that was Kareem. Sam said this family had a great experience with Kareem but were not interested in having anyone else stay there. They certainly didn't need the rent money.

The owner was Brad Marcus, an attorney. Sam thought if Mr. Marcus met me, he might be more willing to allow me to rent the property. Mr. Marcus agreed to see me in the lobby of an office building in Santa Monica where he had a meeting with a client. I would have 15 minutes. I wore a coat and tie, as Sam advised. The conversation was pleasant, but we didn't even sit down. He had a wife and three children. He said that after Kareem moved out, they had turned the guest house into a play area for the two younger kids. His older son was now using the bedroom for a photo darkroom. It had been almost three years since Kareem left, and the family was used to being alone again. I got the feeling the family really connected with Kareem.

Mr. Marcus asked me why I no longer wanted to live in the dorm and why I thought the coaches wouldn't let me continue to share an apartment with Marvin. I told him we didn't bring out the maturity in one another and he laughed out loud. I hoped he was starting to like me. He said he knew Sam more professionally than socially, that they were friendly but not close friends. I figured that was his way of telling me that he was not going to be pressured. Mr. Marcus said he would discuss the matter with his family and get back to me.

A few days later they invited me to dinner. I drove to the Marcus home in the San Fernando Valley and was met at the door by Mr. Marcus (who told me to call him Brad) and his wife, Marsha. She too greeted me warmly. I was introduced to their children, Craig, Mitch, and Karen. We talked, just getting to know each other. It was a typical family dinner with plenty of food and conversation.

After dinner Brad and I talked. He told me he had called the "Housing Department at UCLA" to ask how much it cost per month for a student to live in the dorm so he had an idea what my scholarship check would be each month. I didn't even know that yet! He said if the family agreed to let me stay with them, I would need to pay my rent by check promptly at the beginning of each month. I had never had a checking account, but I would figure out how to start one.

Checks would be proof that I paid rent. Having rented to Kareem, who was as high profile as an athlete can be, he was aware that the NCAA might someday review our arrangement. Brad set the rent just high enough to leave me something for gas and food. When I told Coach Wooden I had the opportunity to live in this guest house he didn't ask a lot of questions, but Frank Arnold, the assistant coach who had replaced Denny Crum, asked for all the details. I may or may not have given him the impression the guest house wasn't much larger than a tree house.

Brad told me that in addition to paying my rent, I would be required to help out around the property, specifically cleaning the swimming pool. I did sometimes skim leaves off the surface, but I was in the pool almost as often as I cleaned it. Brad further made it clear that they did not want their children exposed to loud music or parties or having female visitors coming and going at all hours. Kareem had not done anything to jeopardize the children's innocence. Craig was now in junior high school, while Mitch and Karen were in elementary school. It all sounded good to me. I still had not even seen where the guest house was, much less what it was like.

The very next day Brad called me and told me the family had voted and it was unanimous—they would allow me to move in. I was overjoyed! I drove to Encino to meet with Brad and Marsha and finally get a look at the guest house. Brad told me the first time I met with the family to park on the street, so I parked there again. There were huge hedges in front of their address on Woodley Avenue, perfectly placed so you couldn't see the house from the street.

The first time I went there was at night so I couldn't see much. What I saw now when I walked around those hedges and up the circular driveway was . . . WOW.

Well-placed trees framed an immediate view of the large, ranch-style house that was painted subtle yellow, accented with wood and stone. The landscaping was amazing. I learned later that actor Rod Cameron lived in the white two-story home next door. He was best known for his many roles in Hollywood westerns in the 1940s and later for TV parts, including guest appearances on *Bonanza*, *Laramie*, and *The Virginian*. I was told much later by Tony, Rod's son, that the Jackson Five had lived up the road when they first moved to California.

Marsha and Brad walked out and met me on the circular drive. We walked to the right side of the house and down a part of the driveway that was attached to the circle but led to the back of the main house. There, for the first time, I saw the guest house. It was a smaller replica of the main house. There was a professionally built basketball hoop right behind the main house so I would be able to walk out of the guest house and step onto an outdoor court. The backyard of the main house had a perfect lawn and big ferns, plants, and flowers. The expansive patio had wrought iron furniture covered with bright cushions. Up on a slight hill was the large swimming pool. I had seen places like this before, but only in movies.

Brad opened the front door to the guest house and we walked into the living area. There were large picture windows on both sides of the door. To the right I could see a small kitchen table with two chairs on a tile floor. Beyond the table there was a door that opened to the outside. To the left was a bathroom and a bedroom. The entire house consisted of four rooms.

After two years of sharing a dorm room and a summer sharing an apartment it felt spacious. The kitchen had a window above the sink facing hedges that provided privacy from the backyard next door. The bathroom was small but very nice. The last room I saw was the bedroom. The walls and the ceiling were painted completely black! There was a window facing the main house, covered with a thick black curtain. When they said the bedroom had been turned into a darkroom, they weren't kidding.

Brad told me I would definitely have to paint the bedroom so it didn't look like a room in a haunted house. I said that would be no problem.

Brad asked me what furniture I already had. I told him I had used money from my construction job to purchase a brand new king-size mattress and a 32" color TV. I had a really nice cassette player with two 12" speakers my parents had given me for high school graduation. I assured them again that I wouldn't be playing my music loud. They both smiled. I told them that my parents had sent me two sets of monogrammed bath towels. We all laughed as I acknowledged that towels really didn't qualify as furniture. They said we could treat this as a semi-furnished apartment. They would bring back an old dresser with a mirror that Craig had taken out to make room for darkroom equipment. They had a couch that they weren't using. I might need a chair, and maybe a coffee table. Those items would come much later. Brad gave me a key and told me to just let myself in from now on.

Over the next two years my relationship with the Marcus family would grow. I was very fond of their children, who visited with me a lot. I went to a bar mitzvah and celebrated a Passover Seder with the family. I was invited to join them for Hanukkah. They were great people, and they truly made my living experience a good one. My younger brother, Aubrey, came out to spend a part of the next summer with me, and the Marcus family embraced him as well.

I told Brad and Marsha that I would come back the next day to paint the bedroom and move the furniture. When I left the Marcuses I drove to a pay phone to tell Sam how great the guest house was and that I would be painting the bedroom. Sam said he had already spoken to Brad and would be sending over three cans of off-white paint as a housewarming present. I remember thinking I probably would just need one can of paint.

Marvin had to work the next day so I called another buddy, Craig Impelman, and told him I needed him to help me paint. I had met Impelman at the beginning of my sophomore year when he was a freshman. We became good friends. Craig was a gym rat who came from an affluent and influential family in San Francisco. He belonged to the historic San Francisco Olympic Club. "Imp" lived in Sproul Hall, as I did. He was an excellent student. He was always playing basketball and trying to get in the UCLA team's pickup games. More often than not, we wouldn't let him play. He tried out for the UCLA freshman team but had the bad luck to be a freshman at the same time as Bill Walton, Keith Wilkes, and Greg Lee.

Because Craig was a guard and a trash talker, he had butted heads with Greg during tryouts. When it came time to select the last non-scholarship player for the freshman team, the players voted for the other guy. Craig was crushed. I've always thought Craig's getting cut made our friendship closer. His basketball life became more wrapped up in following me and the varsity team. I chose Craig as one of my assistant coaches when I was made head coach.

The next day I picked up Imp and went to the guest house. Like me, he thought this whole set up was unbelievable. When I opened the door to the guest house, I saw that someone from the main house had left an upright vacuum cleaner. In the bedroom we found a stepladder, three cans of paint, two rollers, paint trays, and two brushes. There was also a large tarp, which we spread over the carpet. It was soon obvious it would take more than one coat of white paint to cover those black walls. We got the first coat of paint on, then went out to get some food and a six-pack of beer. We were there well into the night.

This beautiful little house would be my home for the next two years. I would eventually hang posters of Bruce Lee and Jimi Hendrix on the walls to complete my decorating.

CHAPTER 10

The Best Team Ever?

In the never-ending debate about which college basketball team was the best ever, I go with our 1971–72 UCLA team. Some go with the 1972–73 UCLA team. Or the 1967–68 UCLA team.

Bruins can usually keep the debate "in-house" by discussing all three of Kareem's national championship teams, both of Bill Walton's championship teams, and the Walt Hazzard and Gail Goodrich teams.

Others will even try to say it was Indiana's 1975–76 team with Kent Benson, Scott May, and Quinn Buckner. That Indiana team was honored at the Final Four in Atlanta in 2013 as the best college team of all time. But facts are facts. The statistics speak for themselves.

Look beyond our 1971–72 record of 30–0 and beyond defending our national title. We scored more than 100 points in each of our first seven games. We did that with no three-point shot and no shot clock. Over the course of all 30 games our average winning margin was 30.3 points. That's an NCAA record I doubt will ever be broken.

At the annual Picture Day our only returning starter, Henry Bibby, posed with four pairs of sneakers, symbolic of our need to find four players to fill the shoes of the starters who had moved on.

We went into the season ranked No. 1, but there was no consensus we would defend our national title.

The media could not get Coach Wooden to make any predictions. Coach said that not as much would be expected of this year's team. Asked if we would defend our title, he said, "Maybe." Asked about filling empty shoes, he said, "We have talent. I would rather have talent without experience than experience without talent."

Most of that talent was coming up from the freshman team. Bill Walton was an extraordinary player and would replace Steve Patterson as the starting center. There was even talent behind Walton. Swen Nater, a 6-foot-11, 250-pound junior college transfer student, would give Walton strong competition every day in practice. Eventually, after never starting a UCLA game, Nater would be a first-round NBA draft pick.

It was my first opportunity to play with, and sometimes against, Bill Walton. Bill played basketball during basketball season, but when the season ended he'd go hiking, ride his bike, and just be himself. He did not play in our pickup games.

The dominance of the team began with Walton. He was smart, fundamentally sound, and an excellent passer. Bill could score from anywhere from 15 feet on in. He was an extraordinary shot blocker who had great timing and was quick off the floor. He would start on the left post, near the basket.

Bibby would not be challenged for his starting position. He was a senior and our most experienced player, as well as being a natural leader. The other two seniors, Andy Hill and Jon Chapman, would add maturity to the young team, but their playing time would be limited.

Henry was a lights-out shooter with deep range. Coach Wooden would start him on the left wing. By putting Henry and Bill on the same side of the floor, Henry's defender could not help on Bill.

Another sophomore who would step into a starting position was Keith Wilkes, later Jamaal Wilkes. He was amazing and silky smooth. He stood 6-foot-7 and would start his jump shot with the ball held slightly behind his head. In practice, I tried my damnedest to block his shot, but never could. He could make shots from 18 feet or battle and score around the basket. He was skinny, but surprisingly strong, and an outstanding rebounder. He would start on the right post.

The third sophomore who would break into the starting lineup was Greg Lee, the son of a high school basketball coach. Greg was clever and fundamentally sound, but locked in a battle with Tommy Curtis for the starting point guard position. Tommy was quick and a great ball handler. He talked trash, but he could back it up. Greg would eventually win the starting position, but Tommy was right behind him.

Larry Hollyfield and I, both juniors, were in a similar battle for the right wing position. Hollyfield was a streak shooter, left-handed and flashy. He could play at guard or forward, and was a better shooter, but I could score from midrange and around the basket to produce just as many points. My lateral quickness allowed me to defend smaller players, and I was also very athletic.

I became the starter, with Hollyfield nipping at my heels.

Our starting five consisted of three sophomores, one junior, and one senior. The media called us "The Bibby Bunch."

We became a good defensive team. We ran a 2-2-1 full-court press after every made basket to speed up the opposition's tempo. If an opponent managed to get through our press and tried to attack the basket, there was Walton. He would block shots, retrieve the ball, and make the outlet pass that started our fast break.

Teams that tried to play more deliberately would sometimes find themselves behind very quickly. A turnover against the press or a missed shot would initiate our fast break. We were the best fast breaking team in the country, and could go from defense to offense in the blink of an eye.

Bill would sometimes rebound the ball with two hands and while still in the air, spot one of our guards and throw the outlet pass that started our fast break. We would score and immediately get back in the press, sometimes scoring 8 to 10 points in a row before the other team could call a timeout.

Our fans called this the Bruin Blitz.

During our second weekend of play, our opponents were Iowa State and Texas A&M. Bill called Jamaal and me over during warm-ups and told us that he wanted us to merely box out our men on defense, and allow him to get the defensive rebound to start a fast break. He felt we were getting in his way, and our fast break would be better if we gave him more room to operate. That was fine with me, because the faster I could get down the floor, the greater my chances were to score points. Jamaal felt the same way, so we both agreed on the spot. Problem was, we had not cleared any of this with Coach Wooden. Very early in the game, a shot went up and, as Coach Wooden always taught, we assumed the shot would be missed. We also assumed Bill would get the defensive rebound. Jamaal and I took off running down the floor. Henry and Greg positioned themselves for the outlet pass. Bill tipped the rebound but couldn't control the ball because it took an unexpected bounce off the rim. Suddenly it was five against one under the basket. Coach Wooden was furious, and yelling at all of us about not leaking out. I was not about to tell Coach that it was Bill's idea! It was the last time we left that early, but the three of us always knew that if Bill was close to getting a defensive rebound, we were going to stay out of his way and run out early to start our explosive fast break. It was new, fun, and one of the luxuries of playing with a great center.

We loved that all of our home games were tape-delayed for TV in Los Angeles. That allowed us to get something to eat after the game and be back in our rooms in time to catch the tipoff. We would watch the game in groups of four or five and bet on how many times broadcaster Dick Enberg would say, "Oh, my!" for a Bruin Blitz. We would all say it with him.

We opened the season by beating The Citadel 105–49 and also scored more than 100 in our next six games. Coach Wooden liked to play a Big Ten team before our Pac-8 schedule started. We beat a very good Ohio State team 79–53 in the eighth game of the season. We then opened our league competition with a 78–72 victory over a tough Oregon State team coached by the great Ralph Miller. That game in Corvallis was one of the closest games we played all season.

We beat Oregon in Eugene before coming back to Pauley Pavilion to play Stanford, Cal, Santa Clara, and the University of Denver.

I was the only one excited to play Denver. My hometown team had several players I had played against in high school. Denver played both a 2-3 zone defense and 1-3-1 zone to stop Walton from scoring. By collapsing around Bill, Denver made it difficult to get the ball to him, so he scored only scored 8 points in that game. Henry Bibby and I scored 19 points each and we beat them 108–61. That game demonstrated that focusing only on Bill might not be the best strategy!

During our midseason break from Pac-8 games we always played at Loyola of Chicago and Notre Dame. Hollyfield and I were particularly interested in getting back to South Bend for a bit of payback for the only loss we suffered the year before.

Coach Johnny Dee had left and Richard "Digger" Phelps was in his first of 21 years as Notre Dame coach.

Coach Phelps decided the only way to avoid another 58-point blowout like the 114–56 loss at Pauley Pavilion just before Christmas was to slow the game down. An all-out stall. Limit our possessions. Gary Novak, Notre Dame's 6-foot-7 center, would stay out near half-court dribbling in place. Walton was guarding him in a "cat and mouse" fashion. At one point Novak dribbled more than three minutes off the game clock before finally driving to the basket.

It was frustrating, but for the most part we kept our composure. We scored a couple of baskets right at the end of the first half to take a 12-point lead. Coach Phelps met us with the same stalling strategy in the second half. We had to deal, mentally, with playing defense for long periods of time. We would eventually win the game 57–32. A 25-point loss was, for Notre Dame, a big improvement over their first loss to us. They also beat our average victory margin. By "taking the air out of the ball" Phelps took the fun out of the victory.

We would not face an all-out stall for the rest of the season. We had reason to expect to see it in our next game, against USC. Coach Bob Boyd had used that tactic to beat UCLA in the past, but USC didn't hold the ball and we beat them 81–56.

We continued pressing, fast breaking, and sharing the ball and none of our remaining conference games were even close. We remained even keel, as Coach preached "avoid the highs and the lows." We did. The attention to detail never wavered. Anyone watching our practices would have been bored to tears. We did some combination of the same drills every day. In our defensive segment we might work on an action we would see in an upcoming game, but Coach never mentioned any team by name.

Our last three conference games were on the road against Cal, Stanford, and USC. Once again, we were undefeated and Pac-8 champions. Our first NCAA tournament game was in Provo, Utah, against Weber State, from right up the highway in Ogden, Utah. We beat them 90–58. My 15 points in just over 20 minutes of play would be talked about years later when I was head coach at Weber State.

Once more we would have to go through Coach Jerry Tarkanian's Long Beach State team with All-American Ed Ratleff to get to the Final Four. The hype for this rematch had begun immediately after our tournament victory the year before. Long Beach State complained about a call late in the game and because the margin of victory for UCLA was just two points, made on free throws by Sidney Wicks, Long Beach State fans had spent a year feeling cheated. The matchup was made more personal because both UCLA and Long Beach State had so many players from Southern California.

There was not a lot of time between tournament games to make anything other than subtle adjustments. Given that Coach focused only on us throughout the year, a quick turnaround was not usually an issue. But as we approached the Long Beach State game, Coach Wooden was considering one change to start the game. Long Beach State returned four players who had played us in the tournament the year before. UCLA returned only Henry and me.

To no one's surprise, Coach was going to start me on Ed Ratleff. "Easy Ed" was 6-foot-5 and averaging 20 points per game. He finished his college career as a two-time first-team All-American. I'm not sure how he got his nickname, but Glenn McDonald, one of his Long Beach State teammates, has said it was for the way he made every move on the court look effortless. Ratleff would be the key matchup and I was looking forward to the challenge. He was a point guard but had absolute freedom of movement in their offense. Guarding him was not going to be "easy."

There was just one way for me to guard Ratleff. I needed to be physical with him, bounce him around a little bit, try to get in his head. He was going to score, but I needed to make him work hard to get his baskets. As we settled into the game, I took every opportunity to put a forearm in his chest or back to let him know I was close. If he tried to post up, I would beat him to the spot. If I couldn't get a forearm on him, I'd be pulling on his jersey from behind. Neither tactic could be done forcibly, because I would be of no use if I fouled out. I did it just enough to make him uncomfortable. These were tactics I learned from pickup games at Harrington. I was starting to frustrate Ed, and we led at halftime 34–23.

When the second half started, I was able to get away with a few more bumps and pushes. Ed started to complain about me to the referees. Coach Tarkanian did, too. At one point early in the second half when Ratleff tried to cut toward the ball, I stepped into his path, blocking and knocking him to the floor. The collision wasn't hard enough to hurt him, and I think he "acted" a bit to draw the referees' attention. I got called for a foul. Ed and Coach Tarkanian both yelled at the official that it was about time!

As Ed was getting up, I was confronted by his teammate, Leonard Gray, who was a big fella. Leonard was in my face suggesting that if it happened again he was going to kick my ass. Just as this confrontation was coming to a head, Hollyfield came walking over. Larry was tough and not to be messed with. Larry stepped in between us and said, "What's the problem, Leonard?" Now safely behind Hollyfield, I said, "Yeah, Leonard, what's the problem?" Leonard and Holly jawed at each other for a few seconds until Leonard walked away. I said, "Damn, Holly, what took you so long?" I decided to finally forgive him for not passing me the ball in the Notre Dame game the year before.

We beat Long Beach State 73–57. I had played 36 minutes and was called for just three fouls. Ratleff scored 17 points on 7-of-19 shooting. Coach Tarkanian was quoted in the next day's newspapers saying UCLA played dirty, and Ed had never been knocked to the floor that many times! I took that as a compliment. I wasn't a physical or dirty defender, but I couldn't let Easy Ed just go off.

Now it was on to the Final Four! The Final Four was going to be played at the Los Angeles Sports Arena.

Right away there was a buzz about tickets, how many could we get, and much we could get for them. It was legal to sell your tickets. My family was in Colorado and not coming out, so it was all about being a good capitalist.

The media started building up our trip to the Final Four. In truth, if we weren't playing at Pauley Pavilion, playing at the Sports Arena was as close as we could get to having a home court advantage. We had beaten USC on this court a month earlier. Coach Wooden could treat our preparation as if we had a home game, practicing at Pauley, and staying at the Bel-Air Sands Hotel.

Next up for us, in our semifinal game, was the University of Louisville, led by a coach we knew well.

The UCLA team that had won the national championship the year before had lost not only four players from the starting lineup, but also Denny Crum from the coaching staff. Frank Arnold, who had been an assistant at Oregon, had replaced Coach Crum when he became the head coach at Louisville.

In his first year, Crum had led Louisville to the Missouri Valley Conference championship and to the Final Four, winning 11 of its last 12 games. After playing for UCLA and serving as the top assistant for Coach Wooden, Crum taught the UCLA system at Louisville, and taught it superbly! There had to be mixed emotions for Coach Wooden to be coaching against a former player and assistant. Coach Wooden and Coach Crum had won a national championship together the year before.

When we took the court at the Sports Arena for warmups, I smiled at Coach Crum and he smiled back. He had a rolled-up program in his hand, just as Coach Wooden always had. The game was tough and hard fought early on and we led by eight points at halftime. The second half was a different story. We hit Louisville with the Bruin Blitz and put the game out of reach, winning 96–77. Bill had an exceptional game, scoring 33 points. He made 11-of-13 from the field and 11-of-12 from the free throw line. He also had 21 rebounds. I was the second-leading scorer with 15 points in 27 minutes.

After the game Coach Crum's smile and warm handshake assured me that he was happy for me. The question he had asked on his first phone call to me had been answered.

We were on to the championship game against Florida State. The FSU team was tall, had good quickness and could shoot the ball from the outside. Ron King was their leading scorer and was an excellent shooter. Their big men were Reggie Royals at 6-foot-10 and Lawrence McCray at 6-foot-11.

This was going to be a real test, but we were ready.

Bill won the tip to start this championship game. Greg Lee had the ball just beyond the top of the key. I moved into position on the right wing. Greg was getting pressured by the defense and was looking to make a pass to either Henry on the left or to me on the right. He chose me.

Greg had good reason to think that a lob pass to me was a sure basket.

At the beginning of the season Greg and I had developed this pass play and we could read each other well. If I went backdoor to the basket he would lob the ball over the defense. I'd catch it in midair over the basket and drop it in. The fans loved it! We connected on this play several times in two games over one weekend early in the season and the following Monday, Coach Wooden had other players practice this lob pass in a drill. The drill was a disaster. After several turnovers and missed shots, Coach Wooden called the drill off and it was never practiced again. Greg and I would continue to connect and it became a part of our offense.

Through the years Bill would be more closely identified with scoring off the high lob passes, but he acknowledges that Greg and I "invented" the play. Bill told me as I was working on this book that he "stole" that play from me. He said he told Greg, "Hey man, bring that my way!" We both laughed. Jamaal described the play in his book as "the next best thing to the dunk" when the dunk was not allowed. Jamaal wrote, "Larry's execution was pure art." He described how I would "gracefully drop it in the bucket."

So here we are on the opening play of the nationally televised championship game. I go backdoor and Greg throws me a perfect pass that catches the defense completely off guard. I grab the ball about a foot over the basket. As I had done so many times, I softly guided the ball in for the easy basket. But this time the ball hit the heel of the rim and bounced toward Bill. Fortunately, he put the offensive rebound back up for two points. This play had no negative effect on our game, but I haven't gotten over it. To this day, I cringe at the thought of it.

Florida State created a problem for us that was different from any we had faced all year. They attacked our press, and then instead of being content to set up their offense, they passed the ball to the corner before our defense could get set. Ron King took the shot. Pressing teams will give up certain shots in certain areas on the floor. The mindset of a pressing team is that if the opposition attacks and misses the shot or turns the ball over, the defense won that possession. FSU got the ball to the corner and they took the chance of missing that shot. Any miss would have resulted in our fast break. But they kept making that shot, so Coach Wooden took us out of the press and into our normal half-court defense.

That was a first for us. One of our season-long advantages had been taken away.

We led at the half 50–39. We would ultimately win the game 81–76, because of our consistent, disciplined play. That five-point win was the closest game we played all year. Coach used only eight players the entire game. I played 33 minutes. Walton scored 24 and Jamaal 23. Henry, who was coming off a two-point effort against Louisville, had 18 points in his last college game.

UCLA was, once again, the national champion. To my surprise, this championship locker room was much different from the one I had experienced the year before in Houston. Call it youthful exuberance. This was the celebration I had never experienced! Guys were laughing, hugging, giving skin, talking trash (before Coach Wooden walked in), and basking in the moment.

I flew home to Denver for spring break. It was a triumphant trip home. Everyone had seen me play in the championship game. The Denver media wanted interviews. Now I would have some time with my family. My mother was from South America, from British Guiana (Guyana.) She spoke with a British accent and had a tropical look. She had beautiful long, flowing, black hair. My mom and dad had a running joke. Every Sunday after church service she would say, "Mrs. (So and So) looked so good in her wig! I think I should get one." Or "How would I look with a hairpiece"? My father was not about to let her hide one of her finest features. He would end the conversation by smiling and saying, "No wigs."

We were all in the kitchen and Mom was fixing me something to eat when I noticed something different about her. After a few awkward glances, I finally asked if she was wearing a wig. There was absolute silence in the kitchen. Finally, my mother told me that earlier in the year she had been diagnosed with breast cancer. She had a mastectomy along with radiation and chemotherapy. The cancer was under control but with the rigors of the treatment, she had lost her hair. Of course, I was saddened when I heard that my mom had been so sick. What made it even worse was I didn't know.

My parents called me every Sunday morning; that's how we handled my being away from home. I was now realizing how many times I had talked with them when they did not tell me she was suffering. They told me they didn't want to distract me with worry and fear. After some discussion, we all promised we would be transparent from that moment on. And we were.

I was in Denver for about five days. I was still being congratulated for my success, but that wasn't as important to me as it had been. My main team, my family, had put life in perspective.

Back in Los Angeles, I waited a few weeks until I could be alone with Sam and Rose at their kitchen table. I handed him my newly acquired 1972 NCAA championship ring. I told him that I had given my 1971 ring to my dad and that I planned to keep the one we would win the next year. Sam smiled but was speechless. That was a rare occurrence. He gave me a big hug and a kiss on the cheek. Rose was excited, too. She later replaced the blue "glass stone" with lapis. Sam wore that ring every day for the rest of his life.

With the basketball season over, I was living the life of a student. One spring day after my morning classes I had gone to the cafeteria to eat lunch. I wound up in the student union shooting pool. I loved playing 8-ball or 9-ball. Sometimes I earned my lunch money playing the pool hall regulars for a couple of bucks. I was playing when one of the basketball student managers came in and said he had been sent by Coach Wooden to find me. He was to tell me to stop by Coach's office after my afternoon classes. I did have a class that was going to be starting shortly, so I asked the manager why Coach had not given him my lecture hall information to find me. The manager said Coach had given him that information but told him to check the pool hall first.

After class I went directly to Coach's office, curious and nervous. I hoped I wasn't in trouble. I sat down and we talked for a few minutes about school and my plans for the summer. He then got up from behind his desk and came around to hand me a beautiful trophy. It had my name on it. It was the Player Improvement Award, which Coach said was presented to the player who had shown the most all-around improvement in his play and kept a positive attitude. Obviously, there was not going to be an awards banquet if he was summoning us individually. To me, it was a proud moment. I valued receiving that trophy directly from Coach Wooden.

As for my plans for the summer, I knew I did not want to work construction again for my summer employment. If I had learned one lesson from carrying drywall, it was I needed to be a more devoted student because I did not want to work that hard to make a living. So Coach Cunningham got me a job working for Mike Frankovich. Mike had been a football star at UCLA and was now a Hollywood motion picture producer for Columbia Studios. His pictures included *Butterflies Are Free* and *Bob & Carol & Ted & Alice.*

He owned an apartment building in Beverly Hills that he had turned into condos. I worked as an assistant handyman with a retired gentleman named Gus Hardin. I didn't need a ladder to screw in lightbulbs and I had no trouble lifting those unwieldy five-gallon Arrowhead water bottles.

While working for Mike Frankovich, I was able to shoot outdoors at Beverly Hills High School every day during my lunch hour-or-so. I would start and finish each of my shooting workouts by making 10 free throws in a row. My free throw shooting had been horrible. I shot 48 percent as a sophomore and 55 percent as a junior. I was not going to play my last year at UCLA and not improve on that stat. My body was changing, as I added 20 pounds over the summer. I wanted to play more physically inside, and because I added the weight naturally, I didn't lose any quickness or speed. I was even jumping a little bit higher.

CHAPTER 11

The Walton Gang

I went into my senior year at UCLA with great anticipation.

I was a returning starter and I would be surrounded by incredibly talented players. I expected to win another national title, which would be my third, and we were all hoping for another 30–0 perfect season. I was a senior and the team captain and determined to live up to everything that was expected of me.

My ultimate goal, my dream, was to go on to a career in the National Basketball Association, and playing at UCLA meant NBA teams would see me play. We were playing in the franchise city of the Lakers, which meant that not only Lakers personnel, but their visiting opponents would have easy access to our games, plus a lot of our games were nationally televised. I would be on the floor with Bill Walton and certainly the scouts were interested in him. He was the College Player of the Year as a sophomore and his potential was unlimited. No question I would be seen. I realized that the better the team, the better my chances. I needed to be the best I could be in my role.

I knew I had to stay equally focused in the classroom so I could get my degree. Coach Wooden wasn't the only one reminding me of that goal. The importance of getting an education had been preached to me all my life. It was my parents' dream, and I had to make that happen, too.

There would be no senioritis. There was too much work to do, and too much at stake.

At the annual team meeting, I heard everything Coach Wooden said. Not that I hadn't paid attention before, but I knew I was hearing it for the last time, and I knew I needed to get everything exactly right. Dave Meyers, Ralph Drollinger, and Pete Trgovich were all sophomores and would look to me for leadership and as an example. They would be competing for playing time, but they would also be learning the UCLA culture from me, just as I had learned it from Sidney and Curtis.

Jamaal Wilkes and I were once again hotel roommates. Our personalities meshed well both on and off the court, and it helped me that he was relaxed and easygoing before a game, because I was always a little uptight. He often fell asleep after the pregame meal and could even fall asleep on the 10-minute bus ride from the hotel to the arena, then play great and score 30 points! Unbelievable.

Unlike the previous year, when Henry Bibby was the only returning starter, we now had four returning starters and needed to replace only Bibby. Jamaal and I returned at forward, Bill Walton at center, and Greg Lee at point guard. Larry Hollyfield was taking over in place of Bibby at the other guard position.

We opened the season by beating the University of Wisconsin 94–53. Media coverage noted that it was victory #46 in a row. No one had talked about winning streaks the year before, but this was the season we would have the opportunity to beat the record 60-game streak the University of San Francisco had set 16 years earlier with the great K.C. Jones and Bill Russell. In addition to the pressure of repeating as national champions, we had a streak to deal with. The headline for each game we won included its number in the countdown. There was no way to avoid it, or the noise surrounding it.

Coach Wooden didn't talk about the streak until the week before we broke it. He did everything possible to keep us focused on preparing for the next game, and not looking ahead.

Key Games in the Count Down to 61:

Win #47: Bradley University came out in a full-court stall and scored only 10 points in the first half. We had seen this tactic and we were mentally prepared to stay solid on defense and pounce on every mistake. When they finally tried to play us, it was too late. We beat Bradley 73–38.

Win #49: This game was unique in that Coach Wooden had suffered a mild heart attack the week before and was in St. John's Hospital recovering and watching the game on TV. Gary Cunningham coached the 98–67 victory over UC Santa Barbara. Bill was incredible, scoring 30 points on 11-of-13 shooting and grabbing 22 rebounds. With Coach Wooden not there, the reins were not quite as tight and we played with a little more flair. I scored 17 points, including a reverse layup that I spun in off the backboard. By the strictest of Coach Wooden standards, the play was fancy. Clever was good; fancy was bad. On Monday Coach Wooden was at practice, sitting on the sideline with his doctor, who was making sure he worked his way back gradually. During one drill, Tommy Curtis dribbled the ball between his legs and Coach got up and motioned for Coach Cunningham to blow his whistle. After reminding Tommy that "fancy" is not how we did things at UCLA, he told me that the shot I made in the UCSB game was a "Globetrotter play" and those kinds of shots would get me benched. It was the last Globetrotter shot I took.

Win #50: Coach was back for the 89–73 victory over Pittsburgh. Jamaal scored 20 points, Bill 18, and I scored 16. Coach was presented with the *Sports Illustrated* Sportsman of the Year award before 12,500 screaming UCLA fans.

Win #54: We won our first Pac-8 game of the season over Oregon, which came out in a stall. More teams were attempting to keep the score close by limiting our possessions, and we led by only four points at halftime. A quick spurt in the second half was the difference in the game. Jamaal and I led the team in scoring with 14 points each as we won 64–38.

Win #56: We won at Stanford 82–67. Tommy Curtis had moved into the starting lineup, but now he had the flu and Greg Lee was back. Larry Hollyfield, Bill, and I each scored 18 points. When Tommy was starting at point guard, we played faster as a team. With Greg we still had a potent fast break but would more often be in our half-court offense. It was like playing with two different quarterbacks. In Bill's book, *Back From the Dead*, he mentions his preference for playing with Greg and not Tommy, a subject he discussed with Coach many times. Tommy continued to start, making it clear it was Coach Wooden's call.

Win #57: Playing at the University of California was always fun. Their band always marched into the gym playing their fight song as we were warming up. The place was always packed, and my favorite part was when we got the lead and silenced their noisy students. We won this game 69–50, and I scored 18 points, as did Jamaal. Bill had 14 and 18 rebounds. While the game was in progress and we had the ball, Swen Nater leaned down to tie his shoe. Cal forward John Coughran snuck up behind him to reach down and untie Swen's other shoe. Swen straightened up—with both shoes untied—and pushed Coughran out of bounds with a forearm. Since Coughran was supposed to be guarding me, I saw the whole thing. Coughran and I were laughing, Swen was fuming, and no one else even noticed, because there was never a break in the action. The mini drama lasted no more than five seconds.

After this game Coach Wooden spoke publicly, for the first time, about what he had told the team regarding the streak. He said that, yes, he had in fact mentioned it, but just to caution us about not looking ahead. Then he surprised everyone by saying that if we were going to lose a game, he wanted it to be one of the next four games, all against nonconference opponents.

Next up for us was the team that owned the streak, USF. That was causing a surge of interest. Coach was, effectively, easing the pressure of the streak by putting it in a different perspective. Winning 61 games in a row would be a monumental accomplishment, but it was more important for us to win the league and get into the NCAA tournament.

Win #58: This game was a 92–64 victory over the University of San Francisco, the team that had set the record at 60 straight wins in 1956. USF was having a great year and came in with a record of 12–1. This game was tougher than the final score indicated. Bill had

22 points and 22 rebounds. I scored 15 points and Jamaal scored 13.

Win #59: Providence University had two superstars, Marvin "Bad News" Barnes and Ernie DiGregorio. It was an up-tempo game with plenty of play above the rim, and I spent some time guarding DiGregorio, who was an All-American point guard. Because I was taller it was difficult for him to shoot over me, but he had a lot of shifty moves. He wound up with 21 points on 9–18 shooting. We held Barnes to just 12 points. Bill almost had a triple double with 18 points, 24 rebounds, and eight assists. I wound up with a game high 21 points; Larry Hollyfield 18; Jamaal 17. We won 101–77. It proved to be our only 100-point game in this season.

Win #60: This game at Loyola of Chicago might have been the worst game we played all season because we were emotionally flat. Loyola had only an 8–5 record, and we were probably looking ahead to playing Notre Dame on national television to break the record. It took Bill having a phenomenal game to overcome our 27 turnovers. Bill scored 32 points and had 27 rebounds. Jamaal added 16 points. We won 87–73.

In 1998, I became the head coach at Loyola. UCLA basketball came up many times in conversation with fans over the six years I was there, but I was rarely asked about this game that tied the all-time collegiate win streak record, and I never brought it up.

Win #61: It seemed fitting that the basketball gods would make the Notre Dame game the 61st contest to break the record. Only Hollyfield and I had played in South Bend two years earlier in the last game UCLA had lost. That put us at ground zero to start this streak. How fitting was it to break the record on Notre Dame's court? I remember waking up in South Bend on game day and turning on the television. Coach Digger Phelps' TV show was on and he was talking about how they would defend our team. He went through our personnel and when he got to me, he said that they weren't going to concentrate on me at all. I was already motivated, and that comment sharpened my focus.

Notre Dame was going to play a zone defense, and really pack it in around Bill. Their focus on keeping the ball away from Bill gave the rest of us some easy scoring opportunities, especially me. I was getting great shot opportunities both in transition and on midrange jump shots. The game was physical and chippy. When Notre Dame played man-to-man, I was guarded by Peter Crotty. A big part of my game was crashing the offensive boards. Crotty knew this, and on one very physical exchange when Bill took a shot and missed, he literally boxed me out, all the way out of bounds. As we turned to run back down the floor we swore at each other and I tried to elbow him in the chest. The anger and adrenaline pumping through me caused me to throw the elbow higher than I intended and I popped him right in the nose.

On defense, I was guarding Gary Brokaw, a smooth-scoring off guard, so I sprinted toward him. Hollyfield (Holly) was guarding Crotty, and when Crotty finally got down to the other end of the court, Holly laughed about his bloody nose. Holly and Crotty started jawing at each other and the referee blew the whistle. When Coach Wooden saw Holly up in the face of a guy with a bloody nose, he assumed that Holly had hit him and took him out of the game. Our bench was at the other end of the floor, but I could hear Holly telling Coach, "I didn't hit him, Farm hit him!" I, of course, said nothing. Later in the game, Crotty would return the favor with an elbow to my solar plexus. We had a sizable lead, and I was playing well on national TV, so I laughed and said, "That was a good one." We had no more issues.

Late in the game, Bill missed a shot and Jamaal and I went up for the rebound along with several Notre Dame defenders. I got a solid hand on the ball and tipped it in. The announcer said: "Basket by Wilkes." It wasn't Jamaal's fault, but that basket made him the game's leading scorer with 20 points. Bill and I both had 16. But I managed a team high 19 shots. Thank you, Coach Phelps. I was happier that we had beaten Notre Dame than I was about winning 61 straight games. There was no doubt in my mind that we would keep winning, but this would be my last time playing in South Bend. Final score: UCLA 82, Notre Dame 63.

Sports Illustrated had sent Curry Kirkpatrick to cover the win streak. Whether we failed in our attempt to win 61 straight games or succeeded, the magazine would be there to document this historic event. Kirkpatrick spent about a month with us, and Coach Wooden reminded us to be on alert in answering his questions.

One of his questions to me was about how I dressed to go to games. He said some students had told him about my two-tone shoes with gangster hats and suede jackets. This was the mod fashion era, and Curry joked that it was rumored I rented clothes for the weekend. He scheduled a photo shoot on campus to get me in one of my game day outfits, and joining me was Hollyfield, wearing his letterman jacket.

Kirkpatrick wanted to come to my residence to interview me, but I politely declined because I didn't want to explain the guest house and I wanted to respect the Marcus family's privacy. We did the interview on a Sunday morning at Sam's house, and even included the car washing. I thought the interview went well but I was uneasy when he asked me to tell him something that was not fun about playing at UCLA. It seemed to me like he was digging for something negative.

Curry was actually pretty cool most of time, but he was still a reporter, and we would not let him penetrate the inner circle of this close-knit basketball team. The players would compare notes on our conversations with him.

When the win streak was broken, we were all eager to see the *Sports Illustrated* coverage. On the cover was a picture of Bill getting a rebound in the Notre Dame game. Hollyfield and Wilkes were also in that picture. After admiring the cover, I flipped through the pages to see what pictures they used of me, but there were none in this article about "The Record Breaking Walton Gang." I was the only starter not pictured anywhere. I was quoted in the article and there were statements made about me, so at least readers would know that I was on the team. I was crushed.

Kirkpatrick wrote about the elbowing incident with Peter Crotty, and also wrote that when the team arrived back in Chicago (by bus from South Bend) we all sneaked off and got drunk before we boarded the plane to L.A. Not true. We were flying back first class on a 747, and the entire upstairs area of the plane was at our disposal. I did, very quietly, because it was against team rules, have my first celebratory beer somewhere over Iowa.

It was maybe a week later that I received a letter from Kirkpatrick with some 8 × 10 glossies from the photo shoot. He wrote that I had been edited out and he wished me luck in the future. By then I was over it. My focus was needed elsewhere.

We were back to league play and getting better every day. From here on, every game added to the record streak.

January was coming to an end, and that meant my senior season had reached its halfway point. My birthday was January 31, falling between the Notre Dame game and the USC game. On the 31st, while everyone was getting ready for practice, Bill announced that after training table we would all meet at his place to celebrate my birthday. I told him that I had plans to go out to dinner with my girlfriend, Joyce. Bill said I didn't have to stay long so I could do both.

Practice ended precisely at 5:30, as always. We all hustled through showers, dressing, and training table and headed to Bill's place.

Bill lived in a fraternity house just off campus. Social unrest and antiestablishment feelings had led to the decline of participation in the Greek system (and, unfortunately, programs like ROTC). Bill had a huge room, and a stereo system with speakers to match. When I walked in, there were already about six of my teammates there, and Walton was blasting the paint off the walls with some Rolling Stones. I asked him about his neighbors. He said he had warned them and, besides, he played his music like this all the time.

Nobody sang Happy Birthday, but there was cold beer and wine. We were about an hour into this impromptu party when I realized it was time for me to leave. It was a great way to start off my birthday celebration, and I really did appreciate Bill's gesture.

Win #62: Our next game was at the Sports Arena against archrival USC. The Trojans had two really good sophomores on their team—Gus Williams and Clint Chapman. Clint was from Denver and we both had attended Manual High School and though we weren't teammates, we knew each other. I scored 16 points in the game and was, for the first time, named Southern California Basketball Writers Association's college player of the week. Bill was nothing short of spectacular against USC. He made 10 of his 12 shots and had 17 rebounds. Jamaal had 14 points and Hollyfield added 10. When we had balanced scoring the opposition had no chance.

A highlight for me in that game was shooting a technical foul free throw at the end of the first half. I had been concentrating on free throws after shooting 55 percent from the line the year before. Through the first eight games of this season, I had made 18 of 21 (86 percent). So it was a big moment for me when Coach Wooden sent me to the line. I was the only player on the court and I shot facing the USC student body, which was booing like crazy. I swished the shot and smiled at the crowd. We won 79–56.

Counting the nonconference games at Loyola of Chicago and Notre Dame, the game against USC at the Sports Arena, and our games up north against Washington and Washington State, we had five straight games on the road. Every venue was packed and every crowd deafening at the start of the game.

George Raveling, the Pac-8's only African American coach, was in his first year at Washington State. He was an excellent coach and terrific recruiter, but he didn't know what was coming to Pullman when the Bruins arrived. We led at halftime 34–18, so the game was essentially over. Coach cleared the bench in the second half. We shot 56 percent as a team and outrebounded WSU by 25. (Raveling would later become a coaching mentor of mine as well as a competitor and friend.) We then headed over to Seattle, where we played a much closer game, winning 76–67. Walton and I each had a double double in the game. For Bill it was one of a zillion, but my 13 points and 13 rebounds would be the only double double of my senior year.

By a strange quirk of the schedule, we would return home to play both Washington schools again. We won both games easily.

On February 22, 1973, we were *back* on the road headed to

Oregon. The Oregon Ducks had become known as the Kamakaze Kids. Second year Coach Dick Harter preached tough, in-your-face, hardnosed defense. Their gym was called The Pit, and the Oregon student body was nasty and noisy. The Pit had the reputation of being the toughest place to play in the league. The student section loved being called "insane" and did everything they could to intimidate visiting teams. We had beaten Oregon by 26 points in L.A. when they tried holding the ball. There would be no stall this time. Oregon would play, and the game was a brawl. Coach Wooden called it a "wrestling match" in the newspaper. Players on our team were getting undercut on layups and knocked to the floor and hacked. In general, they were trying to beat us up. Swen Nater, our backup center, got some "tough minutes" in this game.

Nater had been playing against Bill Walton every day in practice, and for all intents and purposes, was the second-best big man in the country. He would never start a game at UCLA but would be a first-round NBA draft choice and would play in the NBA for 12 years. A 6-foot-11 pick-and-pop center, Swen was physical and strong and could really shoot. Whenever games got physical, Coach would play our two enforcers at the same time to get things calmed back down. Our two toughest players were Holly and Swen.

When we had won 72–61 and were running off the floor, the Oregon student section was still in a frenzy. To get to the tunnel that led downstairs to an old rickety visiting team's locker room, we had to get through a mob of angry fans. Ushers and security guards stood arm in arm to provide a human pathway for us. I politely raised both middle fingers and waved goodbye to them, as I would never be going back there again. Yes, I flipped off all those idiots.

Three years later I would return to The Pit as a first-year assistant coach at UCLA on Coach Gene Bartow's staff. I clearly remembered the two birds I had waved at the students, but I hoped that the students who had been there then had graduated.

We would beat Cal and Stanford at home to win the Pac-8 championship once again. That guaranteed us a place in the NCAA tournament.

Our last conference game was at home against USC and we had our Senior Night ceremony before the game. My parents had decided that they could not afford to go to Los Angeles for Senior Night as well as to St. Louis for the Final Four so they had to choose. We were fully confident that UCLA would play in the Final Four and I wanted my parents to be there. I asked Rose and Sam Gilbert to walk with me to center court for the Senior Night ceremony.

The Western Regionals were going to be played in Pauley Pavilion. And of course, the first thing that came to my mind, besides winning, was selling my tickets. None of our preparation or routine would change. The first two rounds of the NCAA tournament would be no different from a typical weekend playing two games at home. It gave us a tremendous advantage which, to be honest, we didn't need.

We opened the tournament playing Arizona State University. A win against them would likely put us on course to play Long Beach State for the fourth year in a row. (My third.) The Long Beach State players were already talking about getting revenge for their previous defeats at our hands in the Regional Finals. Their opening game was

WHERE'S MY JACKET?

In 2010, I was an assistant coach at the University of Hawaii. We had flown to Los Angeles to connect with a flight to a game in Boise, and were waiting at our gate when three gentlemen walked up and said they recognized me from my years at UCLA. Some of the players on our Hawaii team started to tease me about being a legend. One of them told me he was from Oregon, and his father had taken him to watch UCLA play at both Oregon State and the University of Oregon when was he was a kid. He told me I was his favorite player. I thanked him and asked if he perhaps had me confused with Jamaal Wilkes. It was a pleasant visit, and they went on their way.

A few minutes later my "fan" came back and asked to speak to me privately. His eyes filled with tears as he told me that something had been weighing on his heart for over 30 years. He confessed that while UCLA was warming up before a game at The against USF, a team we had beaten earlier and a team they shouldn't take lightly.

From the opening tip of the Arizona State game, Hollyfield was on fire! He was hitting jump shots, driving for layups and "dropping dimes" for unbelievable assists. He wound up scoring 18 (of UCLA's 51) points in the first half. It was vintage Holly. We had seen him get hot like this before. When Holly was in his groove, it was showtime! Unfortunately, Holly cooled off at halftime, and when the second half started, he missed a couple of tough shots similar to the ones he was draining in the first half. Coach Wooden pulled him immediately. I remember thinking that Coach wanted to get his attention and would put him back in. But the longer Holly sat, the more we all started to realize that his minutes the rest of this game were going to be very limited. Holly wound up scoring 20 points in the game to go with Bill's 28. We won 98–61.

Holly was really upset after the game, and I felt awful for him. At times, his basketball relationship with Coach Wooden was kind of like his play in the Arizona State game. Really good or really cold,

Pit in 1973, he stole my warm-up jacket off the bench. I had no recollection of losing a jacket. We always traveled with an extra uniform, so I probably used a backup jacket that night and for the rest of the season. He told me that he had taken good care of the jacket, which was in his brother's storage unit in Colorado. I awkwardly assured him that I harbored no ill will and was happy to let him keep the jacket. He, however, believed it was God's plan to bring us together; that he had thought many times about how he could return the jacket to me. He said he was a born-again Christian and he wanted to return it. I gave him my contact information, and a short time later my jacket arrived by mail. My jersey number, 54, was stitched on the inside label at the back of the neck. It was authentic. It truly was in excellent condition! I sat for a moment, choked up, thinking that the Lord does work in mysterious ways. One of those Oregon fans had happened through my life again, after 37 years, to deliver a piece of the past that he had carefully preserved.

with not a lot in between. Coach Wooden loved Hollyfield as a person, but their basketball relationship was tricky at best.

Long Beach State faced off against the University of San Francisco with two-time All-American Ed Ratleff going into the game with an injured hand. Early in the game he jammed his fingers on the other hand. As a result, Ed didn't play well, but the USF guards did. Mike Quick and Phil Smith combined for 45 points. San Francisco beat Long Beach State 77–67 in what the media called an upset. We knew it was more of an even match.

For the first time of my varsity career, we would have an opponent other than Long Beach State in the Regional Final.

We went into the USF game respecting them. It was almost like playing a conference team for the second time. Something else Coach Wooden preached was: Respect your opponent, but don't fear your opponent.

It was a close game in the first half but we got a nice boost from our bench in the second half, particularly from Tommy and sophomore David Meyers. Meyers was a 6-foot-8 whirling dervish of energy. He was a tremendous athlete destined for greatness at UCLA. At one practice early in the season I went up high above the rim to get a rebound. A long white arm took the rebound from me, right over the top. I assumed it was Bill. No one else on the team could outjump me, and sometimes Bill couldn't. I was surprised it was not Bill who took that rebound from me, but Meyers.

We held USF to just 17 points in the second half and won the game 54–39. I led the team in scoring with 13 points, Jamaal and Tommy each had 12. I stayed on the court for a television interview after the game so I was alone as I walked off the Pauley Pavilion court for the last time as a UCLA player, and I suddenly felt sad. When I went into our locker room and sat in front of my locker, everyone was laughing and happy, with the noticeable exception of the two seniors, me and Hollyfield. We were both happy that we were heading into the Final Four, but Holly's playing time was once again limited and he didn't score in the game. I was sad for him. I also was sad that my collegiate career was two games away from being over.

The Final Four was in St. Louis, and my mother and father were really excited. This was the first time since high school that my mom and dad would see me play in person. Sam was, of course, going to the championship games, and he was excited about meeting them. He asked me if my brother Aubrey was coming to St. Louis. (Sam had met my 13-year-old brother when he visited me in the summer.) I told Sam that Aubrey would be staying in Denver with our grandmother, because my parents could not afford three airline tickets. Sam offered to fly my brother out, with the understanding that when I signed my pro basketball contract, I would pay him back. He made that same deal with me regarding Joyce. Sam wanted me to be surrounded by the people who were important to me. I was sophisticated enough not to tell the coaching staff, because I knew that by the strictest of NCAA rules, this was not kosher. But this was no attempt to beat the system or give UCLA some unfair recruiting advantage. Sam merely wanted my family to be with me.

Despite what critics may have said about Sam, my relationship with him was not about breaking rules. He was really like a second father to me. He was, at his core and in his heart, a philanthropist. He loved helping people. I drove to Century City and bought some blue suede pants and an unbelievable gray sport coat with some of my ticket money. My last outfit was going to be a memorable one. We played a tough Indiana team coached by Bob Knight in our semifinal game. This team featured a young Quinn Buckner, who Coach Wooden had recruited out of high school. We expected a tough and physical game, but we were having our way with them and led by 18 at halftime. We led by as many as 22 points in the second half but got sloppy and allowed Indiana to trim that huge lead to just two points. Tommy saved the day, hitting shots from everywhere.

At one point in the second half, I heard Coach yell, "No! No Larry, Gracious Sakes Alive!" and then he sat me on the bench. I was not playing very well on either end of the floor. When he called my name and I ran up to see who I was going in for he asked me if I had regrouped mentally and could return to my old self. Coach Wooden never hesitated to get on me, but nothing like this had ever happened, and certainly not to this degree! The tone in his voice was full of absolute concern for whether I was going to pick it up and play better. That concern in his voice lit a fire under me and I picked up my play. We beat Indiana 70–59. Tommy had come off the bench to lead us in scoring with 22 points.

The practices between games at the Final Four were always interesting. Each team was given a 45-minute block of time to practice at the site of the competition. During the last practice of the season, Coach would allow us to *dunk* in *one* drill only, the final drill. It was absolutely hysterical. The team loved it! My last dunk was a 360 degree with the ball behind my head! A 10 in my opinion!

Memphis State had beaten Providence in the other semifinal game. Memphis State had a terrific basketball team. They also had two Larrys—Larry Finch and Larry Kenon. They had beaten Providence in the semifinal. The Memphis State head coach was "Clean" Gene Bartow, a soft-spoken Southern gentleman who was called clean because of the way he ran his basketball program. At his pregame news conference, Coach Bartow talked about playing an up-tempo game. That was exactly the kind of game we wanted to play. When the game started, Memphis was in a 1-2-2 zone defense. Hollyfield opened with a long jump shot to put us ahead, 2–0. It was a fast-paced game, and we were tied at halftime. I remember thinking I hadn't gotten many shot opportunities. A lot of my manufactured offense was getting to the offensive board to rebound missed shots. Because Bill was on the left side of the basket, when he shot and "missed long," those would come over to where I was. Also, if Jamaal missed the shot from the free throw line area (where he usually was against a zone defense) the ball either hit the front of the rim or came off to the right, and once again that's where I was. But there weren't many misses, certainly not from Bill's side.

Memphis State hit its first shot of the second half to go up by two points, but Bill was on an unbelievable roll! Between Holly throwing the ball over the defense to Bill from the left side of the court, or Greg Lee doing the same thing from the top of the key, Bill was simply on fire. (At one point I believe he missed a shot but got his own rebound and scored anyway!) We would take control in the second half and go on to win the championship game 87–66.

Bill scored 44 points in that game, but even more amazing was his shooting percentage. Official stats had him 21 of 22 from the field, and he tipped in his only miss. He told me years later he considers himself 24 of 25 in that game because three baskets were "taken away from him" for offensive basket interference.

His performance remains one of the most outstanding in NCAA tournament history.

When Coach Wooden took me out of the game with just a few minutes remaining, he gave me a hug and I thanked him for giving me this unbelievable opportunity and for being my coach.

Then I was congratulated by the assistant coaches. Moving further down the bench, I was giving skin to each of my teammates. I was at the end of the bench and about to get some water when I noticed a little bit of a commotion in the stands. It was my mother talking to one of the security guards stationed at about the 15th row behind our bench. A bunch of UCLA fans were talking to him, too, and pointing at me. The security guard stepped aside, allowing my mother to walk down the stairs and approach our bench. I met my mother on the other side and she gave me the biggest hug! Truly a very special moment in my life. (Eight years later, in my first year as UCLA head coach, a photographer who was at that game sent me a picture of that hug.)

After the postgame ceremonies—cutting down the nets, handing out both the runner up and championship watches, etc.—I took my brother into the locker room. For a few minutes, I even let him wear my championship net around his neck.

For the second straight year we were 30–0. As fast as my UCLA career had begun, it was over. I was on the varsity for three years, and we won three national championships. This was the seventh national championship in a row for the Bruins. In my three years, I experienced only one loss in 90 games. I left the streak at 75 straight wins.

For the first time, I kept a championship watch and a championship ring.

CHAPTER 12

The Cleveland Cavaliers

The National Basketball Association draft was April 24, 1973, which was a Tuesday. The American Basketball Association draft was the next day, Wednesday. That's how it was done in those days. Two different leagues; two different draft days.

I was hoping it might help that I was named an Honorable Mention All-American by both the AP and UPI news organizations, probably as a consequence of being undefeated and on a national championship basketball team two years in a row.

I went to class the morning of the NBA draft, then drove back to the guest house to await a call from Sam. There was no ESPN in 1973 so there was no televised selection show. You just had to wait until the team contacted your agent, and of course Sam was representing me. As time went by, I was painfully aware that I had not been selected in an early round. Sam eventually called to tell me I was selected in the seventh round by the Cleveland Cavaliers, and told me not to be discouraged, that we would wait to see where I was in the ABA draft. The next day I was selected in the fifth round by my hometown team, the Denver Rockets. Now we would wait to hear the offers. I was thrilled to have been drafted, but I knew that such a low choice would mean an uphill battle.

Sam had several conversations with both the Cavaliers and the Rockets, and when negotiations were complete, I was summoned. I was drafted higher by Denver, but financially had a better opportunity with Cleveland. If I made the Cavs' roster, I would make $30,000, and somehow Sam had also negotiated an additional $10,000 signing bonus. It was unheard of for a guy drafted as low as I was to get any signing bonus, much less 10 grand! Sam asked me if I wanted to know how he had gotten that deal. I laughed and said no.

I did know that when the check arrived at Sam's office, it was very real. I went by campus photography and found a nice action photo of me. I signed it and wrote a very appreciative message to Papa Sam, thus paying for his negotiations as all the other UCLA players he represented paid. My autographed picture would go on his wall.

After Sam's negotiations, the contract and money management were turned over to a lawyer, either Ralph Shapiro or Fred Slaughter. Unlike Sam, those lawyers charged money! I knew both Fred and Ralph from UCLA events and from functions with Sam. Fred Slaughter was smart and cool and we clicked right away. He had played basketball on UCLA's 1964 undefeated championship team and he was assistant dean of the UCLA law school. Fred was a good man, and he would become a very good friend and advisor to me.

In early May, Coach Wooden informed me that I had been invited to try out for a USA All-Star team made up of college players and members of the various branches of the armed forces. Tryouts would be at the Presidio military base in San Francisco. The team would play in South America for about three weeks.

Coach Wooden told me he believed that I could make the team, but he expressed his concern that missing a month of school would put passing my spring quarter classes in jeopardy. I was only four classes away from graduating.

Assistant Coach Gary Cunningham told me that my best course of action would be to withdraw from school. He said I could still "walk" with my class at the graduation ceremony, and I could make up those classes later. Before Coach Wooden would give me his permission—more correctly his blessing—to go, he made me promise that I would enroll in the summer session.

At the Presidio I competed with about 20 other collegiate/military guys and I made the roster. Also on this team was University of San Francisco guard Mike Quick. I spent a lot of time with him in South America. We were a decent basketball team and I enjoyed playing with this mix of talent. It was like playing in a well-organized pickup game with guys from vastly different age groups and life experiences. We played three games in São Paulo, then flew to Rio de Janeiro to play three more games. There was plenty of time for sightseeing. Whether it was going to Sugarloaf Mountain on a cable car or walking the Copacabana Beach, Brazil was amazing! The trip to take a picture in front of the statue of Christ the Redeemer was unbelievable.

There was another proposal for international travel that summer. The USSR invited our 1973 team to play some exhibition games in Moscow, which would have been the first trip of its kind. Each of us was asked his interest in going, and I told Coach Wooden I thought it would be a great opportunity. A couple of my teammates wanted to know if haircuts would be required, considering the trip would be in the offseason. Coach said those standards would apply because we would be representing UCLA as well as the USA. Haircuts apparently tipped the scale. We didn't go.

When I returned from South America, I decided that I would go down to Beverly Hills Cadillac to consider one day purchasing a new Eldorado Cadillac. There was absolutely no way Sam was going to let me squander any of my signing bonus on a car but I'd never had that much money, and I just wanted to experience what it was like going into a new car dealership to look around. I wore a suit and tie, my shoes were shined, and I had money in the bank. I walked into the show room, and the automobiles were magnificent. I looked at a Fleetwood, a Coupe Deville, and of course an Eldorado. (In the neighborhood we called the Eldorado an L-Dog.) I had been there for quite a while when it dawned on me that no one had come up to offer to help me. The dealership wasn't that busy, and the more I looked around, the more I saw salesmen, white salesmen, essentially standing around not taking my presence seriously. I eventually walked over to one of the salesmen and started a conversation about pricing and extras. He seemed to make an effort to be polite but at best was indifferent toward me. It didn't take me long to catch on that the salesmen didn't think I could afford to be in there so they would waste no time on me. I walked out demoralized.

This reality check was both humbling and humiliating, and I would never forget it.

At the end of the school year I did participate in graduation ceremonies. I was the first in the family to graduate from college. Grandma Ida Farmer, who was in her 80s, had never been on an airplane, so her first flight had purpose. She flew with my parents and Aunt Ola to see me march into Drake Stadium in a cap and gown. There was no way I would not finish those four classes.

I left Los Angeles for rookie camp in great physical and mental shape. I had worked out for the remainder of the summer and played in some very competitive pickup games. When I arrived in Cleveland there were 16 other rookies in training camp. Bill Fitch, the Cavaliers' head coach, told us the franchise was three years old and was built largely on draft choices. Among the rookies were first-round draft pick Jim Brewer from Minnesota, Alan Hornyak and Luke Witte from Ohio State, and John Coughran from Cal.

At our first rookie camp meeting, Fitch had us fill out a questionnaire to help the staff get to know us better. One question asked for a story about something funny that happened during a college game. Coughran looked at me and we both started laughing. We both wrote about the Cal game when he enraged Swen Nater by untying his shoe.

Rookie camp was held on the campus of Lakeland Community College in Mentor, Ohio, and culminated with a scrimmage played in front of fans and media. We were housed in a dorm. There were two practices every day consisting of drill work and a scrimmage. I could tell right away that my fundamentals were far superior to the other rookies. I was scoring like crazy. I knew I was one of the best rookies in camp. I was one of the leading scorers in the game that wrapped up camp. Coach Fitch told me exactly that when he invited me back to veteran camp. The majority of the rookies were released.

Jim Brewer and I had become buddies. Unlike my "make the team" contract, his contract was guaranteed so he already had a Lincoln Continental in Cleveland. I would hang out with him as he drove around looking for a place to live and buying furniture.

I returned to Los Angeles feeling confident. I never stopped training, so I was still in excellent shape when I flew back for veterans camp. Coach Fitch brought only four rookies back: Brewer, Hornyak, Witte, and me. Rookies and veterans alike were assigned rooms at the Holiday Inn in downtown Cleveland.

Meeting the veterans was cool but intimidating. My former UCLA teammate, Steve Patterson, was a third-year player for the Cavaliers, so I had a veteran to show me the ropes. Austin Carr was also on the team. I didn't know him well, but obviously we remembered each other from the UCLA-Notre Dame matchups. Lenny Wilkins was in his 13th season and was already an NBA legend. He would later be inducted into the Naismith Hall of Fame as a player and as a coach. He was again slotted to be the starting point guard. I heard Fitch ask Lenny for his opinion many times. One of the players who extended his friendship was one I was competing against for a roster spot. Bobby "Bingo" Smith, a phenomenal shooter, was in his fourth year with the Cavaliers, and was a fan favorite. When he put up a shot the crowd shouted "BINGO!" as if it had already gone in. Bobby picked me up one Sunday and took me to a park where he flew his remote-controlled airplanes. Many of the veterans made me feel at home, and some treated me like I was already a teammate. Others kept their distance, avoiding getting attached to someone who might be headed for disappointment.

The competition at veteran camp was much tougher than rookie camp. There was a lot more to learn, and the players were obviously bigger, faster, and stronger. These veterans had lots of experience, but I competed well and more than held my own. The Cleveland newspaper, The Plain Dealer, published an article about me with the headline, "No shot a long shot." The article said I was a pleasant surprise and playing well, but it stressed that I was not a long-distance shooter. That was true, but I had no problem scoring against the Cavs' veterans. The skill set the Cavaliers were looking for would determine whether I made the team. I was kept on the roster when veteran camp ended, which once again was a good sign. Several of the veterans were released.

There was just one more cut to survive. I didn't play much in our first exhibition game, which was in Buffalo. In Detroit, where former UCLA teammate Curtis Rowe was the starting power forward, I got in the game early and played very well. I was one of the leading scorers in the game.

In Kansas City, where the star was Nate "Tiny" Archibald, I got to play quite a bit. At one point I switched off the small forward I was guarding to Archibald. It was early enough in the shot clock that he had time to continue dribbling the ball, break my ankles by using one of his signature moves, and score an easy basket. Archibald knew he had a mismatch. But for some reason he decided to pass the ball and continue running the offense instead of attacking. I quickly started screaming "switch back, switch back" so I could get back to a guy that I was certainly more comfortable guarding. I played well in the time I was given.

Our last exhibition game was against the Rockets in Houston. Houston had Rudy Tomjanovich and Calvin Murphy. Their No. 1 draft choice that year was my old nemesis, Ed Ratleff. I didn't get as many minutes as in the two previous games. It was just a matter of waiting for the final cut on the day before the NBA season began.

The next morning I got a call from assistant coach Jimmy Rodgers telling me Coach Fitch needed to talk to me. This was going to be either really good or really bad. Rodgers was in the lobby of the hotel in downtown Cleveland, waiting to drive me to the arena, which was about five minutes away.

I walked into Coach Fitch's office and sat down. He had a "serious business" look on his face. He said the Cavs were releasing me. I would not be on the final roster. He said I had performed well and had two great camps. In any of the previous three years the franchise had existed, he said, I probably would have made the team, but they were already three deep at the small forward position. All three players had no-cut contracts and years of NBA experience. (Bingo Smith had four years; Fred Foster five; Barry Clemens eight.) Other than Jim Brewer, the only other rookie to make the Cavaliers that season was Witte, a 7-foot center.

During the conversation, Fitch told me that Coach Wooden had called him at least once a week since rookie camp to check on my progress. He also told me that Coach had kept a part-time position on his coaching staff open for me in case I did not win a roster spot with the Cavs. I was aware of the graduate assistant (GA) spot being held open. It was the middle of October, and although school had started, the college basketball season was not yet underway. Coach Fitch told me he never had a college coach call to check on one of his players as often as Coach Wooden had called about me. I was so devastated by the news that I had been cut that what Fitch told me about Coach Wooden's concern didn't register until later.

Fitch said his secretary would make arrangements for me to fly back to Los Angeles. I thanked him and we shook hands. I went back to the hotel and called my parents to let them know. Then I called Papa Sam. He knew. He told me that he had already received a call from Alex Hannum, coach of the Denver Rockets. Coach Hannum had told Sam that they would offer me the league minimum, which was $18,000, but I would need to get to Denver as soon as possible to try to earn a roster spot. It was gratifying to know that another pro basketball team was interested in me. I might have had a better chance of making the Rockets' roster, but there was no way I could handle the emotional toll if I were to be cut again. I knew that I had played as well as I possibly could in Cleveland. I told Sam to politely decline the invitation.

I flew back to Los Angeles two days before the NBA season opened on Friday. Brad Marcus had told me when I first left for Cleveland that he hoped I would make the team but if not, and I needed a place to stay for a while, I could remain in the guest house. I was depressed and stayed quiet for a couple of days. I called Coach Wooden the day the NBA season started to say that if the GA coaching position was still open, I would like to take it. Coach said it was, and that I needed to come in as soon as possible to start.

A new documentary film had just been released about Jimi Hendrix and was playing in Westwood. I needed something to boost my spirits and was anxious to escape my reality. I sat through that film four times over the weekend. I thought it would help me and it did. Classes at UCLA had already started, so it was too late to enroll. Instead, I enrolled in two morning classes at Santa Monica City College, planning to take two classes at UCLA the next quarter. Then I'd be finished. Now, I would start learning how to coach.

CHAPTER 13

On the Outside Looking In

Everything about returning to UCLA after being cut by the Cavaliers was awkward and humbling.

Former teammates didn't know how to greet me. If they said they were happy to see me or glad to have me back, that was like saying they were glad I had failed in the NBA. Should they offer condolences? That's not much of a welcome. It was uncomfortable for all of us.

There was no office space in the athletic department for a graduate assistant coach, so I had to sit on the couch in the reception area as if I were a visitor when I showed up for work every day at 2 P.M. Coach Frank Arnold was the head JV coach. My first coaching assignment was as his assistant, so when he came out of his office and gave me the JV practice plan for the day, I'd copy it onto a 3 × 5 card and head down to the floor early.

That timing worked because I needed to dress for practice early, and I didn't really have a locker room since there was no extra space in the small coaches' locker room in Pauley Pavilion. Nor did I have a locker, obviously, in the players' locker room anymore. I did have a locker with the JV players, but I was a coach, so I didn't belong in their space, either. I would get to practice early and leave late to avoid getting in anybody's way. It was awkward.

Playing basketball every day had been my life for the previous eight years, and not playing left a huge void. It had always been easy to find top competition in pickup games, but in October the pros had reported back to their teams and the colleges had started practice. I tried playing in the pickup games I could find, and I even briefly considered an intramural team, but those players considered me a ringer.

I eventually filled the need for physical activity by studying ka-rate. Some days, I would go to the beginners' class in the morning, attend my classes at Santa Monica City College, grab something to eat on my way to UCLA for JV practice, skip training table, and drive back to Sherman Oaks and train again.

Karate required concentration, which took my mind off basket-ball and helped my self-confidence and self-esteem. Karate and my tight schedule helped me stay focused.

I did not take my part-time job lightly, because I knew it for what it was—an opportunity.

Freshman eligibility was only a year old and was problematic for the Bruins. All UCLA players were highly recruited and going there meant taking a big risk. When freshmen were ineligible for varsity competition, they were all guaranteed playing time on the fresh-man team, but with this change freshmen had to deal with thinking themselves a failure if they were playing on JV their first year.

All five recruits that season were high school All-Americans. Coach Wooden rotated three very talented scholarship freshmen between the varsity and the junior varsity—guard Jimmy Spillane, power forward Wilbert Olinde, and wing Gavin Smith, so Coach Arnold and I never knew when we would have any of these guys. It made both practice and game preparation challenging.

Coach Arnold was quick to correct the walk-on players, sternly if necessary, but the scholarship players he handled more gently. I grew to understand he did not want them to become so unhappy that they would think about quitting or transferring.

When Spillane first came back down to the JV team it was obvi-ous he wasn't happy. I tried to encourage him, saying that playing at any level was better than sitting on the bench. He told me: "I would rather sit on the varsity bench and never play in a game all year, than to play one minute on the JV team." Not the conversation I was trying to have.

I knew the time would come when Coach Arnold would travel with the varsity and leave me in charge of the JV team. When that time came, I knew how to deal with the egos.

The two freshmen who were of immediate use to the varsity were Marques Johnson, the Los Angeles Player of the Year, and Richard Washington, a 6-foot-11 center/forward from Portland who had been one of the most sought-after recruits in the country. Marques really stood out to me because he was an amazing athlete, smart, and great-looking, plus they had given him my old number, 54. When you added those two freshmen to returning starters Bill Walton and Jamaal Wilkes, 7-foot-2 backup sophomore center Ralph Drollinger, and the very talented David Meyers, who had gained varsity experience at power forward the year before, it could be argued that this was the most talented front line (all six future NBA players) ever to play at UCLA.

This team had a different vibe. Keeping a clean-cut appearance, fundamentals, great conditioning, and teamwork were still the pillars of the program, but there were some new characteristics. Bill, Greg, and Tommy were practicing transcendental meditation (TM) and vegetarianism. I know the coaches were concerned about how vegetarianism might impact stamina and physical strength. Still, the varsity team reeled off 13 straight wins to start the season.

By the middle of January when the Bruins traveled to Notre Dame, the winning streak was at 88 straight games. UCLA led most of the way and still had an 11-point lead with three minutes and 30 seconds on the clock. From that point on, UCLA went scoreless while Notre Dame scored 12 straight points. UCLA got five shot attempts off before the final buzzer, but none of them fell and we lost by one point. The streak that had started after a loss at Notre Dame, the only loss in my UCLA career, had now ended at Notre Dame.

I took that loss a lot harder than I thought I would. The biggest chunk of that streak, 75 straight wins, took place during my three years. A part of me still felt attached to it.

UCLA had five straight easy wins before losing at Oregon State and at Oregon. *Sports Illustrated* called it the lost weekend. Our 50-game conference win streak also came to an end. I had not even been aware of that streak.

I did not know until many years later, when a friend sent me the clipping, that on the day after the loss at Oregon the *San Pedro News-Pilot* included a quote from Coach Wooden on how his current team was different from his previous, undefeated team. Coach said: "Gracious, there is no comparison. We don't have a player like Larry Farmer this year."

The Monday after the team returned from Oregon I was in my usual spot on the couch when Coach Wooden walked by and said, warmly, "How are you doing, Larry?" After he had spoken with Jean Dunn, the basketball secretary, he walked by me again and said, "Hello, Larry. How are you?" as if seeing me for the first time. I was a little stunned and worried about Coach for the first time ever. As tough and as strong as he was, I was concerned that the losses might be getting to him.

In early March it appeared that UCLA had righted the ship when the Bruins beat USC 82–52 at the Sports Arena. It was a showdown for the Pac-8 title and a berth in the NCAA tournament. Both teams had conference records of 11–2, with UCLA ranked No. 1 nationally and USC No. 7. A record crowd of more than 15,000 packed the Sports Arena expecting a classic game—but it was never even close!

It was full steam ahead into the NCAA tournament to compete for our eighth straight national championship. The JV season had ended, enabling me to attend varsity workouts all that next week, but I knew I would not be making the trip to Tucson for the tournament because the NCAA did not allow graduate assistants to sit on the bench, and UCLA was not going to pay for my travel to be a fan.

Sam Gilbert was going to fly to Tucson for UCLA's first game Thursday, fly back to L.A. for work Friday, and return to Tucson for Saturday's game. That schedule called for a charter flight, and he asked me if I wanted to tag along. The plane was a small Cessna single-engine propeller plane that could comfortably seat four people. It was just the pilot, Papa Sam, and me. I was nervous because I had never flown on anything that small before.

At the game I sat with Sam in the alumni section behind the UCLA bench. I was amazed at how many people knew Sam. At least as many recognized him as me. Before the start of the game he left his seat to wander around our section socializing.

The game against Dayton went three overtimes, with UCLA pulling out the victory, 111–100. There's a notion associated with the NCAA tournament that every championship team will have one big test during the tournament. Every team has to survive a game that they have to scratch and claw to win. I assumed Dayton was our test.

On the flight back, Papa Sam talked a mile a minute about the UCLA alumni he'd told about me. He bragged about the great coaching job that I had done that season. He said he was telling everybody that, eventually, I would be a full-time assistant coach at UCLA. I asked him why he said that, and he said he just wanted to plant the seed. He also reported that most of the people he talked to about my getting a real position on the coaching staff seemed very receptive. I had not asked him to say anything. There were no positions open anyway. But Sam was seriously working the crowd.

After beating the University of San Francisco in the Western Regional finals, UCLA advanced to the championship round in Greensboro, North Carolina. I watched the game on TV from the guest house in Encino. We all expected UCLA to win, but David Thompson led North Carolina State to a come-from-behind double overtime victory. I was sad and disappointed, and after feeling awkward and humbled throughout the season, I could now add frustrated.

In 2012, I took an administrative coaching position at North Carolina State University. On the main wall of their practice facility hung two huge pictures depicting their two national championships. One of the pictures I had to look at every day was David Thompson getting a rebound over Bill Walton. It remained a sore spot!

With the 1973–74 season finally behind me I had time to think about whether I was a coach or a player. Being around UCLA basketball but no longer being a part of the team had been even harder than I thought it would be. Throughout the season I had tried to follow Coach Wooden's maxim: "Things work out best for the people who make the best of the way things turn out." I still wanted to play, but my understanding of coaching had grown more than I thought it would.

I had gained confidence in my ability to teach basketball. I was proud to see a few of the players improve with my help. The JV team started 0–5 but wound up 10–8.

I had gained in my love and respect for the art of coaching. I passed both classes at SMCC, and now I was just two classes away from earning my degree. I thought that, at some point, I would get a teaching credential so I could be a high school coach and, eventually, get a job as an assistant college coach.

My relationship with Coach Wooden changed over the course of this difficult season together. It was like when a son becomes a father himself and gains an understanding and appreciation for all the things his father did for him.

Another year of growing up helped me realize how much Coach really cared about me. He always wanted what was best for me, even when I didn't know what was best for myself. His phone calls to Cleveland Coach Bill Fitch finally made sense to me. For that, I will always be grateful. Loving Coach Wooden was now easier.

I could now picture myself as a future coach, but another thing was also clear—I was not finished playing. I didn't know where I would play, but I was going to get back into great basketball shape so I would be ready to play in the NBA, the ABA, or overseas.

In June, Papa Sam was contacted by a representative from a team in the German Bundesliga. UCLA players Terry Schofield and my former teammate, John Ecker, had played well in the Bundesliga. Through a connection in Southern California, the Koblenz team called Sam to see if I would have any interest. According to Sam, the salary plus a car and an apartment would put me at $28,000 a year, which was almost as much as I would have made with the Cavaliers. A few days later I got a call from Jürgen Stoltz, an international banker in L.A. for Deutsche Bank.

Stoltz and I met for dinner and he told me, in fluent English, all about this city called Koblenz in West Germany. The city was about an hour and 45 minutes from Frankfurt, where the Rhine and Mosel

Rivers joined in the middle of Germany. He made it sound beautiful. He told me that the club had drawn huge crowds in the past, but their level of play was down. The team was looking to invest in an American player to come over and turn things around. Most important, Koblenz wanted to stay in the Bundesliga, a league with 16 teams. After the upcoming season, the league would restructure to 12 teams. This season would determine Koblenz's fate.

Jürgen and I hit it off almost immediately. In mid-July, he took me to the Los Angeles Forum to watch a closed circuit telecast of Germany playing The Netherlands for the World Cup soccer championship. The Forum was packed with transplanted Germans. After Germany won, Jurg and I went to a little hole-in-the-wall beer

DEFINING A ROLE PLAYER

I truly did not appreciate the value of a good role player until I became a coach. Then I was able to see more clearly why Coach Wooden made me captain of the team my senior year. I also understood why he worked so hard behind the scenes to help me become a coach.

It was my willingness to accept that the team comes first and my ability to see how teamwork wins games.

Like every other player who steps on the court, I would have loved to score a lot of points and be a focus of the offense. The extraordinary talent of Bill Walton and Jamaal Wilkes reserved that role for them. Coach Wooden wanted me to play relentless defense, set screens, and score my points off offensive rebounds and fast breaks. Coach wanted me to battle for defensive rebounds and execute the plays that featured the great players surrounding me. So that's what I did. Without sulking. Without once wanting to transfer or let my personal goals transcend the team goals.

When I was drafted in the seventh round, I wondered whether I might have gone higher if I had attended Drake and been a high-scoring standout with a little flair. We'll never know. I was a "team player," a "role player" on an amazing star-studded team.

Coach Wooden acknowledged that his 1973–74 team had

drinking spot called The Fox Inn in Santa Monica.

That night I told Jurg I would play in Germany. The club prompt-ly sent details of my contract to Papa Sam, and he had Fred Slaugh-ter review the offer. I would be paid at the beginning of each month and given my round-trip airline ticket up front, which would allow me to leave if there were problems.

Koblenz was scheduled to play some Friendlies in late August, but they wanted me to come over a few weeks early to begin work-outs with my new teammates. Joyce was aware I needed to get play-ing out of my system. The question was whether we could make our relationship work through a year apart. About two weeks before I left for Europe, I surprised her by proposing. She accepted.

---

more talent than his previous undefeated team and was asked why the team was struggling. A *Los Angeles Times* article dated December 11, 1973, quoted him as saying, "Physically we're as good as last year and we have the potential to be better. But we can't overlook the absence of a player like Larry Farmer, who out-scored, out-rebounded and played in our press better than his replacement has. Which is not to say his replacement isn't doing a good job, because he is. We just miss Farmer right now."

On February 17, 1974, the *San Pedro News-Pilot* wrote much the same thing, quoting Coach Wooden about missing me, but quoted him further to explain my role: "There was, as you know, a great tendency on the part of people to overlook Larry, the things he did for team cohesion, his disposition and amiable manner on the court. He was a definite influence on the team."

In Bill Walton's letter of support for my induction into UC-LA's Hall of Fame, he wrote: "Our coach . . . made tough deci-sions as to what he thought would be best for team success, and that often left incredibly great players in supporting roles. Larry was one of those guys."

My role was defined by Coach Wooden. I accepted my role and I gave it my best. My UCLA teams won 89 of the 90 games we played.

I thanked the Marcus family for their love and generosity and I moved out of the guest house. On the flight to Frankfurt I was nervous but confident that I was making the right move. I was about to become a professional basketball player.

CHAPTER 14

The Black Pearl of
the German Bundesliga

As my Lufthansa flight was descending into Frankfurt, I was amazed at the beautiful shades of green. There was forest as far as they eye could see.

There were several "get to know your teammates" events planned for me. One was an evening dinner, the second was our first team conditioning outing, and the last was an informal practice with a team meeting. The dinner went great, the conditioning was horrible, and the conditioning fiasco made the first practice contentious.

One of my teammates picked me up for conditioning and drove me to the edge of a forest, where the rest of my teammates were waiting. They had shown up with running suits, jogging shoes, and great attitudes. I had on my basketball shoes, playing shorts, and a tank top. The plan was to start running on a bumpy, winding dirt pathway that was level for about half a mile and then went up the side of a mountain. We were running to the top! Several of the big guys surrounded me and said we would go as a group. One by one, the big guys ran ahead. Of course, at the top of the mountain the drill was to run back down the same path. I was only halfway up when my teammates started passing me on their way down. My roundtrip took about an hour and 15 minutes. When we started up the mountain, we had daylight. When I walked back to join my new teammates it was dark and they were all angry and speaking rather loudly in German. Maybe they were arguing about which of them would form the search party to go back and rescue the knucklehead American?

I was angry, too, because my knees were sore. That night, I told Rudy Liesenfeld, the general manager, that I had come to Germany to play basketball, not to run cross country or climb the Matterhorn. And if this is what they expected from me, they could send me right back to the USA. The phrase "Ugly American" might have crossed his mind.

The team meeting scheduled to be after my first practice was held before practice instead, and we met in a small classroom next to a gym. They spoke in German, so I had no idea what they were saying, but it also prevented me from saying something stupid. For the final minutes they switched to English, and Coach Paul Alilovic said I would work out in the gym with several of my teammates, while those who chose to run would do it on a voluntary basis. I was good with that.

A few weeks later, we played our first friendship tournament. Friendly games are like exhibition games. In this tournament there were three teams, each playing two games. Stoltz was back from Los Angeles for a week of vacation, so he attended the games. We played in a gym that could have held about 1,000 fans, but there were only about 750 there. I got off to a shaky start and missed my first three or four shots. I'm sure my teammates thought the club had wasted a lot of money on a guy who couldn't shoot any better than he could run up a hill.

Once I settled down, I got in a good rhythm and the onslaught was on. I started making jump shots, dunks, layups, and tip-ins. You name it. We won the first game, had the next game off, and played in the evening finale. I scored 36 points in the last game and, in a brief ceremony, was named the tournament MVP.

Stoltz came up to me with a big grin on his face and shook my hand. He said, "I'm so proud of you I could kiss you!" My scowl got a big laugh.

Before the season began we played in one more friendly tournament about an hour and a half from Koblenz, three games in one day. I asked a teammate if the games would be shortened but he said no, three complete games, which I thought was absolutely ridiculous. We won all three and once again, I was the tournament's MVP.

I was learning my way around Koblenz but having difficulty with the language. Rudy's solution was to introduce me to Gerd Clever, a club member about my age. He took me to the market, taught me to read labels and to figure the exchange rate between dollars and Deutschmarks. He showed me how to read the menu, say "please" and "thank you" and order another beer, large or small. What I didn't realize was that he was reporting back to Rudy. Eventually Gerd became such a good friend he told me he was a spy! It didn't matter. Gerd and I are best friends to this day.

When league play started, we played each opponent in the southern division one time at home and one time on the road. There was a lot at stake in these league games, and I could tell the management team was nervous. Coach Paul was still saying, "You need condition." But I almost always played 40 minutes.

The more I scored and the more we won, the more my teammates liked me. They even expected me to hang out with them after every game at a small but really nice pub called The Drop Inn. The owner of the pub gave me my own beer mug. There was a nameplate on the shelf where my mug was placed.

Gerd and a few of my teammates took me to the wine festival one evening in November. Harvesting the grapes and producing the wine was a big deal here. It was like going to a huge outdoor flea market. Every booth represented a different vineyard. The atmosphere was, indeed, festive, and for a few Deutschmarks you could sample the wine at each of the many wine stands. There must have been 30 of these stands. Each stand had a large table, with plastic glasses and open bottles of wine to sample. A "taste" of wine was served as a full wine glass. Behind the table were tents, with cases upon cases of wine. So if you sampled one that you liked, buying a case was quick and easy. We had been there for about half an hour, walking and sampling. We happened upon one booth where an older and rather plump German woman was pouring. She had silver hair, and with a big smile on her face, spoke directly to me in

German. That got the attention of my friends. They all nervously started chuckling, as she continued talking to me. I turned to Gerd, who told me that the woman said she had never seen hair like mine before and if I allowed her to touch it, all of my wine at her stand would be free tonight. So I smiled back at her, walked over to where she was standing and bent over enough so she could reach the top of my head. She touched my hair tentatively, then pressed it a little. She giggled as she touched my Afro and ran her fingers through it, as best she could. She then told the group that *my* wine was free and poured me a glass. It wasn't bad! I only went back by there a couple of times, but each time I did, she smiled and poured me a full glass of wine.

Back at home, a request like that might be taken as insulting, but in this place and this setting, it was simply innocent curiosity.

Joyce came to visit for Christmas and New Year's. Our last game before the Christmas break would be her only opportunity to see me play in Germany. She had seen me play at UCLA, where my freedom to score and my responsibilities were totally different. I was excited for her to see me play here.

From the very start of the game, I wasn't missing anything. I scored 35 points in the first half. That even surprised me! I told her that what she was seeing was why I needed to play basketball again.

One day after practice Heinz Anspach, the team president, and Paul, the coach, told me that they needed for me to do more. More? I was averaging 28 points per game. The team had an overall winning record.

Heinz explained that fans in Koblenz were coming to watch me play. They wanted me to be more of an entertainer and less of a team player. Of course, they wanted to win, but they believed I could become even more of a fan favorite. They wanted more points. The dunking and the shooting with either hand was putting fans in the seats, and they wanted more fans!

Once I started concentrating on scoring, my point totals went up into the 40s.

I was working for those points because defenses were set up to stop me. But I kept finding ways to score. Heinz was right, because our gym was always packed. The local newspaper called me the "Schwarze Perl" or black pearl. There was not much concern about being politically correct in those days.

In February, Koblenz had a weekend where we drew a bye in the league. I used the time to go to Belgium. I had been quietly contacted by a basketball team there and I had spoken to a scout from the team when he came to watch me play. I scored 46 points that game. When I agreed to drive to Belgium to meet with the management of the club he said they would provide me with a hotel if I chose to stay that night, but I planned to drive back because I didn't want my team to know I was shopping around.

I met the scout at a huge cathedral he had suggested as a landmark. I followed him to the gym, where one of the owners explained that in Belgium they had three foreign players on each team. The Bundesliga allowed just one. So this level of play was better than what I was seeing in Germany. Plus, this city had a great team because two Americans on the team had married Belgian women and started families, so they were citizens and didn't count as foreigners. Also, the salaries were much higher.

A "friendship match" was hastily arranged for that evening, even though there had been no mention of a tryout. I was on a team with possible future teammates, while others played on the opposing team. There were referees and a few fans, made up of families of the players.

I played well in the first half but then caught an elbow above my right eye going up for a rebound. It required four stitches. The good news was I played well enough for the Belgium club to say we would talk about a contract at the end of the season. The bad news was I was going to have to tell my Koblenz teammates that I ran into a door.

We finished the regular season in fourth place, which gave us a good seed for the postseason tournament. We would have only two playoff games. If we won both games, Koblenz would be assured of a spot in the following year's 12-team Bundesliga.

I had been following UCLA basketball as best I could. I knew that UCLA had won the national championship and that Coach Wooden had announced his retirement. I usually spoke with my parents every Sunday, but they had called me again early Tuesday morning to tell me of those historic events. I was sad to hear that Coach was retiring, and the only consolation was that he was going out a winner.

A few days later, I was sound asleep in my flat when my phone rang at 4 A.M. It was Papa Sam with a bombshell. "How would you like to be an assistant coach at UCLA?" he asked. "What?" Sam told me he had it on good authority that the new coach, Gene Bartow, wanted to hire one of Coach Wooden's former players, ideally a recent player with some coaching experience. I asked Sam who Gene Bartow was. Sam reminded me that Bartow was the head coach at Memphis State when we played them my senior year for the national championship. I'm wide awake now. Was I interested? Absolutely! Sam said, "I think if you interview, he will give you the job. You need to get back here right now."

Now? I am on the other side of the Atlantic Ocean, and we're about to start the playoffs, which is why the team brought me here in the first place. I thought, I can't leave now.

I called Heinz and told him it was important that we meet right away. When he came to my flat, I told him this was an opportunity of a lifetime, and I was trying to figure out how I could go to Los Angeles for the interview and still make it back for the playoffs. My goal was to do both, but I told him that if we couldn't make it work, I was going to leave anyway. It wasn't a threat. I was sincerely explaining to Heinz how important this was for my future.

We had a friendly game scheduled for Saturday and our first playoff game would be the next Tuesday. I proposed that if I could skip the friendly game I could get to Los Angeles, interview, and get back in time for the playoff game. Heinz agreed. He said the team would buy my round-trip ticket, and he called the team secretary and told him to come to my flat to work out the details. Heinz would drive me to the airport himself for an early flight on Friday. I would have to arrange my interview for Saturday.

I called Sam back and gave him the scenario. It all came together quickly. Heinz picked me up early Friday morning in his beautiful 911 Porsche SC. It was canary yellow and one of the hottest cars in the city of Koblenz. At first I thought only of the stretch on the autobahn where there was no speed limit. I was looking forward to seeing what that Porsche could do. But then it dawned on me that Heinz had driven his smallest car to make sure I wasn't packing up all of my things. Even though I had a round-trip ticket, I think he was still fearful that if I got the job I would not return.

Sam and Rose picked me up at LAX. The meeting with Coach Bartow was the next day at 1 P.M., and I'd be flying back to Germany that night. And, of course, I would be spending Friday night with the Gilberts.

My hair was long, and I had a mustache, befitting my job as a pro player! We hadn't made it to the freeway before Sam told me that I would have to get a haircut in the morning. I was about to argue when he said I could take his car, drive into the city for a haircut and then drive to UCLA. Take Sam's Mercedes over to Crenshaw and Jefferson (the city) to get my hair cut, and then drive to UCLA? I was good with that!

I had brought a nice conservative suit for my interview, but once Rose saw my tie, she replaced it with one of Sam's. I had a wonderful evening getting caught up with Rose and Sam. And, of course, getting pointers about how to handle myself in the interview. Sam told me that I would probably also meet with J.D. Morgan, the UCLA athletic director. Regardless of the salary I was offered, I was to act excited and tell him that salary would be no issue. Papa Sam reassured me that we would figure out a way for me to live on that salary. Whatever I was offered, I was to take it.

I was 30 minutes early for my interview. I waited on the same couch that used to serve as my office, and because it was Saturday, no one else was around. Coach Bartow came around the corner not expecting me to be there yet. When he saw me he said, "Larry Farmer! The last time I saw you, the national championship game had just started and you hit that first shot against my Memphis State team and we were down, 2–0." I just smiled and shook his hand. I did not want to start my interview by correcting him, but it was actually Larry Hollyfield who hit that first shot.

When Coach Bartow and I sat down in the office, I tried not to show how strange it felt to me to be in Coach Wooden's office when Coach was not there. I managed to focus. He told me that he had already hired Lee Hunt, his longtime friend and assistant coach who had been with him at Memphis State and most recently at the University of Illinois, and that he had talked to a lot of UCLA people about me, and they all had nothing but good things to say. And then he said that he liked the fact that I had recently played for Coach Wooden, because he wanted a link on his staff to help him understand and navigate the UCLA tradition. I knew exactly what that meant. He didn't want me to come in every day and talk about the old days, but he did want someone familiar with UCLA's way of looking at things. This was now his program, but it was going to be a difficult transition. We also talked about loyalty, the first responsibility of every assistant coach. Which was exactly the message that Coach Wooden gave me when I became his graduate assistant coach.

We talked about my upcoming marriage, when I would be earning my college degree, and many other things. Then he told me J.D. Morgan wanted to talk to me. When I stood up, he shook my hand and said, "If you want it, the position is yours." I said, "Absolutely, Coach. Thank you."

Mr. Morgan greeted me with a big handshake and told me he was thrilled to see me back at UCLA, and excited that I was coming on board. Mr. Morgan asked me how things were going in Europe, and with the small talk out of the way, he said, "Now, about your salary."

J.D. Morgan had a very distinctive baritone voice. He spoke slowly, and in this instance very precisely. He said because of my lack of experience, and the opportunity for growth, my starting salary would be $11,000 a year. He added that this opportunity would be a great start for my career. I told him I understood and salary was not an issue. Altogether the meeting lasted only about ten minutes, and when we finished, I stood up, shook his hand, and thanked him. I wasn't asked to sign anything. With two handshakes, I was hired.

When I landed at the airport in Frankfurt, Heinz was waiting for me just outside of customs. I believe it was relief I saw on his face when we made eye contact. I thanked him for allowing me the opportunity to secure my coaching position.

It was odd to think of myself as a coach. A few weeks earlier my plan was to play the next season in Belgium. I also had heard rumors that I would be offered more money to play another season in Koblenz. Not now.

Word had spread among my teammates when I wasn't at our game on Saturday that I had gone back to America. But they also knew I planned to return for our playoff games. At practice there were handshakes and expressions of happiness about my future.

The first playoff game might have been the best 40 minutes of basketball I played all season. I scored 46 points and I didn't take a lot of shots to hit that total. We played our last playoff game on Friday, and we won that game, too. There was Sekt (German sparkling wine) in the locker room, and we were all drinking from the bottles and hugging! It reminded me of the NBA celebrations I'd seen with the champagne in the locker room, except nobody in our locker room was wasting a drop. We hadn't won a championship but we had accomplished our goal!

Rudy told me at the Drop Inn that the team wanted to have one last friendly match the following Saturday in my honor. They would advertise the game, and it would give the fans in Koblenz one last chance to watch me play and properly say goodbye. I told Rudy to go ahead and set it up.

A week would give me time to get all of my business affairs in order.

Gerd came to town to help me pack and send some things back by mail and showed me articles written in the local newspapers about this final friendship game. It really did say basketball fans were invited to say goodbye to me. The club was charging an entrance fee, so it was about making a few Deutschmarks, too.

When we got to the gym the fans were gathering early. By game time, we had a nice crowd.

There was a microphone at center court for a pre-game ceremony. As The Lord Mayor of Rheinland-Pfalz (the state Koblenz was in) walked out to begin the ceremony, the fans and my teammates all stood and started clapping.

When the Lord Mayor said "Larry Farmer" the gym erupted in applause and Heinz and Rudy walked me out to center court. I tried hard not to cry but my tears flowed. What had started in my basement with a tennis ball and a coat hanger was coming to an end halfway around the world. I wasn't moved to tears by the honor, but by the realization that this would be the last time I played competitive basketball.

My teammates later translated the highlights of what the Lord Mayor had said: "Larry became a part of our city . . . He made all of us in Koblenz proud . . . The team would remain in the Bundesliga . . . He was the most exciting player in the Bundesliga . . . We will never forget this man from America . . ."

Among the dignitaries at center court there was a lady with a proclamation declaring it Larry Farmer Day in Koblenz. She handed me the document and we kissed on both cheeks. Rudy held it for me. The mayor said some more words, the fans cheered, and another lady handed me a small silver plaque with a symbol of the city etched into it. Again we kissed on both cheeks and Rudy took it from me. A third lady handed the mayor a beautiful beer stein with a pewter top. On the front of this beer stein was a map of early Koblenz. The pewter top had fine artwork on it. The mayor handed me the mug, which was a personal gift from him to me. We shook hands and I smiled through tears as photographs were taken. Rudy took the beer mug and we walked back over to our bench where I was greeted by my teammates. I glanced down at the team we were going to play the friendly game against and they, too, had been standing and clapping for the entire ceremony.

By tipoff time I was emotionally spent. I might have had my

lowest point total of any game I played in Germany. But I really didn't care. The event was truly a special way to bring my basketball career to an end. After the game, the opposing players as well as my teammates all shook my hand. A few of my teammates hugged me. I waved to the crowd, blew kisses, walked off the court crying again.

When I started playing basketball I didn't know how far the game might take me. Well, it took me all over the United States and now to Germany, where I received a paycheck to play basketball. That made me a pro, by definition. Now it was over. My last game wasn't in Madison Square Garden or the L.A. Forum. It was a small gym in West Germany. I can't imagine I would have been any more proud than I was right where I was standing. I had played a lot of basketball in a very short period of time. I knew in my heart of hearts that I turned out to be a pretty good player. Jazz legend Miles Davis once said, "You have to play a long time to be able to play like yourself." In Germany, I played with freedom and creativity.

I left knowing that I had played the game the right way. I respected the game, and the game respected me.

The next morning Rudy, Coach Paul, and Gerd picked me up at my apartment and we drove together to the Frankfurt airport. In saying goodbye, I shook hands with Rudy and Coach Paul. I hugged Gerd. I knew when I walked away that day he would always be one of my best friends and one of the best people I would ever meet.

CHAPTER 15

"Clean Gene" Bartow

Coach Bartow was similar to Coach Wooden in many ways. He was a man of great character in addition to being a successful coach. Coach Bartow, like Wooden, was simply a nice man who didn't drink or use bad language. A family man, he had earned the nickname "Clean Gene" because of the way he conducted himself and ran his basketball programs. UCLA's athletic director, J.D. Morgan, hand-picked him to follow Coach Wooden.

The announcement had come in April, and UCLA was to play its season opener on November 29 in St. Louis in a much-anticipated showdown against Indiana University, coached by Bob Knight.

It was going to be a busy seven months for all of us. Joyce and I married and moved to Culver City. I did some work on a movie starring Jamaal Wilkes, and, of course, we were always recruiting.

Coach Bartow got great news on the recruiting front on May 16 when three big recruits—Brad Holland, Roy Hamilton, and David Greenwood—committed to UCLA. The fans who were worried about recruiting now that Coach Wooden was gone had their concerns put to rest for the time being. Our team was loaded with talent. We returned four starters from a group that had just won a national title, and Marques Johnson and Richard Washington were coming off outstanding sophomore seasons. Center Ralph Drollinger and guard Andre McCarter, who would be seniors, provided a solid foundation on which to build. We also had guards Raymond Townsend and Jimmy Spillane coming back. I couldn't wait for practice to start!

Coach Bartow assigned me to the team's academics and scheduling, and I would also oversee the junior varsity program. He wanted me to hire a graduate assistant coach and make him primarily responsible for the day-to-day operation of the program, but I wanted to be more hands on in practice as Coach Frank Arnold had been when I was his assistant. I wanted the experience. I proposed we start the JV practice earlier so I could run my practice and then come to the varsity side. Coach Bartow agreed, and I hired former teammate Bob Webb to assist me.

The JV team practice would be at 2 P.M. The varsity started at 3 P.M. It kept me on my feet a little longer, but I was only 23 years old. The week before the Indiana game I asked if I could skip the trip to St. Louis so I could coach my JV team's first game against Santa Monica City College, which had a really good junior college program. I wanted game coaching experience, and Coach Bartow reluctantly agreed.

Anticipation for the UCLA-Indiana game continued to build. At the end of the previous season Indiana had gone into the Midwest Regional with a record of 30–0 and great expectations for meeting UCLA in the NCAA championship game. They were considered invincible in their Regional—until they lost by two points to Kentucky, a team they had beaten soundly earlier in the year. Indiana had been favored, despite having a star player, Scott May, playing with a broken arm. Kentucky fans were the only ones who did not consider the final game spoiled.

UCLA had won Coach Wooden's last title with a victory over Kentucky, so this year's opener, a made-for-television game between UCLA and Indiana, was a de facto national championship game, and it was Coach Bartow's debut as UCLA's coach. Knight had the core of his team back, including May, center Kent Benson, and guard Quinn Buckner. The game was close in the first half, but Indiana blew us out in the second half and beat us 84–64.

Angry reaction was immediate. UCLA's spoiled diehard fans had no interest in being patient with a new coach. I felt just awful for Coach Bartow. I could not have been more demoralized myself. My JV game was a complete blowout. SMCC jumped out to an 18–0 lead and the students in their packed gym were chanting for a shutout as I burned three timeouts in the first half. We lost 84–55 but it wasn't even that close. Incredibly, the worst part of this weekend was yet to come. In the '70s, there were only a few black head basketball coaches in Division 1, although it was becoming more common to have a black assistant coach on the staff. For the most part, it was assumed that the one black assistant was there to recruit black players. That was the perception. I was the first full-time black assistant basketball coach at UCLA. My hiring had made national news, so when UCLA played Indiana on national television and I wasn't sitting on the bench, red flags went up. It was noticed. On

GOING HOLLYWOOD

Hollywood is a fun perk for an athlete in Los Angeles. As much fun as it was to recognize celebrities, it was even more fun being recognized. At a Lakers game, when I was a junior, I said to the man sitting next to me, "Aren't you Walter Matthau?" And he said to me, "Yes. Aren't you Larry Farmer?"

Gene Kelly introduced himself to me in a VIP lounge at LAX when I was the head coach. He said we had played well the night before.

Celebrities sometimes came to campus, hoping to play in our pickup games. We didn't let just anyone play. J.J. Walker showed up regularly at noon looking to play. Dorian Harewood also was a regular until he got a part in the TV series Roots. Craig Impelman told a guy with Marvin Gaye that our game was for UCLA players only, so Marvin shot some baskets on an empty hoop and left.

There were also opportunities to be a part of a movie.

I was just back from Germany when Fred Slaughter, a former UCLA basketball player who had been my lawyer and was now Jamaal's, called me about the movie Cornbread, Earl and Me, starring Jamaal, a very young Laurence Fishburne, and Rosalind Cash. The script called for Jamaal's character, Cornbread, to dominate a 3-on-3 game. I "choreographed" the game. The extras who played in the game included Marques Johnson, Bob Webb, Wilbert Olinde, and André McCarter, all UCLA basketball players.

Monday, both J.D. Morgan and Coach Bartow received angry phone calls from African American fans asking why I had been hired only to be left behind. I was alone with Coach Bartow in his office when he told me I would be traveling with the team from now on. I apologized, acknowledging the whole thing was my fault.

The varsity won its next 11 straight games, but our fans were grumbling about everything from who we played in our lineup to how we played.

Many of those victories were blowouts, so Coach Bartow was able to use 13 players. That gave him the opportunity to see which

---

When a basketball player was needed as an extra, UCLA usually got the call. For football players, the call went to USC. Athletes were considered "special talent," so they were paid at a higher rate than other extras.

I played basketball in another film, *Fast Break*, starring Gabe Kaplan, from the hit TV series *Welcome Back, Kotter*. Craig had a role as a player, too. The script called for him to goad me into hitting him so I'd be kicked out of the game. In discussion with the director about what Craig should call me, Mike Warren (a former Bruin who also was cast as a player and who later starred in *Hill Street Blues*) said the surest way to get punched was to insult a guy's mother. It was decided that Craig would direct a racial slur at my mother. Craig was so uncomfortable with the line he called my real mother in Denver and apologized before we shot the scene.

I also had a speaking part in an episode of *The White Shadow*. I played one-on-one against the show's star, Ken Howard, opening and closing the scene with dunks. When the episode aired we were both drenched in sweat at the beginning of the game. That was because we did so many takes. Ken kept missing the shot he was supposed to make.

I even have an IMDb (Internet Movie Database) listing. "Hooray for Hollywood!"

combination of players worked best, plus playing time keeps players happy.

Freshman Brad Holland did not travel with the team to play against Indiana. The next game, at home against San Jose State, he came off the bench to score 17 points. That, of course, was considered an example of Bartow's poor judgment of talent by some vocal fans. Guards Andre McCarter and Jimmy Spillane were not shooting consistently well. Raymond Townsend, a tough guard who played good defense and was a capable shooter, still lacked confidence. Roy Hamilton continued to work hard in practice but was behind the other guards.

The front line was by far more reliable. Richard Washington, at 6-foot-11, was an excellent jump shooter and was comfortable shooting from 18 feet on in. He was a matchup nightmare for most teams. He was also an excellent rebounder. Marques Johnson played hard and above the rim. He was a capable jump shooter, but a spectacular scorer around the basket. He and Richard were not only our two starting forwards, but they were best friends and roommates. Our center, Ralph Drollinger, was a 7-foot senior and the world's nicest kid. He had a nice shooting touch and could be described most accurately as a finesse player. Those three big guys were the backbone of our team. They gave us stability as we searched for a combination and a rotation with our guards.

We experienced a jolt of reality as we tried to take the court at Pauley Pavilion for our game against Denver on January 2. Instead of hearing the band playing the fight song and seeing cheerleaders lined up to greet the players, we were met with the sight of the football coach at center court. Coach Dick Vermeil had just given UCLA a Rose Bowl victory with an upset of Ohio State. A student at the microphone was leading the cheer: "ONE, TWO, THREE, HAPPY NEW YEAR COACH VERMEIL!" The student section was cheering like crazy for him as our team reached the basket at the other end of the floor, and the coaching staff stopped at the near edge of the court. When Coach Vermeil realized that the tribute to him was overshadowing our team's entrance for a game, he thanked the fans as quickly and quietly as he could and told them to root for the basketball team tonight as hard as they had rooted for the football team yesterday! Coach Bartow smiled uncomfortably and whispered to me: "I thought we were a basketball school." We beat Denver 111–79.

The last victory in that 11-game streak was at Oregon, where we won a dogfight 62–61. We then got blasted at Oregon State 75–58 and came home to beat Stanford, 68–67. That one-point victory was like a loss to UCLA fans. Stanford had not beaten UCLA in L.A. since 1952. A loss on the road, sandwiched between one-point wins, had UCLA followers in an uproar.

In late January, we headed to South Bend to play Notre Dame. Coach Bartow and Coach Hunt had never been to the Athletic and Convocation Center. Although I had been there three times to play games, I hadn't seen much more than the corridors from the bus into the arena, so I went along when Bartow and Hunt left the locker room to stroll through the beautiful building packed with Notre Dame sports history. We happened upon the Notre Dame football coach, Dan Devine, who invited us to his office where Bartow and Devine compared notes on what it was like to follow a coaching legend. Devine had replaced Coach Ara Parseghian, who had recently won two National Championships and 84 percent of his games in his 11 years at Notre Dame. Coach Bartow was following Coach Wooden, who had won 10 National Championships in the previous 12 years. If there was one common theme it was that no matter what you did it never seemed to be good enough. Lee Hunt and I sat quietly, taking in what we knew was a truly rare conversation.

The game at Notre Dame was, of course, on national television and still there was a packed house. Adrian Dantley, Notre Dame's star forward, had not played well in our first meeting but he made a big comeback with a 30-point performance. Richard Washington was equally outstanding, scoring 30 points on 14-for-17 field goal shooting. Notre Dame won 95–85. The loss was UCLA's third in a row in South Bend. This was now a full-fledged rivalry.

Our season record went to 14–3, and all three of our losses were on the road.

Coach Bartow was really struggling with negative press. Local sports talk shows were relentless. He started to privately refer to those folks who were openly and unreasonably hostile as "kooks." He had noticeably lost weight, and his hair seemed grayer.

We beat USC, Washington, and Washington State to take the outright lead in the Pac-8. We reeled off six straight conference wins in February before hitting another historic bump when we lost a game (a conference game!) at home. It broke a streak of 98 straight home victories. UCLA's home record, over 11 seasons, was 166–2.

The stunning loss in Pauley Pavilion was to Oregon. We expected Oregon to play well after we barely escaped disaster in Eugene earlier, but we weren't expecting our own team to get off to such a horrendous start. We shot 22 percent in the first half. I had never seen anything like it. Greg Ballard, Oregon's future NBA star, did a great job defensively against Richard Washington. Richard missed his first six shots. We lost 65–45.

It was at about this time the rumors of the NBA's interest in Richard Washington grew louder. But he was a junior. Since 1971, the NBA had allowed players with remaining college eligibility to declare themselves available for the draft in what was then called the "hardship" draft. No UCLA basketball player had ever "gone hardship." If Richard did leave early, he would be the first.

We won our last three games to finish the regular season 24–3. We won the Pac-8, but the fans just expected that. Our players were genuinely happy about winning the league, and the coaches were relieved.

Talk of losing Richard Washington to the pro draft now included the possibility of losing Marques, too. They might both leave UCLA early to enter the NBA or the ABA draft. I would get to the bottom of that very quickly merely by talking to Sam Gilbert since he would probably be representing both of them. We were certainly losing seniors Ralph Drollinger and Andre McCarter. They were terrific players, but if everybody else came back, we would be loaded once again. We needed to recruit several talented front-line players, just in case!

TOM TELLEZ

One of the advantages of coaching at a university like UCLA is the availability of resources—including world class coaches. I learned from many. While I was an assistant coach I had the good fortune to have an office just down the hall from Tom Tellez, an assistant track coach at the time. Coach Tellez went on to coach the University of Houston track and field team for 22 years and has since been inducted into the U.S. Track Coaches Association Hall of Fame. He coached a long list of Olympic athletes, including Carl Lewis and Dwight Stones.

Coach Tellez also loved basketball. I had always been a big fan of track and field. We had been talking sports since I was a player at UCLA.

Many times when I walked past his office, I would see him in there with the lights off watching his athletes on a small 8 mm film projector. I poked my head in one day and asked if I could watch. He invited me in and began my lessons. He was breaking down the film, frame by frame, of one of the UCLA long jumpers. He explained exactly what he was looking for. Stride length, head up or down, position of arms, lift off, and placement of hips—every little thing that you could think of that would go into someone running down the runway and trying to jump as far as he could. Then I watched him break down one of the high jumpers, using the same process of analysis. Coach Tellez was literally teaching me how to break down film. I knew the fundamentals of basketball after playing for Coach Wooden, but this showed me how to see techniques more precisely and intricately. This would come in handy. I would watch film, spot a technique that was being done incorrectly and use that film to walk the player through the correct technique for executing fundamental skills.

It was exactly what Coach Wooden used to do without film. I just wasn't aware of what a good eye he had. It explained his insistence on correcting and repeating and correcting and repeating. He knew what he wanted to see and he wouldn't settle for less. I would use this teaching tool to help basketball players improve for the next 44 years.

Richard Washington was a first team consensus All-American. He had become a consistent 18' jump shooter and was better facing the basket than posting up and playing with his back to it. Certainly more of a "finesse big," not a "power big." Richard averaged 20 points per game as a junior, and if the three-point shot had been in college basketball at the time, he would have averaged more. He was a good offensive rebounder and could score in traffic. NBA scouts' assessment was that you couldn't defend him with a typical power forward, because at 6-foot-11, he could shoot over most of them. Richard was also quick and agile for a man his size, so if you tried to guard him with a center of equal size, he was capable of driving around a slower player.

Marques Johnson was one of the best players in the country around the basket. He was a good 12' to 15' jump shooter. He was very explosive offensively and his athletic ability allowed him to play well above the rim. He was terrific running the lane and attacking the basket on the fast break. Marques could score both facing the basket and in post-up situations. He was UCLA's best rebounder and best shot blocker. I often wondered, if the dunk rule had been reinstated when he was a junior, how many more points we would have scored. There were many situations where Marques would "power" the ball up to score near the basket, and if challenged by a defender (instead of going through that player to score), Marques would resort to finesse and shoot it with either his right hand or his left hand, attempting a much more difficult shot. Because he was so talented, he made most of those shots anyway, but if he could have dunked, he would have averaged more than the 17 points per game he did average. His NBA stock was rising too.

The Pac-8 title made us an automatic qualifier for the NCAA tournament. Our first three postseason games were played in Pauley Pavilion, where we beat San Diego State, Pepperdine, and the University of Arizona. The Final Four was in Philadelphia at the fabulous Spectrum, and Indiana, the Big Ten champion, was our semifinal opponent. The perfect rematch.

We were certainly a better version of ourselves than we were when we lost our opener to this team, but there was no doubt Indiana had improved as well. They were again going into the NCAA tournament undefeated.

At the start of the game, Indiana's 6-foot-11 center, Kent Benson, was trying to guard 6-foot-11 Richard Washington. Richard was much quicker and Benson picked up two early fouls. Coach Bob Knight called a timeout. As the teams headed to their benches, Knight launched a verbal assault at referee Irv Brown. Irv was from Denver and I'd known him since I was in high school. Coach Knight's complaint was one of the most amazing uses of profane language I had ever heard! When Irv Brown didn't hit Knight with a technical foul, I knew we were in trouble! Benson was important to everything Indiana did, both on offense and defense, and a third foul on Benson would have given us a huge advantage. But Benson didn't pick up his third foul until well into the second half. Coming out of the timeout, Knight put Benson on David Greenwood, and Indiana took control of the game.

Indiana played smart, packing their defense inside and allowing our guards to shoot. Our guards did shoot, but not well, making just 4 of 24 from the field. Indiana played only six players the entire game and beat us 65–51. Indiana beat Michigan for the third time that season to win the national title.

We beat Rutgers 106–92 in the consolation game, and our season had come to a merciful end. Our record was 28–4, which by UCLA standards, was not a good year. Going to the Final Four and winning 88 percent of your games would be cause for celebration at most universities.

Right after the season both Richard and Marques let Coach Bartow know that they were petitioning the NBA to be included in the draft. I spoke to Sam Gilbert, who was representing both of them, and he confirmed that he was hearing from NBA general managers that both players would be top 10 picks. Sam also explained that the ABA and the NBA were planning to merge in 1977, so this was the last chance for a player to negotiate one league against the other.

The Denver Rockets of the ABA had offered Marques Johnson

a five-year million-dollar contract in a deal that had already been negotiated, but Marques' deal fell apart when the NBA told four ABA franchises that they could join the NBA as solid franchises, meaning that they would not have their players made available in a dispersal draft. If they chose to come in whole, they could not compete against the NBA for that year's college players. The four franchises were the Indiana Pacers, the New York Nets, the San Antonio Spurs, and the Denver Rockets.

At the 11th hour, Denver had to withdraw its offer to Marques. The Detroit Pistons were interested in Marques, and they had the fourth pick in the NBA draft. But the money was nowhere close to what Denver had offered. Marques decided to play another year at UCLA.

This all happened on June 6 and June 7. For Marques to take his name out of the NBA draft, a document with his signature had to be received at NBA headquarters in New York before the draft began. It was the only way to safeguard his college eligibility. FAX machines were not a household item in 1976, but the *Los Angeles Herald-Examiner* office in downtown L.A. had one and J.D. Morgan had arranged for us to use it.

Coach Bartow asked me to pick up Marques at his apartment, which was near my home in Culver City, and get him to the *Herald-Examiner*. When Marques climbed into my car he was noticeably quiet. I tried to have a conversation with him, but he really didn't want to talk. We listened to music. Just 48 hours earlier, he was celebrating being a millionaire, and now he was back to being a college student again. He tried to put on a good face while at the newspaper office, but he was clearly disappointed. Coach Bartow met us at the *Herald-Examiner*. He and I were thrilled that we would have the best player in college basketball back for his senior year, but we didn't make a big show of it out of respect for Marques' feelings. All three of us smiled for a picture. There was not much conversation on the drive back, either. When he got out of the car he simply said, "Thanks, Coach."

Kansas City made Richard the third player picked in the first round of the NBA draft.

Coach Bartow's second year started off exactly where his first year left off. We had a talented team that was expected to do well. Timing may not have worked out for Marques as far as the draft, but there was a good timing element for his return to college basketball. After a 10-year ban on dunking, the NCAA brought it back just in time to give Marques a spectacular stage.

David Greenwood would replace Richard Washington in the starting lineup alongside Marques.

The JV team looked very promising. Coach Bartow was more open to occasionally sending one of our scholarship varsity players down to the JV team to get some playing time, and we were better at managing it now. I convinced my friend Craig Impelman to quit his job in retail management to come back and help with the JV. The NCAA had added a coaching position but it was part time. To make ends meet, Craig had to take a job in the morning washing dishes at Dykstra Hall, but he loved basketball so much he took that deal. I knew he would be both a tremendous coach and a terrific influence on these walk-on players.

UCLA opened the season with three straight wins over San Diego State, DePaul, and Jacksonville University. In the middle of December, we played Notre Dame at home. We were ranked No. 3 in the nation at that time, and Digger Phelps' team came in ranked No. 7. We led for the majority of the game but went without scoring a basket for the last six minutes and wound up losing 66–63. The press noted that Notre Dame's Rich Branning, a freshman guard from Huntington Beach, California, had been recruited by UCLA but got away. Rich was a terrific player and we had, in fact, offered him a scholarship, but he decided against UCLA because of possibly playing behind sophomore guards Roy Hamilton and Brad Holland. Branning hit a key basket late in the game to help win it for the Irish.

Once again, the record book was dusted off to show how far we had fallen. UCLA had never lost to a nonconference opponent in Pauley Pavilion. Ever! It was only the fourth loss of any kind in the history of Pauley Pavilion.

We would then run off seven straight wins, all at home, leading up to our first conference game against Oregon.

It was around this time that a popular and controversial radio sports talk show host in Southern California decided to take the criticism of Bartow's coaching to a new level. He told his listeners that if they had a problem with the coaching at UCLA, they should tell Gene Bartow directly—here's his home phone number. The next morning Coach Bartow was visibly shaken. Unfortunately, before he had made it home the night before, his wife answered a lot of the phone calls. Bartow changed his number to one that was unlisted and private.

On January 9, while the varsity was beating Oregon State, my junior varsity team played Santa Monica City College (SMCC) in the preliminary game. SMCC returned most of the players that had destroyed us the year before. Most of our players were back so this really was a rematch. The JV team played an absolutely flawless game, and we beat SMCC 63–62.

Later in January we traveled back to South Bend and beat Notre Dame. This was a nice stretch for us. After beating Notre Dame we flew back to beat USC at home and then the University of Tennessee at the Omni Arena in Atlanta. Both the Notre Dame and Tennessee games were nationally televised.

USC proved to be no match for us and Marques Johnson could not have been more spectacular. He had 26 points including five dunks. He also had 15 rebounds. We won 77–59. More importantly, we moved into first place in the Pac-8 conference.

During the week before one of our home games Coach Bartow received a call in his office from a guy who said he was going to bring a rifle to the game on Saturday. Coach Bartow talked to J.D. Morgan about it, and the Los Angeles Police Department was notified. Lee Hunt and I were given an overview of the call. Our players were never told about it. There would be plainclothes policemen at a couple of the main entrances watching people as they entered. There were no metal detectors in those days. Two plainclothes policemen would escort us from the locker room to the court, sit close by and escort us back.

Coach Bartow, Hunt, and I were sitting silently in the coaches' locker room waiting for time to give the pregame speech. I was always nervous before games, but this time I was scared. I assumed they were as well. I asked Coach Bartow if he would mind if Hunt and I sat at the other end of the bench next to Ducky in case this guy was a bad shot. That made Bartow laugh. We won the game, and there was no incident. It was a sobering moment in my young coaching career. In February we faced our toughest stretch in the race for the conference title with four straight road games. The game at Oregon was crazy!

When we had played at Notre Dame at the end of January, their fans were particularly noisy and rambunctious. We won, and when Marques Johnson was asked during the postgame interview if Notre Dame was the craziest place he had ever played, Marques said, "No." He cited the fans in The Pit in Eugene. Marques said: "They aren't insane; they are deranged!" Marques' comments were published in *Sports Illustrated*. Two weeks later we were in Eugene.

The students, now embracing the "deranged" label, were holding signs and screaming obscenities at us. Security around us was tight, but there was still a sense of physical intimidation that was not normal, even for Oregon. The first half was really tight. Coach Bartow was up yelling at the officials, saying Oregon was getting away with playing dirty. Dick Harter, Oregon's coach, stood up and flipped him "the bird" while mouthing, "F...you!" I was shocked. Coaching decorum (in my experience) was more gentlemanly than that. The officials gave Harter a technical foul, and that made the Oregon fans go even crazier. At halftime, when we headed to the ancient locker room downstairs, their fans waited by the exit, shouting obscenities and flipping us off. Oregon won the game 64–55. Still, the officials needed a police escort after the game.

After that loss we were tied with Oregon at the top of the league with records of 8–3. But our schedule was favorable, putting us back at home for two of our last three games. Oregon would be at Washington and at Washington State. We returned to the friendly

confines of Pauley Pavilion, and immediately beat Stanford 114–
83. Marques scored 30 points and David Greenwood had 28. We
cleared our bench. Washington State helped us out by beating Oregon and giving us our one-game lead back.

The Senior Night game, against Cal, was the last home game for
Marques, Jimmy Spillane, and Wilbert Olinde. Marques was now
a lock for College Player of the Year honors. He scored 37 points
and had six dunks in the game. It was his career high. I would tease
Marques about wearing the No. 54, which was my number when I
played at UCLA. I would tell him I was letting him borrow it. I think
it was on this night that I told him it was officially his.

In 1996 his No. 54 was retired.

Oregon beat Washington, so all we needed to do was win at
USC the next weekend to win the conference. The Trojans were
2–11 and in last place in the Pac-8. But this was one of those "throw
out the stats" rivalry games. USC played its best game of the year.
Marques played Superman, scoring 25 points (with six in-your-face
dunks) and pulled down 16 rebounds. UCLA won 78–69.

My JV team squared off again against USC's still undefeated JV
team. They continued to use the same three scholarship players in
every game. We would play this game with all walk-ons. We handed
USC its only JV loss of the season 82–74. UCLA's JV team had its
first winning record with 12 wins and 6 losses.

Coach Bartow saw the last five minutes of the game. When I
wasn't standing up coaching, I was sitting down talking to my players on defense, just as I had talked on defense when I played. When
the varsity game got tight that night, Coach Bartow turned to me
and said: "I need you talking to our guys like you talk to those JV
kids, because this team is where Hunt and I earn our salaries!" The
comment was made half-jokingly, but I started talking every time
we were playing defense.

This year, our first round of the NCAA tournament was in Po-
catello, Idaho. We beat Denny Crum's tough Louisville team and
moved on to play Idaho State in Provo, Utah. Idaho State was
coached by Jim Killingsworth. His nickname was "Killer," but he

could not have been a nicer or more respected coach. Idaho State played in the Big Sky conference and had proven they could play with the big boys by beating Jerry Tarkanian's Long Beach State team in the first round of the tournament.

The day before the Idaho State game, Marques Johnson was in pain with what he described as a toothache. He told us he had been aware of it for a couple of days, and it was a nuisance. By the next morning (game day) he was in so much pain our trainer, Ducky Drake, took him to a dentist. Marques had an impacted wisdom tooth. The pain was so extreme we had no other option but to get the tooth removed. The extraction of the tooth required a hammer and a chisel. Marques would later describe it as "the worst dental experience in my life." Our concerns were how bad his pain would be, how to get the bleeding stopped, and how any pain medication might affect him. Marques had made it clear he intended to play.

When the game started, Marques played like the All-American he was. He scored 19 points and had 10 rebounds in the first half and UCLA had the lead. But by the time the second half started, we knew we had a problem. He was in pain and the wound was bleeding. He would score only two points in the second half. Marques told the media after the game only that he had a wisdom tooth infection. No mention of the horrendous extraction or the pain or the bleeding. The rest of the team struggled in the second half and we did not play well at all against Idaho State's zone defense. We were behind by five points with 37 seconds left. We pressed and fouled and ended up losing 76–75.

After Coach Bartow had spoken to the team, the players sat at their lockers for a long time. Coach Bartow, Coach Hunt and I sat in the training room area with Ducky. We decided to stay out of the way until the players had showered and dressed. Marques got dressed and joined us in the training room, sitting on the taping table between me and Coach Bartow. Tears came as he told Coach Bartow he was sorry for losing the game. Coach Bartow told him he had done no such thing. I put my arm around him, thinking, "It takes a young man of great character and humility to feel responsibility for this loss and be concerned about letting down his team instead of blaming emergency surgery or looking forward to a lucrative pro career."

This was the year college basketball came up with the equivalent award to football's Heisman Trophy. It was called the John R. Wooden Award, and Coach Wooden had designed it himself. Coach had recruited Marques to play at UCLA. Marques starred on the team that gave Coach Wooden his last championship before he retired. It was fitting that the first Wooden Award would go to Marques. Truly a storybook ending—except for the outcome of the tournament.

The media focused on how Coach Bartow was bringing about the end of the UCLA dynasty. In early June, Coach Bartow went on the Bud Furillo radio show, one of the most popular call-in talk shows in Southern California. He wanted to address some of his critics head on, but after a few calls he stormed out of the studio while the program was still on the air.

On June 10 Bartow asked J.D. Morgan for permission to talk to the University of Alabama Birmingham (UAB). UAB was starting its program and needed both an athletic director and a basketball coach. When news of UAB's interest leaked out, it put pressure on Coach Bartow to make a quick decision, and he chose to leave UCLA.

In his two years at UCLA, Coach Bartow's record was 52–9. An 85 percent winning percentage. Yet he felt like he was being run out of town. His longtime assistant coach, Lee Hunt, told me Coach Bartow said coaching wasn't fun anymore. Coach Bartow had told me at the start of the process that I had a job with him at UAB should he accept that position. He told me that I could wait to see if the new coach at UCLA might rehire me, but he would hold a position open until that was known. It was a very kind gesture, and I appreciated it. I had a wife and a mortgage and no guarantee of a job.

Coach Bartow served as head basketball coach and athletic director at UAB for 18 years. During one stretch, the team went to seven straight NCAA tournaments. In 2009, he was inducted into the National Collegiate Basketball Hall of Fame.

I learned a great deal from Coach Bartow. He loved the game and treated his players with dignity and respect. He taught me patience and humility. To a large degree, he taught me how to compartmentalize my emotions after winning or losing. After watching what he went through, I promised myself if I ever got a job as a head coach, I would never read the newspaper or listen to sports radio talk shows.

CHAPTER 16

Superman Is Really Gary Cunningham

There was plenty of speculation about who would be hired as the next UCLA coach. Names being floated included North Carolina's Dean Smith, Louisville's Denny Crum, and Wyoming's Don DeVoe. Another name that kept coming up was Gary Cunningham. After spending 10 years as Coach Wooden's assistant, Gary had retired from coaching when Coach Wooden retired. Gary had moved to the building next door as director of the UCLA Alumni Association.

Although Coach Wooden had not publicly pushed it, he had let it be known that when he retired he wanted to turn over the reins of the program to either Cunningham or Crum. Both had played for him and both had been outstanding and loyal assistants.

One morning a little over a week after Coach Bartow resigned, UCLA Athletic Director J.D. Morgan came into my office and told me he was going to be interviewing Gary Cunningham that day. I was thrilled! I thought Coach Cunningham would be a great hire, and a UCLA fan favorite. Also, I knew I would have a great chance of being retained if he got the job.

That afternoon, Coach Cunningham interviewed with J.D. They talked behind closed doors for well over an hour. When the interview ended, Coach Cunningham poked his head into my office and said he thought the interview had gone great! A short time later, J.D. Morgan walked into my office and shut the door. He told me he thought the interview had been awful. He was frustrated because he couldn't tell whether Gary wanted the job or not! I told J.D. that I was certain Gary wanted the job, and that I would speak to him, which J.D. encouraged me to do. He told me he had planned to talk to Gary again after interviewing some others.

Like Gene Bartow, Gary Cunningham was one of the world's nicest human beings. Unlike Bartow, he was a John Wooden disciple and a UCLA native son.

I could understand why it might be hard to read him, especially when he was in his office demeanor. When I was on Coach Cunningham's freshman team, the players used to joke about his transformation every day at 3 P.M. At his desk he looked like Clark Kent and was very affable. When he took off his glasses, popped in his contact lenses, and changed into basketball gear, he became strict and forceful, like Superman.

I called Coach Cunningham and asked him to stop by my townhouse the next day. I knew I had to hit him between the eyes to make him understand the impression he had given Mr. Morgan. I told him, very directly, to leave no doubt that he was passionate about wanting to be the next UCLA basketball coach.

Coach Cunningham immediately started floating word of his interview and his excitement about the job throughout his extensive UCLA network, and he made sure the talk reached the *Los Angeles Times*. It wasn't long before there was an article in the *Times* about his desire to become the next head coach.

He was hired about a month later.

Coach Cunningham had let me know early on that if he got the job I didn't have to worry about keeping mine. He would, however, need to hire another assistant coach to replace Lee Hunt.

He chose an old friend, Jim Harrick, who had coached Morningside High School in Inglewood. One year Harrick's Morningside team had been ranked the No. 1 high school team in the country, and he was currently an assistant coach at Utah State. On the day Jim interviewed, he walked into my office and sat down so we could talk. We spoke for about 10 minutes before it was time for him go across the hall and talk with Coach Cunningham. My first impression of Jim was that he was confident and knowledgeable, and I could learn a lot from him. Harrick eventually would become the head coach at UCLA and win its 11th national championship in 1995.

Coach Cunningham rehired Craig Impelman to head the JV

team. Seven years after he had been cut from that team he was being named coach. With Coach Cunningham, I was back in familiar territory. He was going to run practice exactly as Coach Wooden had. Same philosophy, same drills, same defense, and even the same offense. At our initial team meeting, the handouts for the players were essentially the same sheets Coach Wooden used. The only difference was that Coach Cunningham did not show our guys how to tie their shoes.

We opened the season at home against Brigham Young University, which had a talented freshman named Danny Ainge, and the Cougars gave us all we could handle. With the score tied at 73, David Greenwood missed a short jump shot, but James Wilkes tipped it back in. Gary Cunningham's stint at UCLA began with a two-point victory.

We were still undefeated when Notre Dame came to Pauley Pavilion early in December and beat us on our own court for the second straight year. They had many of their stars back from the previous season along with their "enforcer" Bill Laimbeer and some new talent in freshmen Kelly Tripucka and Orlando Woolridge. Not only did we hate losing to Notre Dame anywhere, but Digger Phelps (who had already recruited Rich Branning from Southern California), got a boost in recruiting in our backyard any time he beat us.

Our fans were disappointed but there were no cries to bring out the tar and feathers. Not even close to what we experienced with Coach Bartow.

We won our next nine games before going to South Bend to play Notre Dame for the second time. Coach Digger Phelps loved to make UCLA's visits to South Bend uncomfortable. He would always hold a student pep rally the night before our game at the exact same time we were scheduled to practice in the adjacent auditorium. Digger would often invite the broadcasters who were in town to do the national telecast to come to the rally to address the students. (I always felt it was to nudge them toward being more complimentary to Notre Dame.) When the rally was over, Digger would walk into our practice, basically interrupting it, to say hello to the coaches.

He would always ask how our stay in South Bend had been thus far.

This time Notre Dame beat us 75–73, completing the season sweep. Those were the only two losses we had during the regular season.

We won the last 11 games to finish with a regular season record of 24–2.

The first 10 games in that streak were conference games. We beat USC once, Stanford twice, and Cal twice without much difficulty to take a two-game lead over both USC and Oregon State.

But we would be tested in our next game, at home, by George Raveling's Washington State Cougars. We were trailing by one point with 10 seconds left to go in the game and WSU was shooting a one-and-one. Terry Kelly made the first free throw, making the score 60–58. But the whistle blew and the referee signaled that WSU's Stuart House entered the lane too soon. This violation nullified the basket and gave us the ball out of bounds. Coach Raveling was beside himself and would vehemently disagree with the call. But it was UCLA's ball, and we would have to go the length of court to score and win the game. WSU extended their defense, but we inbounded the ball to Roy Hamilton, and he took off. I thought he had a chance to drive the ball to the basket, but his attack drew an extra defender. Roy opted to pass the ball to our center, Gig Sims, who missed a very makeable shot for him. But in the scramble to stop Hamilton, Greenwood found himself open for an offensive rebound and a put-back dunk. An improbable win, but such was the magic of Pauley Pavilion.

Of the games we had left, my favorite was the game at The Pit in Eugene, Oregon. We were met by the usual screaming students, most of them proudly wearing buttons identifying them as "deranged idiots." It was Coach Bartow who added "idiots" to Marques Johnson's description "deranged." I told Cunningham and Harrick about UCLA's last two visits to The Pit, and how ugly those games were, resulting in losses. But not this time. Their fans couldn't muster enough hostility to hold off the inevitability of the butt whooping we were about to put on the Kamikaze Kids! We blew it open in the second half and won 83–57. Toward the end of the game, I

took a moment to watch the student section. There were a few obscenities still being shouted, but most of the students were sitting in
silence. I thoroughly enjoyed that.

We finished the conference run by beating USC to remain undefeated in the Pac-8 (14–0) and earn the NCAA berth. We were
ranked No. 2 in the nation.

The next day we played Michigan in a nationally televised game
in Pauley. It was Raymond Townsend's last home game and he went
out scoring a game-high 29 points. We handed Michigan its worst
loss of the season 96–70.

We found out right before the Michigan game that our first-
round NCAA opponent would be the Kansas Jayhawks, the Big
Eight champion. The game site would be MacArthur Court in Eugene, Oregon, aka The Pit. I was curious how we would be greeted
at The Pit when we weren't playing Oregon. We were representing
the Pac-8 in the tournament. There were fans from UCLA and Kansas at the game, but most of the crowd was local. Some rooted for
good basketball plays, but a small portion of them definitely rooted
for Kansas!

ROY HAMILTON AND CBS

Roy Hamilton and I had a great working relationship when I was
an assistant coach at UCLA and he was a player. From 1975 to
1979, I not only worked with Roy during practices and games, I
also helped him schedule his classes and monitor progress toward
his degree.

Roy and I also had a great working relationship about 18 years
later when Roy was an experienced TV producer and I was in my
first year of broadcasting.

I was getting good reviews for my work on ESPN and I was
subsequently selected to work for CBS during the first two rounds
of the NCAA basketball tournament in 1993. There was a huge
staff meeting in a hotel ballroom in New York. At this gathering of
producers, directors, sideline reporters, play-by-play announcers,
and analysts, we learned our assignments.

The game was nip and tuck, with Kansas leading most of the way. It felt to me like we were playing catch-up but could never take the lead and control of the game. Late in the second half, I thought this game might get away from us. Kansas committed a few untimely turnovers that would ultimately cost them the game. We definitely got the better end of the officials' whistles. The Jayhawks were called for 30 fouls, and we were called for just 14. Valentine fouled out with more than eight minutes left, which crippled the Jayhawks' chances. Raymond Townsend had 22 points including 6-for-6 from the free throw line. Final score was 83–76 UCLA.

I shook Coach Ted Owens' hand at the end of the game. I thought he would be angry because of the way the game had been officiated. There were some questionable fouls called against his team. But he was very gracious in defeat and wished each of us luck. I went into the media room to listen to his press conference. I was impressed with the way he walked off the court, and I wanted to see if his attitude would stay the same. Coach Owens was humble. He talked only in positive terms about both teams and did not say anything negative, not even about the officiating! This was an NCAA

The man in charge of the Western Regional was Roy Hamilton. Now our roles were reversed. He was telling me what I needed to do and how I needed to do it. For TV interviews and newspaper articles about our new collaboration, we took some jabs at each other, all in fun.

In truth, Roy was invaluable to me. I had several private tutoring sessions in which Roy and I watched video tape of my work for ESPN. He would pause the tape every now and then to explain to me what he liked or didn't like. He really helped me improve as a broadcaster.

I was available at tournament time because I was coaching the Kuwait national team during the spring, summer and fall when international competitions are usually held. I would come back during the NCAA regular season. I worked NCAA Regionals for CBS three times and for two of them, Roy was my producer.

tournament game, and we had just ended the Jayhawks' season. Losing games is never easy, but how you conduct yourself when you lose is something you can control. Coach Owens was both a fierce competitor and a gentleman. He set the standard for me that day, demonstrating how to behave after a game.

I had never been to Albuquerque, New Mexico, but that's where we played Arkansas in our Western Regional semifinal game. Coach Eddie Sutton played a three-guard offense, unique in those days, and those guards were sensational! All were terrific scorers and with Ron Brewer at 6-foot-4, Sidney Moncrief at 6-foot-3, and Marvin Delph at 6-foot-4, they presented matchup issues.

Our game against Arkansas was probably the worst we played all season. Raymond Townsend, who had been shooting the lights out in our previous four games, went ice cold, making just 1 of 11 shots from the floor. Arkansas got 23 points from Delph, 18 from Brewer and 21 from Moncrief. It was as if they took turns scoring baskets at the most critical times. Our season ended with a 74–70 loss. Cunningham finished his first season with a record of 25–3.

For the second straight year, UCLA had been eliminated in the semifinal round of the Western Regional. I braced myself for the avalanche of criticism. Our fans were extremely disappointed, but it seemed like they were willing to give us a "mulligan" this time around.

Former UCLA All-American Walt Hazzard (Mahdi Abdul-Rahman) gave us a heads up on a forward out of DeRidder, Louisiana. He told us this kid was a terrific all-around player and would fit perfectly into the UCLA system. Mike Sanders was 6-foot-6 with long arms and soft hands. He could rebound in traffic. We made contact with Mike, evaluated some of his game films, and immediately set up a campus visit.

Recruiting was one of my strengths, but Mike Sanders was the victim of my most horrendous few hours as a host. Craig Impelman, now the JV coach, went with me when I picked Mike up at LAX. We thought we would dazzle him with a drive up the Pacific Coast Highway. I stopped in Pacific Palisades to show him the ocean, the beautiful beach and the California girls. We had just stepped out of the car when Mike told me it "smells funny" here. The fishy smell of the water had put a very unpleasant look on his face and I feared he might throw up, so I made my apologies while getting him back in the car to head for campus. As we drove around Westwood so I could point out the movie theaters and restaurants that enhance the UCLA community, I asked Mike where he would like to have lunch. I showed him restaurants for Italian, Chinese, and Mexican food. Mike's face once again had a pained look as he told me, very politely, he doesn't eat foreign food. I changed the subject and took him straight to Coach Cunningham's office. I went to Harrick's office to tell him about Mike's aversion to "foreign food" so he and Coach Cunningham could figure out where to go to lunch while I showed Mike the campus.

I took Mike into the old Men's Gym and told him of its history, pointing out buildings as we strolled through campus. The sky was getting a little overcast but it was still a pleasant Southern California day. A highlight of my tour was taking recruits to the top of the building named for Dr. Ralph Bunche, UCLA's Nobel Peace Prize winner (and former UCLA basketball player). It has a spectacular view of campus as well as Westwood and Beverly Hills. As I was telling Mike all about the university I love, I tried to ignore sprinkles of rain. Mike's body language was saying we need to get off this roof. By the time the elevator reached the ground floor, it was pouring. I had no umbrella. Who carries an umbrella in Southern California? From Bunche Hall back to the athletic department is usually a 15-minute walk. We made it back in 10 minutes. When Coach Cunningham saw us, both literally dripping, his mouth dropped open. I tried to dry Mike off with paper towels from the restroom, which proved to be a fruitless effort.

The itinerary was adjusted to get Mike to the hotel for a change of clothes before lunch. I was sure I had blown it with this kid before he had been in Los Angeles for two hours. He hadn't even seen Pauley Pavilion.

Mike was dry when we took him to get a hamburger and french

fries. The rest of the visit went well. Mike told us before he flew back to Louisiana that he wanted to come to UCLA, despite my efforts!

Coach Cunningham's second season opened at home against Boise State and DePaul. Boise State posed no problem, but DePaul was a very good team led by Hall of Fame Coach Ray Meyer. I was the coach who scouted DePaul and my biggest concerns were seniors Gary Garland and Curtis Watkins. While going over personnel with the team, I told David Greenwood (our first team All-American) that he would be guarding a freshman named Mark Aguirre. I really didn't know what he was good at because he had no college stats or past game film footage. I watched him warm up and he appeared to be slightly overweight, had soft hands, a nice-looking jump shot, and a big butt. So when David asked me about Aguirre again, during warmups, I told David he was good jump shooter, and he looked to be a step slow.

Aguirre's first basket in a college game was a dunk that was close to being on Greenwood's head. The look Greenwood gave me as he ran past our bench said: "How could you lie to me, Coach?" Aguirre was the No. 1 pick of the 1981 draft and played 13 years in the NBA. In this game, Greenwood scored 29; Aguirre 28. We beat DePaul 108–85.

We beat Santa Clara a week later, then had a week to prepare for Notre Dame. Notre Dame had swept us the previous year and we were looking for a measure of payback. This game was in Pauley Pavilion, and we felt good about our chances. Notre Dame Coach Digger Phelps showed up for the game dressed in a beautiful sport coat, a white dress shirt with three buttons open, no tie, and several gold chains. He looked very Hollywood. When we shook hands before the start of the game, I mentioned how dapper he was dressed, and he looked me square in the eyes and said, "Yes, I know, and I also knew you would appreciate it!"

In all my time at UCLA, this was without question the most talented Notre Dame team I had seen. It was a classic struggle and they beat us 81–78.

Notre Dame had beaten us three straight times in Los Angeles.

Larry's parents, Clarice and Larry Senior, on the trip he was able to give them when he became head coach at UCLA.

Larry Farmer conducts an inspection as an ROTC officer at Manual High School.

Coach Wooden presents the Seymore Armand Award for the most outstanding freshman to Larry Farmer at the awards banquet in 1970.

The UCLA team that has just won the NCAA title in Larry Farmer's sophomore year. It is the fifth straight NCAA title win for UCLA. The team finished the season with a record of 29–1. Larry is in the back row on the left.

Coach John Wooden's birthday was October 14, which was also the date of the annual Picture Day before practice could begin on October 15. A cake for Coach became a tradition. Larry Farmer (No. 54), Henry Bibby (No. 45), and Tommy Curtis (No. 22) were up close for the cake cutting.

Coach Wooden instructs Larry Farmer during a practice at Pauley Pavilion.

UCLA's vaunted 2-2-1 press, with Larry Farmer (No. 54) and Henry Bibby (No. 45) in the foreground. Jamaal Wilkes and Greg Lee are in the second row of the press, with Bill Walton protecting the basket.

Larry Farmer goes to the hoop as a Buckeye defender stops short.

Larry Farmer (No. 54) and Bruin teammate Bill Walton battle University of Texas players for a rebound in a game UCLA won 117–65 in 1972.

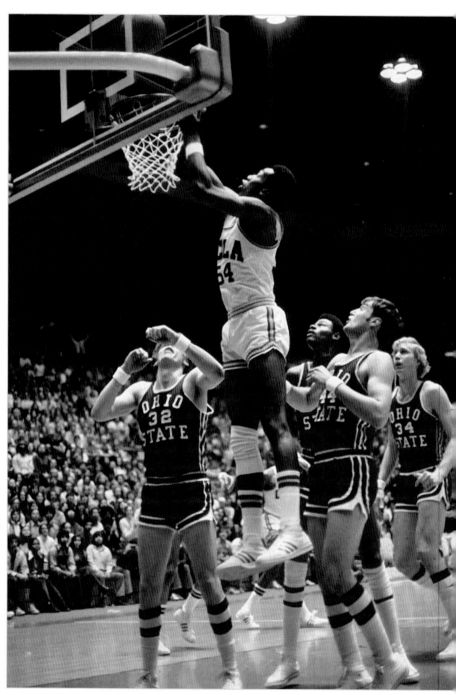

Larry Farmer goes up to score, surrounded by several Ohio State defenders, in a game at Pauley Pavilion on December 4, 1971. Ohio State arrived ranked No. 6 in the country and lost to the Bruins 79–53.

Larry Farmer (left) plays a game of Spades on a bus trip in 1972. In the foreground is Gary Franklin and across the aisle is Vince Carson. Bill Walton is in the background.

Larry Farmer advances the ball against the press during an NCAA tournament semifinal game against the University of Louisville in the Los Angeles Sports Arena.

The UCLA team that has just won its sixth straight NCAA championship with a victory over Florida State. This is the team Farmer thinks is the best college basketball team ever. Their average winning margin was 30.3 points per game, which still stands as an NCAA record. Farmer is standing in the middle of the photo with his arm around Jamaal Wilkes. The team finished 30–0 and was ranked No. 1 in the country all year.

Larry Farmer goes up to score over Ernie DiGregorio, a consensus All-American who would go on to be named NBA Rookie of the Year. Providence came into Pauley Pavilion ranked No. 7 in the country and lost to the top-ranked Bruins 101–77.

Larry Farmer takes
the ball up over
Dwight Clay in
UCLA's record-
breaking streak
game No. 61 at the
University of Notre
Dame.

Larry Farmer walks
off the court after
UCLA's record-setting
61st straight victory
alongside Coach
John Wooden, who is
carrying the game ball.

Coach Wooden and Larry Farmer have a serious exchange before Farmer goes back into the game against Indiana University in an NCAA semifinal game in 1973.

After UCLA's seventh straight NCAA championship victory, Larry Farmer got a boost from teammate Swen Nater as he cut down one of the nets. Teammate Bob Webb joins in the celebration.

The UCLA team that has just won its seventh straight NCAA title. The team finished 30–0 and was ranked No. 1 in the country all year. Larry Farmer is wearing a net around his neck and kneeling in front of Coach John Wooden. Farmer has just played his last game for UCLA, finishing with three NCAA titles and a record of 89–1.

Larry Farmer's NCAA championship rings from 1971, 1972, and 1973.

Larry Farmer scores on a dunk during a game in Germany.

Assistant coach Larry Farmer, All-American forward Marques Johnson, and Coach Gene Bartow watch NBA draft results come in at the *Los Angeles Herald-Examiner* office.

Larry Farmer, as an assistant coach, on the bench with Head Coach Gary Cunningham (center) and assistant coach Jim Harrick, while Chancellor Charles Young (leaning in) and Athletic Director J.D. Morgan stop to visit before a game at Pauley Pavilion. Both Farmer and Harrick later became head coaches at UCLA.

Coach Larry Brown (right) confers with his assistants, Kevin O'Connor (left) and Larry Farmer during a timeout.

JOE KENNEDY / Los Angeles Times

Larry Farmer made his introduction as UCLA basketball coach a family affair by sharing the moment with his wife, Joyce, (right) and his parents, Larry and Clarice Farmer, who flew in from Denver to help celebrate son's promotion.

This is a clipping from the Sports section of the *Los Angeles Times* when Larry Farmer was introduced as head coach.

Larry Farmer's first team as head coach at UCLA.

Coach Larry Farmer huddles with his assistants, Kevin O'Connor and Craig Impelman, before speaking to his team during a timeout.

Coach Larry Farmer and point guard Ralph Jackson confirm strategy.

Coach Farmer directs his team during a game.

Los Angeles Times beat reporter Tracy Dodds talks with UCLA Coach Larry Farmer in a photo taken in Pauley Pavilion in 1983.

Coach Larry Farmer delivers an encouraging message to forward Kenny Fields.

Coach Farmer directs his team.

UCLA Coach Larry Farmer kneels on the side of the court at Pauley Pavilion.

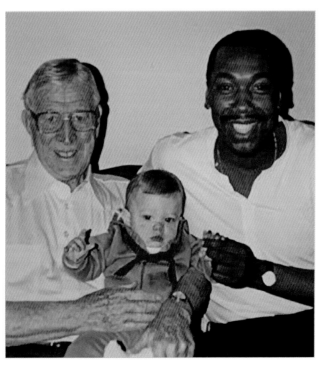

Coach John Wooden holds his great grandson, John Lawrence Impelman, who is named after both Wooden and Larry Farmer. Larry also is his godfather. John Impelman grew up to become a basketball coach himself.

Varsity Captains

1949 - *Ronnie Pearson
1950 - *Alan Sawyer
1951 - Eddie Sheldrake
1952 - Don Johnson + *Jerry Norman
1953 - *Barry Porter
1954 - *Ron Livingston
1955 - *John Moore + *Ron Bragg
1956 - *William Naulls
1957 - *Dick Banton
1958 - *Ben Rogers
1959 - *Walt Torrence
1960 - *Clifford Brandon
1961 - *John Berberich + *Bill Ellis
1962 - *Gary Cunningham + *John Green
1963 - *Jim Milhorn
1964 - *Walt Hazzard + *Jack Hirsch
1965 - *Keith Erickson + *Gail Goodrich
1966 - *Freddie Goss
1967 - *Mike Warren
1968 - *Mike Warren
1969 - *Lewis Alcindor + *Lynn Shackelford
1970 - *John Vallely
1971 - Steve Patterson, Curtis Rowe, Sidney Wicks
1972 - *Henry Bibby
1973 - *Larry Farmer
1974 - *Bill Walton + *Keith Wilkes
1975 - David Meyers

Coach Wooden kept a handwritten list of his team captains in his desk.

Coach Larry Farmer poses with the team he coached in Kuwait. The Kuwait Towers are in the background.

Larry Farmer's warm-up jacket was taken from the UCLA bench during a game at The Pit, stored in Colorado, mailed to him in Hawaii, and moved with him to Illinois.

Larry Farmer with Bill Walton.

Larry Farmer holds the trophy after being inducted into the Colorado High School Activities Association Hall of Fame as a player for Manual High School in Denver.

Larry Farmer at his induction into the UCLA Hall of Fame with his daughter, Kendall, and his son, Larry III.

At his induction into the UCLA Athletic Hall of Fame, Larry Farmer (center) is joined by his brother Aubrey, his sister-in-law Ora, his daughter Kendall, and his son Larry Farmer III.

Teammates Jamaal Wilkes, Greg Lee, Larry Farmer, and Bill Walton got together at Farmer's induction into the UCLA Athletic Hall of Fame. The four were starters for two perfect seasons, going 60–0 and winning national titles in 1972 and 1973.

Larry Farmer with Jamaal Wilkes, who was among those who recommended Farmer for the UCLA Hall of Fame.

Rich Branning and Tripucka scored 21 points each for the Irish. Branning seemed to enjoy coming home to Southern California to play his best games.

I had a lot of respect for Digger Phelps as a coach. He certainly had turned the Notre Dame program around, and with this win he had done something no other coach had done before. No nonconference opponent had ever won three times in a row at UCLA.

My relationship with Digger Phelps was a complicated one. In my second year as JV coach we played a game right after Notre Dame had beaten UCLA on national TV. Our fans had all but filed out of Pauley Pavilion and the Notre Dame players were still showering and dressing when Digger came out to watch the JV game. He sat right behind our bench. With the exception of our JV players' families or girlfriends, Pauley Pavilion was empty. I could hear every word of Digger's running commentary. To my surprise, he was saying complimentary things about how we were executing on offense. As he was leaving, he told me I was doing a heck of a job. I was flattered!

Just after Christmas we began league play with a loss at Stanford that was a sign of things to come. The Pac-8 conference was now the Pac-10 with the addition of Arizona and Arizona State. Winning the conference title was going to be more of a challenge, and we seemed to have too many single-digit margins, whether we were winning or losing.

At Stanford, senior guard Wolfe Perry had a career night, scoring 34 points. We played sloppy, and our shot selection and passing were not very good against the Stanford 2-3 zone defense. Still, we were actually leading by one point when Stanford held the ball to take the last shot—which they made at the buzzer. We were 0–1 in the conference.

After a comfortable victory over Cal, our next three conference games were perfect examples of how tight the conference race was going to be. We beat Oregon State 65–63, Oregon 74–71, and USC 89–86.

As a team, we had been struggling from the free throw line. It took a 23-of-29 exhibition of free throw shooting to win the USC game! Their superstar center, Cliff Robinson, had 32 points and 14 rebounds (18 of those points coming in the first half). The good news in all of these close games was that we had a veteran team and the team reflected the personality of Coach Gary Cunningham. We played calmly and with confidence. There was no panic.

At one of our home games I was on the court early, watching our team warm up, when I noticed a young lady wearing a distinctive T-shirt walking down the stairs in the student section. My eyes were then drawn to the tall, attractive young lady with her. I was struck by a strange sense of connection. I knew at that moment that I would someday get to know her. I did not see her again until years later, but when I saw her on campus I recognized her immediately. I learned that her name was Chris O'Brien. She would become my second wife and we would have two beautiful children.

It was January before we went on the road for our first games against the newest members of the conference. We played first at Arizona, where Fred Snowden was in his seventh year as coach, and played in front of a packed house. When David Greenwood missed a 20-foot desperation jump shot at the buzzer and Arizona beat us 70–69, the arena erupted. Fans swarmed Coach Snowden and his players. All I could do was wave at him and mouth the words "Congratulations, Coach."

Snowden was a friend and coaching role model for me, as one of the original African American head coaches in Division 1 basketball. When Arizona became a part of the Pac-10 he was the second black head coach in our league. George Raveling, at Washington State, was the first.

We salvaged a split out of that trip by winning 95–79 at Arizona State.

We beat Washington State and Washington at Pauley and followed up with victories at Oregon and at Oregon State, so we went into our game against USC with a conference record of 9–2. USC was 8–3. Bob Boyd had already announced he would be resigning as USC coach at the end of the season. (Boyd's most famous victory came at Pauley Pavilion, in 1969, when his USC team beat UCLA with Kareem Abdul-Jabbar by using a stall.) His current team was talented and playing with a lot of emotional energy. It was a typical UCLA-USC game and we won in overtime to take sole position of first place in the Pac-10.

There was no time to recover from the stressful overtime victory over USC on Friday evening, because we had to travel to South Bend on Saturday for a Sunday afternoon game. Historically, we had played Notre Dame and USC back-to-back, but in previous years we played Notre Dame in South Bend and came back to Los Angeles to play USC with five days in between.

For this game, Notre Dame was ranked No. 1 in the nation with UCLA No. 4. Statistically, we were the two best shooting teams in the country, with UCLA shooting 56 percent and Notre Dame 55 percent. UCLA had lost three straight to Notre Dame, which meant there were four sophomores on the Notre Dame team who had never lost to UCLA. When UCLA won 56–50 it was called an upset. Our overall record was 18-3 as we returned to league play.

Our victory over Arizona State in Pauley Pavilion was one of the craziest ebb-and-flow games I have ever been involved with and it had a crazy ending. With nine seconds on the clock, Arizona State led 83–79. They were inbounding the ball, needing only to get it in to force us to foul. ASU's Tony Zeno, who had been playing great, inbounded the ball against our press. He attempted a home run pass that went out of bounds without touching anyone, so it's our ball, under our basket. We inbound the ball to Roy Hamilton, who gets fouled immediately, and the clock hasn't moved. He makes both free throws to put us within two points. The next inbounds pass is stolen by Kiki Vandeweghe, who drives to the basket and gets fouled as only two seconds tick off the clock. Kiki makes both free throws and now it's tied with seven seconds left. ASU can still play for the last shot, and if they miss, the game goes into overtime. We back our defense up, wanting to make it difficult for them to score without fouling. ASU inbounds the ball, brings it up the floor quickly and gets off a tough shot that misses! Brad Holland comes down with the rebound, and in the chaos, a referee blows his whistle and calls an over-the-back foul on ASU. The clock is showing 0:00. After a brief huddle among the officials at the scorers' table, it was determined that Holland was fouled before the horn went off. With no time left on the clock, Holland sank both free throws. Final score: UCLA 85, Arizona State 83.

While ASU was leading, with about a minute to play, Jim Harrick was up yelling at the referees. Coach Cunningham told him to calm down because we didn't need a technical foul. Jim whispered to me that this "bleeping" game was over and a "T" was not going to make any difference. When the game was over and Coach Cunningham had addressed the team, Jim and I had a private moment. We laughed and agreed that nobody else could have sat on that bench as calmly as Coach Cunningham to pull that one out!

We had a two-game lead in the conference but the roller-coaster ride was not over. We lost at Washington by one point before scratching out an overtime victory at Washington State. Our last two games were at home. We beat Cal 79–68, marking the 1,000th victory in UCLA's 60-year basketball history. Then we won our 13th straight conference championship by blowing out Stanford two days later 99–71.

The Stanford game was Senior Day for David Greenwood, Roy Hamilton, and Brad Holland. They had been recruited by Coach Wooden (and Gary Cunningham). They had played two seasons for Bartow, who signed them, and two seasons for Cunningham. All three were first-round NBA draft picks.

Winning our conference and finishing 23–4 gave us a first-round NCAA game at home against Pepperdine University, which was just a few miles down the Pacific Coast Highway. Pepperdine had some great players, and we were sluggish after eight days without a game, but we won 76–71 to advance to the next round in Provo, Utah, to face the University of San Francisco.

USF, led by 7-foot-1 All-American center Bill Cartwright and a 6-foot-9 freshman named Guy Williams, would challenge us with their height. We thought our speed would give us an advantage, and it did.

We trailed USF throughout the first half. They were hurting us on the boards. The offense that we ran at UCLA, the high post, had a 2-3 alignment, with our guards at the top. We had a play, called "the letter play," that involved our center setting a screen at the top of the key for one of those guards. Because Roy Hamilton was left-handed and Brad Holland was right-handed, we would set them up in our two-guard front specifically so they could use their dominant hand. We ran it to perfection and USF had no answer for it, or for our guards. Whoever Guy Williams was guarding, Brad or Roy, could attack him on this play. Cartwright, who was guarding our center, was pulled away from the basket so he couldn't block shots. Roy Hamilton scored a career-high 36 points and Brad Holland added 22. Cartwright had 34 points and 9 rebounds. He was terrific, but it wasn't enough.

We beat USF 99–81 to set up a rematch with DePaul in the Regional final.

We had beaten DePaul in our second game of the season, which seemed like ages earlier. DePaul was much improved as was freshman Mark Aguirre. They beat Marquette 62–56 to set up our rematch. We watched the Marquette game and we had watched them beat USC. They were good!

There's always a day in between the semifinal game and the regional final. The remaining teams would each get an hour to practice. DePaul practiced first at the arena, and then Coach Ray Meyer had his required meeting with the media. We practiced next, and when we finished Coach Cunningham instructed the team to go back to the hotel. He didn't know how long his interviews would take. As our team walked out to board our bus, we came upon Coach Meyer, who also had sent his team back and now he was stranded. He asked if he could hitch a ride on our bus. We, of course, said yes. He could not have been nicer to our players. He was the grandfatherly type, and for the 15-minute bus ride to the hotels, he talked and told stories. He simply mesmerized our players, and me as well.

In Los Angeles, back in November, we had beaten DePaul

108–85. To this day I'm not sure how much that easy victory might have affected our mental preparation for this tournament game. Our performance in the first half of this game was so bad one newspaper report called it "abysmal."

But it was worse than that! We committed 14 turnovers in the first half alone and trailed by as many as 19 points. DePaul led, 51–34, at halftime. It was not the first time these players had been behind. We very recently had come back from a bad start to beat USF. But this was a much deeper hole!

We played at the Marriott Center Arena in Provo, which is on the campus of BYU. For most of the game the 13,000 fans had largely been cheering for UCLA. BYU put on an elaborate halftime show, with different themes and many participants. The entertainment went long, and as our team left the locker room to warmup for the second half, the court was still being occupied by the final dance routine. Our band leader, Kelly James, didn't know what to do, but our chancellor, Charles Young, told Kelly to play our customary fight song when the team took the floor! Our players recognized that with the festivities still going on, they should probably wait until this last song and dance number was finished before taking the floor. But the music for the dancers was getting drowned out by the UCLA fight song, and the fans in the Marriott Center started yelling at our band and quickly turned against us. When our coaching staff walked out of the locker room, all we could hear were boos and it wasn't until later we were told exactly what had happened. And the fans cheered for DePaul for the final 20 minutes.

We shot 61 percent from the floor in the second half, which helped us fight our way back into the game. But our outside shooters struggled, as Brad Holland shot 6–15 and Kiki Vandeweghe shot just 7–17. Their outside shooting would have really helped open up DePaul's 2–3 zone defense. We could never get any closer than four points. Gary Garland scored 24 points for DePaul and would be named the MVP of the Western Regional. Curtis Watkins also scored 24 points and Mark Aguirre added 20 for DePaul. David Greenwood scored a career high 37 points in his last college game.

Brad Holland scored 19, Roy Hamilton added 16.

The DePaul Blue Demons beat us 95–91.

Once again our season ended abruptly with a loss in the Regional. Coach Bartow lost to Idaho State. Coach Cunningham lost to Arkansas and DePaul.

Four days later, Coach Cunningham organized a team dinner, which I assumed was to end the season on a more positive note. Before driving to Westwood for dinner, the coaching staff would meet in Cunningham's office. Jim Harrick had been hired at Pepperdine to succeed Coach Gary Colson, who was retiring. I was happy for Jim and thought the dinner would give him a good opportunity to say goodbye to the team.

But I was shocked when, during the brief coaches' meeting, Gary Cunningham told us he was stepping down after two years as UCLA's coach. I did not see this coming. The players were just as shocked when Cunningham told them a short time later. Gary and I were very close but throughout this whole process he never once hinted that he was thinking about quitting.

Gary Cunningham's record at UCLA was 58–8, putting his winning percentage No. 1 on the list of UCLA coaches. In preparing for this book I asked Gary why he quit. He said, as Bartow had said, it just wasn't fun anymore.

Shortly after his resignation, J.D. Morgan summoned me to his home in the San Fernando Valley. Mr. Morgan had undergone open heart surgery the previous December and was convalescing at home and working mostly through his assistant, Bob Fischer. I left the office and drove directly to Mr. Morgan's house. He greeted me at the door wearing pajamas and a bathrobe. It was about 7 P.M. and he jokingly asked that I forgive him for not getting dressed up for my visit.

He first asked me how I was doing, and I told him that I was still getting over the shock of Gary stepping down. Mr. Morgan told me that discussions had been taking place for some time, so he knew Cunningham would probably leave. He asked me about our returning players, and I told him that I had been in contact with all of them and would stay in contact to make sure none of them considered transferring. Mr. Morgan then asked me about recruiting. The national signing date was in early April, and we did not want to lose any recruits because of this coaching change. I told him that we had verbal commitments from two guards. J.D. told me to make sure I kept those relationships warm, as he was going to move quickly to replace Cunningham.

J.D. then started asking me questions about myself, and how I was growing as a coach. He asked me about my coaching philosophy and my thoughts on future recruiting. We talked for another ten minutes before it dawned on me that he was interviewing me for the job.

I knew my name had been mentioned for the position, but that, in my opinion, was just a courtesy. I was a 27-year-old kid with two years of junior varsity head coaching experience. I had been a full-time assistant coach for only four years.

Mr. Morgan's attention then shifted to Larry Brown. He asked me if I knew him, and I said I did because of our commonality with Denver, my hometown. He was head coach of the Denver Nuggets. We knew many of the same basketball people. Mr. Morgan asked me if I thought hiring an NBA coach would hurt our program in any way. I told him I didn't think so and that it might add some excitement to the program.

A new approach might be good. Two winning college coaches had walked away in just four years.

Before I left, Mr. Morgan told me that if he hired Larry Brown, he would strongly recommend that Larry keep me on his staff.

Gary Cunningham would go on to become an athletic director. His first stop was Western Oregon State, followed by Wyoming and Fresno State and, finally, 13 years as the athletic director at UC Santa Barbara. He retired in 2008. He had appeared on the cover of Sports Illustrated as a player in 1962 and he was inducted into the UCLA Hall of Fame in 2001. I was sincerely sad to see him go. It was Gary who had flown to Denver when I signed my letter of intent. He had planned every class I took at UCLA. He was my friend, and when he was hired to be the head coach at UCLA, he gave me a job and entrusted me with a great deal of responsibility. I learned to plan and execute practices from the assistant coach who for 10 years did the same thing with Coach Wooden. He was an exceptional teacher. My approach on the court would most resemble his.

After UCLA's own Jackie Robinson had retired from Major League Baseball he said: "The game had done much for me, and I had done much for it." He could just as well been talking about Gary Cunningham's relationship with UCLA. Gary Cunningham had given much of himself to UCLA.

CHAPTER 17

Larry Brown: The Birth of Cool

Larry Brown was the coolest coach in the history of UCLA basketball. He dressed the part, he looked the part, and he acted the part. He was charming, polite, and sophisticated, but also shrewd and very smart. He loved basketball, and he knew the game. If you were around him for any length of time, he made you love basketball, too. He respected the history of the game, had played and coached at the highest levels, and taught some of the greatest players. I was excited to learn from him.

I first met him shortly after he was hired by J.D. Morgan. We met at the Holiday Inn in Westwood. I assumed he had already discussed my place on his staff with Mr. Morgan and he had agreed to keep me, but during our friendly conversation it was made clear that my rehiring would be completely his decision and his alone. Our conversation remained cordial and exploratory, but I went to work on selling myself much harder than when I thought I was a done deal. I'm not sure when Coach Brown decided to hire me, but I think it had to be before he asked me to talk with Eddie Fogler and Kevin O'Connor and give him my opinion on how they would fit into our staff.

Fogler was one of Dean Smith's assistants at North Carolina, and O'Connor was an assistant coach at the University of Colorado.

When I met Eddie Fogler, I immediately liked him. He loved Dean Smith the way I loved Coach Wooden, so we talked about our special bonds with those coaching icons. After about an hour I knew he would remain at North Carolina. He couldn't turn down a chance to at least talk to UCLA, but his heart was in Chapel Hill.

Kevin O'Connor was personable, funny, and a great storyteller.

O'Connor had been an assistant coach for seven years at Virginia Tech, VMI, and the University of Colorado. He was a family man, and we knew many of the same people and places in Denver. When Coach Brown told me that he was going to hire Kevin I, too, believed that Kevin would be a terrific hire.

With the staff set, getting our team set was the top priority. Recruiting through a coaching change is an art unto itself, and Coach Brown knew we would have to work closely, as a staff, to try to hold on to the young men the previous staff had been working with.

He also made time to meet the people he needed to know in his new position.

Larry Brown was a magnet. There were always people coming and going. He had a big circle of friends and associates, and a smaller inner circle of NBA buddies. Two of his most trusted friends were lawyers Joe Glass and his son, Keith. Joe was Larry's agent and negotiated his contracts and had that New York swagger. He was rarely seen without his trademark cigar. Joe's family and law practice were back in NY, but he came out to Los Angeles to help Larry get situated. When he went back to New York, Coach Brown talked Keith into putting his law practice on hold and becoming a member of our coaching staff. Keith had a quick wit, was very smart, and had a way of keeping Coach Brown grounded. Joe and Keith were more like father and brother to Larry Brown.

Coach Brown had heard a lot about Sam Gilbert and he told me he looked forward to meeting him. They met at Coach Brown's hotel and as soon as their meeting ended, Sam called me. He was, of course, impressed by Larry and couldn't help but like him, and thought he would be very good for UCLA. But then Sam shocked me by saying he thought Larry wouldn't be at UCLA for very long. I had just survived two coaches leaving, and Sam is telling me that Coach Brown will be the third? I asked Sam why he thought that. He said Coach Brown would enjoy coaching at UCLA but would grow tired of his modest salary and lifestyle in Southern California. Eventually he would use his being unhappy as an excuse to leave for a much larger payday. Sam told me to watch and see. I really hoped he was wrong.

One of our largest support groups was the Bruin Hoopsters. The president of the Hoopsters was Matt Suddleson, a very successful businessman who ran his own land title company. Some of its members were Jewish (including Matt) and because Larry was also Jewish, there seemed to be an instant connection. They wanted to look after him, answer his questions and get him settled in. There was always a small group of boosters that got close to a head coach. Coach Bartow had a group of friends that he trusted and embraced, as did Gary Cunningham. Larry had this group, all good people, getting things done for him behind the scenes to make his transition to Southern California easier.

Larry also was terrific with the UCLA students, who quickly grew to love him. It was customary before big games at UCLA for the students to camp out the night before the game to be the first to claim seats when the doors opened on game day. The student section at UCLA was first come, first served. There could be up to a couple hundred students with sleeping bags lined up outside Pauley Pavilion a full 36 hours before a game. The first time Larry Brown saw the students in line, he was so impressed that he went around talking to them and shaking hands. In the morning he came back with dozens of donuts from the donut shop in Westwood. He did more visiting while passing them out. I'd seen students lining up for UCLA games since I was a player. It never crossed my mind to do anything that thoughtful. I would talk to them, as all the other coaches I worked with did when we walked by. But Larry took it a step further, and the overnighters loved him. That was cool!

Larry was just as charismatic with recruits. Recruiting at UCLA was easy and yet complicated. It was easy because a player's talent level was usually pretty obvious and it wasn't hard to sell a young man on a program as strong as UCLA's. The complexities came in when the other schools recruiting him ganged up and directed their negative recruiting toward UCLA and not each other. During our glory years the only negative thing to say about us was that the competition would be so great the recruit might never get a chance to play. When Gary Cunningham stepped down, the young men we had been recruiting were told by our competition that the UCLA program was unstable and the head coach recruiting you might not be the head coach at your graduation. This was a real problem. With Coach Wooden retiring, followed by Bartow and Cunningham re-signing after two years each, that angle had a lot of traction.

Things were happening very quickly, and there was a looming deadline. We had about two weeks before national signing day. As a new coach, Coach Brown needed to meet with our current team. I filled him in on who they were, how they were doing in school, and how they played. I also filled him in on our prospects and the positions the previous staff was trying to fill. Roy Hamilton and Brad Holland were both graduating so we had recruited guards, getting early verbal commitments from two—Mike Chavez, a 5-foot-9 point guard from Downey, and Leon Wood, a 6-foot-2 shooting guard from Santa Monica.

Coach Brown asked me to set up home visits with both families, and he intended to honor the scholarship offers that had been made. He also wanted to introduce himself to these recruits and their families to take the fear of the unknown out of the coaching change.

Coach Brown was a sharp dresser and I tried to hold my own in that department. When I picked him up at the hotel to go to the Chavez home, he had his jacket over his arm. As I started to get back into the driver's seat of my car, he told me, "Coach Farms, you probably want to take your jacket off, so you don't get the back all wrinkled up." He then opened the back door to my car and laid his jacket on the seat, so I did the same. When I got back in the car he noticed that I had my initials monogrammed on my left shirt cuff, and I saw that he had his shirt monogrammed on his left shirt pocket. Coach pointed at my sleeve, and said with a sly little smile, "You know, Coach Farms, only pimps and hustlers wear their initials on their shirt sleeves!"

I realized he could teach me more than basketball.

At the Chavez home, his mom and dad were very polite and

seemed genuinely excited about meeting Coach Brown. But Mike told us early in the conversation that he had reopened his recruiting and was strongly considering Cal. When we left, I told Coach that Mike's enthusiasm for UCLA had taken a 180-degree turn. Based on the vibe he was giving off, we weren't going to get him. He did, in fact, sign with the University of California.

The next day we made the in-home visit with Leon and his mom, Evelyn Wood. (No relation to the speed-reading guru!) I had explained to Coach that Leon had grown up around UCLA basketball, and since junior high he had been coming to the Men's Gym to watch the games. Occasionally the guys would let him play. I was close to Leon and his mother. A couple of years earlier, when Leon was about to start high school, Evelyn had asked me where I thought Leon would be best served both academically and athletically. I recommended Saint Monica Catholic High School over the larger public school, Santa Monica High School. That worked out well for him.

I told all of this to Coach Brown, thinking he could expect a much better reception here than from Chavez. I was wrong! Evelyn

YOU DON'T EAT CHICKEN IN BED, DO YOU?

Larry Brown had stories to tell and I never tired of them. Especially his stories from his days in the NBA.

When he and I traveled to Pittsburgh to watch the Dapper Dan Classic, a high school All-Star game that was ideal for evaluating talent, we spent a lot of time together.

We took a redeye and when we finally arrived at the hotel, I discovered we were sharing a room. All the other coaches I had worked for would get their own room on the road. I'm not sure if we were sharing because we planned our trip at the last minute and couldn't book two rooms or if Coach wanted to get to know me, but there we were—roommates.

Coach Brown wanted to get some rest before the game that night. As the sun was coming up in Pittsburgh, we had all of the shades pulled down to make it as dark as possible. We put the was skeptical of Larry Brown from the minute we walked into her house. What I failed to realize was that despite the fact I could be a role model to Leon, so could Coach Fred Snowden, from the University of Arizona. Evelyn had done a terrific job of raising her son, but like many single parents, she was looking for a coach to assume the role of a surrogate father when her son left home. Arizona had been behind UCLA in recruiting Leon, but since the coaching change, Evelyn was focused on Arizona. The home visit did not go well. Evelyn was polite but distant and the questions she asked had undertones of concern. Leon sat quietly while she listened to everything Coach Brown had to say. As we walked to the car, I told Coach I would follow up with a phone call to Evelyn as soon as I got home. Evelyn had been told that NBA coaches were accustomed to coaching grown men and may not be as sensitive to the needs of a teenager, and also that Coach Brown would probably be going back to the NBA and would not stay for Leon's four years in college. Arizona had done a great job of recruiting Evelyn. I believed Leon still wanted to come to UCLA, but Evelyn had the final say. Leon signed a letter of intent with Arizona.

Do Not Disturb sign on the door. I was lying there in the dark, trying to fall asleep, when Larry interrupted the silence to ask if I remembered a guy who played in Denver. I told him of course I remembered that guy. I had actually played in some pickup games with him when I was home from UCLA for summer.

Larry tells me that when he roomed with this guy, he liked to eat Kentucky Fried Chicken while sitting in his bed watching television. He said this guy would eat a piece of chicken and then try to throw the bones in the wastebasket, wherever that might be in the room. The funny part of the story was that he would miss most of the time, covering the floor with chicken bones. Larry didn't like living in a room littered with chicken bones, and he really didn't like getting out of bed and stepping on a bone. I'm laughing, trying to figure out if this is a true story, and Larry ends with: "You don't eat chicken in bed, do you?"

I assured him that I did not.

We also had been recruiting front line players Cliff Pruitt from
Verbum Dei High School and Darren Daye from John F. Kennedy
High School for a couple of years. Neither had committed to UCLA.
We signed them both, giving this new staff immediate credibility.

Now we just needed to find another pair of really good guards.

Shortly after Coach Brown took the job, I got a call from a Pasadena High School guidance counselor telling us about Michael
Holton. She told me that he had written a letter expressing his interest. UCLA had never responded. He had visited several schools
and it appeared he would select either Oregon or Oregon State and
play against us. She was reaching out because she felt his heart was
at UCLA.

Holton was a tremendous player that we had become aware of
later in the year. The problem for Michael Holton was that Leon
Wood and Mike Chavez had made verbal commitments to us in
the fall of the previous year, essentially ending our recruitment of
guards. Now, however, we were seeking guards.

Michael made his campus visit the next weekend. He was a
6-foot-4 athlete, handsome, articulate, outgoing, dressed nicely, and
seemed excited about his visit. I thought it would be a pleasure to
get to know him during our drive from Pasadena to the campus. But
he immediately brought up his disappointment that UCLA had ne-
glected him. I felt I was being put on the spot, and he didn't seem to
accept my explanation. Finally, I told him that despite any error that
might have been made, he was now on his recruiting trip and if he
didn't go to UCLA, it would now be his decision, not ours. Holton
had a great weekend and bonded with Coach Brown. When I drove
him back Sunday, he resumed the conversation we had on the way
to campus. I ended it the same way, telling him the ball was now in
his court.

Michael chose UCLA and we were all thrilled to get him!

Rod Foster was a 6-foot-2 lightning-quick guard out of New
Brunswick, Connecticut. He attended a small Catholic high school
and put up incredible scoring numbers. Rod came highly recommended, and once we got him to campus for his visit, he instantly

won us over. He, too, would commit to UCLA.

When we received Rod's unofficial transcript, he had good grades, but in one of his core classes, we couldn't tell whether his grade was a B- or a B+. We phoned St. Thomas Aquinas High School and talked to a nun who was Rod's guidance counselor. She asked, "What do you need it to be?" We knew then the Good Lord was on our side.

When we met as a staff just before the start of the season, Coach Brown told Kevin O'Connor and me that a lot of what he planned to teach would come from Coach Dean Smith's system at North Carolina. He would also infuse some of the UCLA high post offense, and he thought the combination would work well for our current players. I was personally excited because I was going to be learning from an NBA coach. NBA coaches play an 82-game season. That's almost three college basketball seasons. I could only imagine the amount of information that Coach Brown would be sharing. I planned to be a sponge.

The system of offense that we were putting in relied on spreading the floor with good spacing between our players, with a lot of screening and freedom of movement. Players had to be smart and unselfish. The player's job was not only getting himself open but working just as hard to get a teammate open. It was really good stuff, and Coach Brown was teaching me how to teach it to our players. We would also put in some of the UCLA high post action, out of our old 2-3 formation. I was certainly comfortable with that and spent a lot of time with Coach Brown showing him how Coach Wooden and Coach Cunningham ran the offense. I showed him how Coach Wooden broke down drills to teach in the whole-part-whole method. Coach Wooden would often show his team a play or action using five players, then teach it in smaller pieces using two or three players, and then put it back together and run it with five players again. It was time consuming, but a great way to teach. This was practiced every day and repeated until the action was second nature. Coach Brown loved it, and our team seemed to be all in. In our defense we had pressing, and we included the run and jump and trapping the ball. That went along with our straight up man-to-man defense. It was quite a bit to teach, but we had five weeks before our first game. We would have everything completely in before we played our first league game. Coach Brown approached every day like an NBA coach. He wasn't a real fan of all the office work that went on with college basketball, but he got that done. His real enthusiasm would start when we met, talked basketball, and planned our practices. Some of his NBA buddies came around early, and I enjoyed meeting and talking with them as well. Doug Moe and Donnie Walsh were a part of Larry's coaching inner circle, and we talked hoops. Coach Brown never really distanced himself from his NBA coaching buddies.

Coach Brown was different from anybody else I had worked with because he operated by feel. If he had delegated 10 minutes to run a drill, and he felt the team had gotten it, that drill might last only eight minutes. But if the team wasn't getting it, that 10-minute drill might be 15 minutes or even longer, until he was satisfied! Kevin O'Connor and I learned to follow his lead and focus on having a terrific practice. Coach Brown started giving me more and more responsibility in practice. There were days where I would recommend something and he would just say "OK, put it in and teach it." I had never done that before with the varsity. It was great for my development as a coach.

We kicked off the Larry Brown era at UCLA by blowing out Idaho State 82–40. The fans were excited. We followed that up with blowout wins over Hofstra and Santa Clara. Our first real test would be against Notre Dame. I had prepared Coach Brown and Kevin O'Connor for what to expect in South Bend, telling Coach Brown about Digger Phelps and his antics. UCLA was on the floor warming up when Coach Phelps walked out of the tunnel and stared at the student body, encouraging them to yell louder. He had his crowd going nuts and he was still motioning with his arms to get louder. Once he had the student body in an uproar he stepped out of the way and the Notre Dame team came running out. The student body showered the court with rolls of toilet paper, just as they had the year before. It completely disrupted our warmup. Coach Brown was not happy but pretended not to be bothered.

We played a very good first half and led 36–30. It was a typical UCLA vs. Notre Dame game, and we had a 74–60 lead with two minutes left. Notre Dame had to start intentionally fouling. We made only 8 of 19 free throws. Notre Dame made several quick shots that killed us down the stretch.

With five seconds on the clock and a Notre Dame win guaranteed, Notre Dame's Kelly Tripucka was accidentally hit in the mouth when he ran past a referee at the very moment the ref raised his arms. Tripucka fell to the floor with his mouth bleeding. Digger Phelps started yelling at Coach Brown, thinking that one of our players had punched Tripucka. The crowd followed Digger's lead. There were some ugly exchanges before the official convinced Digger that it was an accident, going so far as showing Digger the teeth marks on his elbow. But the damage was done. Coach Brown was fuming. Notre Dame won 81–78 and now had a five-game winning streak on us.

Our schedule didn't get any easier. We returned home to face DePaul four days later. They, like Notre Dame, had a roster filled with future NBA players. Mark Aguirre, Terry Cummings, and Teddy Grubbs were young but absolutely sensational. Coach Ray Meyer was going for his 600th career win. They had beaten us the year before to end our NCAA tournament bid, and we knew this game would not be easy.

DePaul mixed up its defenses, got great scoring from Aguirre and Grubbs, and took control of the game in the second half. We didn't play well and lost.

Back-to-back losses had us doing some soul-searching. We had lost to two very good teams, but we had a chance to win both. We just didn't get it done. Our record was 3–2. Some of our upperclassmen were not leading on the floor, and at times lacked passion. Our younger kids were playing hard but making mistakes, as you would expect. Our teamed looked confused at times.

UC Santa Barbara provided a much-needed win not only for

our players' confidence, but for the coaching staff as well. We beat them 102–58. The next night we beat up on Colorado State 86–63.

On Christmas Eve, *Sports Illustrated* came out with an article about our back-to-back losses, and it was a gut punch! The headline was: "The Bruins Are In Ruins." The article was about a once-great UCLA program now in serious decline.

Merry Christmas!

After the break we opened our Pac-10 competition with easy victories over California and Stanford at home. Our next three games were all conference games, all on the road.

Oregon State was favored to win the conference and we lost there 76–67 after committing 27 turnovers. Coach Brown got hit with his first technical foul of the season. When he sat back down, he told me he made a mistake, because you should never get a technical foul when your team has the ball. He said, "You always wait till the other team has the ball. That way you don't lose possession of the ball and give up the technical foul free throws."

That was the first I had heard on the strategy of the technical foul. I had been an assistant at UCLA for four years, and that was the first time our head coach got a technical foul.

Heading into the game at Oregon I told Larry and Kevin about The Pit and its "deranged" student body. I had them prepared for madness. We jumped out to a 7–0 lead, which kept their crowd from getting crazy early, and we never looked back. We won 76–62. Coach Brown told the media after the game that he had enjoyed playing at The Pit.

We were running the North Carolina motion offense with some of the old UCLA set plays in. We were disrupting teams with a variety of different defenses, but there were times when our players were thinking about how to play, instead of just playing.

USC ended its 10-year losing streak to UCLA by beating us 82–74. When basketball historians start digging up facts like that, it's never good.

Coach Brown got another technical foul in the USC game when he was up screaming at Charlie Range, a good official who was not having an especially good day. Larry was yelling "BULL." When the officials looked at him he would quickly say "BULL-oney." He never said "bulls#*t." When he got hit with a technical foul he was up complaining that he didn't do anything to deserve it. Coach sat down and told me, "If you're going to get a technical, always try to get it in the first half, or early in the second half. That way you have a chance to get those points back." I was learning how to work the referees, but we had lost again!

Arizona State came into Pauley with what I thought was the most talented team in the conference. Despite all that talent, we were leading by four points with under two minutes left to play. We went into our four corners delay game to run out the clock, but we turned the ball over twice, allowing ASU to beat us 78–76. Coach Brown talked openly with the media about changing our lineup.

We played our last nonconference game at home against Notre Dame.

We knew we were in for a battle, and Coach had told us that he was going to start playing the young players more. We were going to take some lumps. Notre Dame beat us 80–73 but the game wasn't as close as the score might indicate.

They had beaten us five out of the last six times we played. Coach Digger Phelps joked that maybe Notre Dame should place a shamrock on one of the 10 national championship banners hanging in Pauley.

I could tell that Coach Brown was really down and just needed to be with his staff. I suggested we meet at the San Francisco Saloon, a bar in Santa Monica. It was frequented by off-duty LAPD, so the clientele was not rowdy and was not likely to bother us. Tonight, it was just Coach Brown, Kevin O'Connor, Keith Glass, and me.

The mood was pretty somber. All we could talk about was our team, and how bad things had gotten. After about an hour, when I had a couple beers and a couple tequila shots down, Coach Brown said, "We are eight and six and I don't think Chancellor Young or Mr. Morgan are going to put up with this for much longer." I never felt like I had to mince words with Coach Brown, and I wasn't a "yes man." But I was always diplomatic. I avoided comments that had an edge or seemed confrontational. That's how I was. But I knew our players. I had helped recruit them. I knew we had good players! And I had just enough liquid courage in me to say: "Coach, I think we're doing too much. Our older guys were used to running a very simple system, the UCLA offense. They've run it for three years! All of the North Carolina stuff is good, but it's not working for us. We need to simplify everything so these guys can just play, and not think about what we're running."

Nobody said anything. My gut instinct was to apologize to Coach Brown before he fired me. I took another big swallow of beer instead. His response was, "You're right!" His mood changed instantly! We were going to keep it simple and just run the UCLA offense. No more motion offense. And we would simplify our half-court defense. A good head coach is willing to listen to the guys he has hired, trust his own judgment, and then make decisions. That's what he did.

When Coach Brown decided that we would run the old UCLA high post offense, he wanted it to fit his new starting lineup. So I taught the center position to 6-foot-5 Mike Sanders, who had played only at forward. I specifically taught the footwork. Steve Patterson and Fred Slaughter had both played this position as undersized centers for Coach Wooden in the '60s and '70s. Sanders would be perfect in that spot, because he was such a terrific shooter and passer. (Mike was the kind of player who would do exactly as you asked him to do, a requirement for the execution of the center position in the offense.) Defensively, we were already getting by just fine with 6-foot-7 James Wilkes defending the other team's best big man. James was strong, quick, and fundamentally sound defensively. He also was our best defensive player, guarding anyone on the other team. Those subtle changes would make starting a smaller front line efficient and quicker. Plus, we were leading the Pac-10 in rebounding despite being undersized. Coach Brown was starting two freshmen at guard, Rod Foster and now Michael Holton. Darren Daye (6-foot-8) was also now rotating in at guard. Our big subs were

Darrell Allums, Gig Sims, and Cliff Pruitt, another freshman. Kiki Vandewegh's role didn't change! That was our core group of players. Man-to-man in the half-court was still our primary defense, no more run and jump or double teaming in the open court. And we played an aggressive zone as well. So this was how we made our stretch run.

We won six of our next seven league games, including a 93–67 blowout victory over the No. 2-ranked team in the country, Oregon State. That win was so decisive that the UCLA student body kept chanting for Larry Brown and the team to come back out of the locker room for a curtain call, which they did!

Our only loss during that stretch was at Washington State to a team that had been ranked nationally and was third in our league.

We lost on the road to Arizona State in the middle of February when they were ranked nationally, and then returned home to beat Washington State. It helped your strength of schedule rating to have ranked teams in your conference. Winning or losing to ranked teams could be positive in the long run. Our only bad loss during that stretch came against the University of Washington on Senior Day. Coach Brown started all five of our seniors—Kiki Vandeweghe, James Wilkes, Gig Sims, Darrell Allums, and Chris Lippert. It was an emotional game. Coach Brown didn't play them long, but while all five of them were out there, the seniors played well. It was when we started to substitute that the level of play dropped off. We lost when Washington hit a shot at the buzzer.

Our last two league games were victories at Stanford and at Cal.

We finished fourth in the Pac-10 and had a good chance to get into the NCAA tournament. Our overall record was 17–9 including 12–6 in the Pac-10. Of our nine losses, seven were to ranked teams.

Then there was that intangible reason for the NCAA to want UCLA in the tournament. The UCLA Bruins had won 10 national championships. Do you really want to leave them out of the tournament? There were 25 automatic bids into the 48-team tournament, and the NCAA selected 23 at-large teams.

We flew back to Los Angeles after the Cal game knowing only

two things for sure: The coaches would attend a retirement party for J.D. Morgan that night, and we would practice Monday not knowing if we were going to the NCAA tournament or the NIT.

The NCAA took four teams from our league, and we were the fourth. Our opening round game was against Old Dominion in Tempe on Arizona State's court. That was the good news. The bad news was that if we advanced we would again be facing DePaul, which was back in the No. 1 spot.

We beat Old Dominion 87–74. Kiki Vandeweghe scored 34 points. Our players were nervous and made a lot of mistakes as indicated by 23 turnovers. Old Dominion was in a press, which we would break and then attack the basket. Another key to our success was that we did out-rebound them. Getting that game under our belt really helped settle our team's jittery nerves.

DePaul had a record of 26–1 and Coach Ray Meyer had been named the national Collegiate Coach of the Year. DePaul's only loss was at Notre Dame, by two points. Mark Aguirre was averaging 27 points a game, and they were basically playing eight players, four of them averaging in double figures.

Our team was ready and playing with a whole new level of confidence. We led at halftime by two points.

Late in the second half, when the game was on the line, we desperately needed a defensive stop. DePaul had just taken possession and headed up the court.

Coach Brown was up clapping his hands and stomping his feet to motivate his team to play defense when he sprinted over to me and Kevin and told us, "We've got to use The Power." I had absolutely no idea what that was. He told us that we had to call upon this mystical basketball force to help us. To summon The Power, he explained: "Take your right hand and squeeze your left testicle! Squeeze until they miss and we get the rebound!" Kevin immediately leaned forward in his chair so he could follow these instructions without detection. I crossed my arms over my lap and managed the maneuver by leaning forward and reaching.

Coach Brown has now jumped back up and he's cheering as

loudly as before.

Kevin and I are holding and squeezing. DePaul takes a shot and they miss—The Power has worked! Except that DePaul got the offensive rebound and we have to keep squeezing. Coach Meyer is up calling out another set play, and DePaul is taking its time getting into a different formation. Coach Brown looks over at me and Kevin, and says, "Sorry guys, but keep squeezing!" DePaul shoots again and they miss. UCLA gets possession, and Kevin and I can let go. In the last minute and 30 seconds our guys made 10 straight free throws, including six in a row by freshman Cliff Pruitt.

We beat DePaul 77–71. We had just taken down the No. 1 team in the country and yet, in my jubilation, I had empathy for the Blue Demons. They felt now the way we felt when they eliminated us the year before in a game we were favored to win. I remember seeing Mark Aguirre outside the arena long after the game was over, still in his uniform, sitting with both hands covering his face. But UCLA was off to the Western Regional.

I knew Coach Brown respected superstition even before he invoked The Power. About halfway through the season, Coach Brown had been approached by a male grad student who was an assistant instructor in the UCLA dance department. He told Coach Brown that he could eliminate a lot of the minor muscle strains and pulls by putting the team through a stretching routine they used for dance. Coach Brown decided to give it a try. This gentleman came out the next day dressed in a leotard, tights, and leg warmers. He set down his extra-large portable jukebox, a "ghetto blaster," turned on some really nice Motown music, organized the team into lines, and led a 15-minute stretching routine. Well, we started winning after that and with the winning came superstition. So our dance instructor became an everyday part of our pre-practice routine. That, too, was a first at UCLA!

The opening rounds of the Regional were in Tucson on the campus of the University of Arizona. Coach Fred Snowden allowed UCLA the use of the Arizona locker room, which was much nicer than the visiting team's locker room. It was a courtesy he extended to our team representing the Pac-10. I ran into Leon Wood outside the athletic training room before our first practice. I gave him a hug and asked how he was doing and how school was going. Our team was heading to the court and, of course, Leon knew everybody. When Michael Holton and Rod Foster walked past, I tried not to let my facial expression show any reaction. I was thinking Leon could have been a freshman guard about to play in the NCAA tournament for UCLA. Our two freshman guards were starters. Leon had played a lot during his freshman year at Arizona, but their season was over. I had known Leon since he was a middle school kid, and I sensed his disappointment.

Our first game was against Ohio State. The Buckeyes had a record of 21–7 and were coming off a victory over Arizona State. We had a tall mountain to climb to pull off another upset!

Just before we left for the game, some of our players were out relaxing at the hotel pool. James Wilkes, our starting forward, noticed that a child had separated from his parents and accidentally jumped in the deep end of the pool, and was struggling to get out. Wilkes jumped in the water and pulled the youngster out, getting his basketball shoes soaking wet. Shoes would dry in the desert heat, but James had literally saved this kid's life. That might have been his most important rescue of the day, but we needed him to save our team, too.

Coach Brown assigned James to guard 7-foot-10 Herb Williams, who was averaging 18 points per game. Not only did James hold Williams to 10 points, but he hit two clutch free throws late in the game to help us pull off another upset. Mike Sanders and Rod Foster scored 19 points each. UCLA had gone from a program that was always expected to win a national championship to a team that was grateful for an at-large bid and was now, (like butter), on a roll! The final score was UCLA 72, Ohio State 68.

We were one win away from a trip to the Final Four. A month and a half earlier we were worrying about keeping our jobs!

The Western Regional final matched us against Clemson, which had a record of 23–8 and had finished fourth in the ACC.

Once again UCLA's quickness bothered a much bigger team. We led by 18 points twice in the second half before Clemson made a final run that was too late. We beat Clemson 85–74. Mike Sanders had 22 points and 10 rebounds against Clemson and was named the Western Regional MVP.

The worst-kept secret during the Western Regionals was the make-shift artwork on Kiki Vandeweghe's shoes. Kiki had a very wide foot and had complained throughout the season that the PONY brand shoe that the team wore hurt his feet. Coach Brown had a deal with PONY that paid him for our team to wear their shoe. But Coach had to allow Kiki to wear Adidas. The problem was that with so many of our tournament games on TV, the folks at PONY noticed that our leading scorer was in a different shoe. Still, they had let it go until UCLA got to the Regional Finals. Now something had to be done. Coach Brown got one of our managers to skillfully tape over the three adidas stripes with white athletic tape (the same tape used for ankles) and draw on the PONY Chevron with a felt tip marker. From a distance it looked like Kiki was wearing PONYs during warmups. But as soon as the game started, that athletic tape got stretched and rolled up, and Kiki's shoes had stripes going in every direction! He would be wearing custom-made PONYs soon, because UCLA was headed to the Final Four.

When we returned to Los Angeles there was a new *Sports Illustrated* on the newsstands, and this headline declared: "Up From the Ruins Come the Bruins."

The Final Four was in Indianapolis and we were going to play Purdue. UCLA was being called the Cinderella team in the Final Four. I was also very happy to see my old friend and coach, Denny Crum, whose Louisville Cardinals were in the Final Four.

In our semifinal game against Purdue, our young team once again had to grow up quickly. I had seen no signs of jitters since the game against Old Dominion, but with two and a half minutes to play against Purdue our 10-point lead had been cut to just one, 59–58, and nerves were showing. Coach Brown called a timeout and went off on the whole team. Not just the guys that were in the game, but the guys that were on the bench as well. It was almost as if our players had forgotten how we had made it to the Final Four. Coach Brown ripped into the mistakes we had just made, and then challenged their courage. The team responded. We beat Purdue 67–62.

Louisville beat Iowa 80–72 to set up the championship game.

We would face Coach Crum and Dr. Dunkenstein, the Cardinals' All-American Darrell Griffith. If you happened to be a John Wooden fan, you would enjoy this game since both teams ran the same UCLA offense. Coach Crum had a few more wrinkles in the Louisville version, but I knew them all and there would be no surprises. The basic UCLA offense was not a secret. Defending against the execution of the offense would be the problem, for both teams!

Neither Louisville nor UCLA played well the first half. We were ahead 28–26 but had been shooting the ball terribly. I had an uneasy feeling because Louisville had played much worse than we had.

THE ROAD TO KUWAIT

It was not uncommon for a foreign country to send representatives from its sports federations to the United States to observe our Final Four tournament. Some delegations would immerse themselves in the organization and pageantry of the tournament. In 1980 when we were at the Final Four, Coach Larry Brown asked me to sub for him and meet with a group from Kuwait. You really don't know how legitimate some of these requests might be. They might want just to shake hands and tell the folks back in their home countries that they met a coach whose team was in the Final Four. To say I was less than enthusiastic might be a slight understatement.

The Kuwaitis had requested similar audiences with the other three teams, probably resulting in meetings with their assistants. My meeting with four Kuwaiti representatives was pleasant and lasted about half an hour. We talked about the basketball history at UCLA, Coach Wooden and Bill Walton. They were more like interested fans than officials. It was fun and I stayed longer than I had planned. When the meeting concluded I handed each of them

After the game, Coach Crum would tell the media that he yelled at his team and said they were choking. He said he had not done that all year, and actually apologized to them as they were leaving to start the second half.

The game would come down to one key play. We were up 54–50 with four and a half minutes left to play. We had just created a turnover and breakaway opportunity for our leading scorer, Kiki Vandeweghe. He was dribbling quickly toward our basket for a sure two points that would put us up by six. Louisville guard Jerry Eaves chased Kiki down and cut in front of him to try to slap the ball out of his hands. Kiki changed the angle of the ball as he started to take his two steps to go in for the layup. When Eaves cut in front of him, Kiki's rhythm was thrown off and he took an awkward step, attempted a tougher shot and missed it.

Louisville's next basket cut our lead to two and we never scored

one of my UCLA business cards. One member of the delegation said, "One day, Coach, we will invite you to come to Kuwait and teach UCLA basketball to our players." I thought he just said that to be nice. Honestly, I didn't know where Kuwait was at the time. I knew where Saudi Arabia was. I could locate Israel and Egypt on a world map. But I knew nothing about Kuwait.

Remarkably, the Kuwaitis followed my career. Eight years later, when I was living in Utah having just been unceremoniously let go as the head coach at Weber State, they called. Somehow Fahmi (pronounced FAM-mee) got my unlisted home number. He asked if I would come to Kuwait to coach a club team. I was looking for work, but I had concerns about going to the Middle East where turmoil and conflict were common. It became my mission to learn about this small, oil-rich country and locate it on the map.

It always pays to be nice to people. The brief meeting I had attended so reluctantly provided me with a coaching job for seven years—two years with the Qadsia Sporting Club before the Gulf War and five years with the Kuwait National Team after the war.

again. We shot 36 percent for the game, which was our lowest shooting percentage of any of the games in our tournament run. We lost 59–54 and my friend Denny Crum and the Louisville Cardinals were national champions.

As the clock ran down, Coach Brown, who was sitting on the bench, started to get emotional. Kevin O'Connor got up and stood in front of him. It was the first time as a coach I had to fight off my emotions. This had been a long and difficult season. The weight of it was hitting all of us. I told myself that I was representing UCLA, this team, and my family. I would give in to my emotions privately, but not now.

In the days after the tournament, Cal State Fullerton offered me my first Division I head coaching position. I was extremely flattered, and I was leaning toward taking the job. When I talked to Coach Brown about it and told him how my interview had gone, he showed very little enthusiasm about the position. Coach Brown asked me, "Do you think this is the best job you can get, leaving UCLA?" Then he added, "If you think we are *not* going to win and have a good year next year, then maybe you should consider leaving, but I think we are." I had no answer for that one, and his reaction made me believe that if I stayed at UCLA, I would get other job offers. He was also telling me, rather indirectly, that he did not want me to leave.

After I had politely turned down the Fullerton offer, Wilt Chamberlain pulled me aside one evening and talked to me in a serious, big brotherly way. He reminded me of how difficult it was for African Americans to get coaching jobs, much less to be offered a D1 head coaching position. He warned me not to be so quick to turn down such an offer. I thanked him for his advice.

CHAPTER 18

Larry Brown: Exit Stage Right

Before Coach Brown's second season even began, a cloud of controversy, issues, and rumors was beginning to form. That scenario would continue throughout the season.

An article in the *Los Angeles Times* on July 27, 1980 was accompanied by a photo of players' cars parked in the driveway and in front of Coach Brown's home in Brentwood. The news was that the National Collegiate Athletic Association (NCAA) had begun an investigation in April into the "circumstances" of the car purchases and whether athletes were getting an "extra benefit" based on the sale price. Pictured were cars belonging to Rod Foster and Cliff Pruitt. The article also raised questions about Michael Holton's and Darren Daye's cars. All four cars belonged to our celebrated freshmen.

More questions came up later about why the players were even at Coach Brown's house when he and his wife were out of town. We were blindsided by the story. It felt to me like a "hit job" and, of course, I always assumed USC was behind it. I didn't know the players were at Coach Brown's house, so how did the *Times* know?

I had no immediate answers for our athletic director when he called to ask what was going on. During my years as a player and during my years on the coaching staff, we had dealt with questions about perceived irregularities in the program several times. When allegations were made, the NCAA would send out a representative who asked questions and requested information, and we would comply. In my experience, our answers were satisfactory, and that was always the end of it. I had no reason to think this would be any different.

From that day forward, of course, there was speculation about whether the NCAA would find wrongdoing and, if so, whether penalties might include probation. Even the possibility of probation can be damaging in recruiting, and an obvious distraction. We wanted this dealt with and out of public discussion as quickly as possible.

Coach Brown himself raised other minor issues publicly, and he was starting to let it be known when he was annoyed. For example, there was that thing about his partially painted office. A crew had painted one wall and had not come back to paint the other three. It had been weeks. Once he mentioned this issue to the press, the other walls were finally painted. And there was the shoddy cleanup outside Pauley Pavilion after a weekend rock concert. Besides some trash that was missed, there were signs of overindulgence splattered on the walkway. He didn't want to look at it, nor did he want parents and recruits grossed out by it on their way into Pauley Pavilion. Both of those stories were printed in the newspapers.

Coach Brown even made public statements about our alumni not being as enthusiastic during games as he thought they should be. He said UCLA fans were too "sophisticated." I knew our fans were spoiled and laid-back; the teams I played on helped create that attitude. Some of UCLA's fans would come late, making an entrance and then leaving early. This was not uncommon for L.A. crowds. When I was a player, we said the fans leaving early must have dinner reservations. No head coach had ever complained publicly about our fans, and I wondered whether calling them out might backfire.

Still, there were many reasons to feel positive about the season.

Going to the Final Four the year before had helped us sign two very promising freshman recruits. High School All-American Kenny Fields from Verbum Dei High School had committed to UCLA before our previous season ended, and All-American guard Ralph Jackson had made his selection known right after UCLA played for the NCAA title with two freshman guards in the starting lineup. It says a lot about Ralph's skill and confidence that he did not shy away from that competition. We were, once again, loaded with talent.

We opened the season by beating VMI and then played Notre

Dame at Pauley Pavilion in the second game of the year.

We were starting Mike Sanders, Darren Day, Rod Foster, Michael Holton, and Kenny Fields. Ralph Jackson was coming off the bench but playing about the same amount of time as the starting sophomore guards.

We beat Notre Dame 94–81 despite being down by 12 points at halftime. When we needed it most, Ralph Jackson just took over the game with his ball handling and passing wizardry.

Mike Sanders scored a career high 24 points and Rod Foster added 22. Darren Daye scored 17 points. Notre Dame's John Paxson had 21 points but its other star, Kelly Tripuka, was bothered, defensively, by Darren's size.

We then beat Pepperdine, which was bittersweet. Coach Jim Harrick had Craig Impelman on his staff as an assistant coach. It's tough coaching against friends.

Our record was 5–0 when we flew to Tokyo for an exhibition game against the Japanese national team, followed by a regular season game against Temple. The Temple game would be listed as being played at a neutral site but would count like any other game. This was a first, two American college teams playing a game in another country.

The games we played in Japan went very much as expected.

We were particularly effective against Temple's zone defense and we won 73–49. Our game against the Japanese national team would not affect our record, but we blew them out as well, 94–55.

The trip was mostly for fun, for the novelty, and for the overseas experience.

But the carefree mood was interrupted by a jolt of heavy reality early in the flight to Japan when we were informed that J.D. Morgan, the UCLA athletic director for 16 years, had died. It was a loss to me, personally. Mr. Morgan was a fine man and had helped me in my career. I was thankful for our friendship and deeply appreciated the confidence he showed in me. I would miss his deep, booming voice and our talks about the glory days. His death also was a loss to UCLA athletics and would have a major impact on the direction of the program years later.

We returned just in time for Christmas, but December 27 we were off again to play at DePaul. For DePaul, this was a payback game. The Blue Devils were ranked No. 1 in the country, just as they had been when we eliminated them from the NCAA tournament the year before. DePaul beat us 93–77 in a game that was not as close as the score indicates.

Back home, we opened league play with easy victories over Washington and Washington State only to be upset by USC when Maurice Williams hit a shot at the buzzer. We lost again a week later at Arizona State in triple overtime. We managed a split of the trip by beating Arizona.

We beat Cal and Stanford at Pauley Pavilion the next weekend, taking our record to 11–3 overall, 5–2 in the Pac-10.

Rumors were circulating about Coach Brown going back to the NBA. He had denied those rumors earlier but what made these rumors different was that the team was named, the New Jersey Nets. Still, Coach Brown denied the rumors.

Meanwhile, there was tension building between freshman star Kenny Fields and Coach Brown. Kenny had moments of brilliance, but he also had moments, defensively, when he either played soft or his inexperience made him look disinterested. If you played for Coach Brown, you played hard and you played tough. In late January, when we played at Oregon State, their starting center, 6-foot-10 Steve Johnson, was scoring at will over our defenders. OSU was undefeated and had taken over the No. 1 ranking. Johnson was shooting 74 percent from the field, which led the nation. He would soon be a first-round NBA draft choice. Coach Brown even tried Mark Eaton on him, but Johnson scored 10 straight points on Mark, effectively breaking the game open. When Coach tried Kenny Fields on Johnson, it was even more of a mismatch! Nobody was stopping Johnson that night, and Kenny was overmatched. After the game, Coach Brown not only lit into the team, but he singled out Kenny. I thought Coach Brown was jumping on Kenny just to toughen him up. He did need to be tougher, but Kenny was just a freshman and this was the first time that Coach had really gotten on him. He took it personally, which prompted a meeting between Coach Brown and Kenny's father a few days later. It's not a good sign when meetings are being held between a player's parent and the head coach halfway through the season.

At the University of Oregon, the atmosphere of insanity remained at full strength but the team wasn't as strong and we beat them 75–69. We beat USC at the Sports Arena 76–62.

Up next was Notre Dame in South Bend, and we completed that year's sweep by beating them 51–50. Rod Foster hit two clutch free throws with five seconds left to give us the win.

That game featured another incident between Larry Brown and Digger Phelps. At the end of the first half, John Paxson made a shot at the buzzer to end a Notre Dame run that took our 10-point lead down to just two points. Digger Phelps claims to have made a fist in exuberance while staring at Larry. Coach Brown thought the gesture was a fist with one raised finger but couldn't say for sure. Words were exchanged between the two as we headed off the floor for halftime—a sure sign that the UCLA vs. Notre Dame rivalry was alive and well. It was a low-scoring game, and again Michael Sanders led us in scoring with 16 points. Now firmly out of the starting lineup, Kenny Fields came off the bench but did not score. He was visibly shaken from both a bout with the flu and disappointment in his situation.

It was during the week of a home game against the University of Arizona that Coach Brown finally got his whole office painted. At that point, besides not being pleased with the alums' lack of enthusiasm, he now wanted the students to be more raucous! He compared the fans at Pauley Pavilion to an audience attending the theater instead of throwing rolls of toilet paper in the air like the fans in South Bend. The student body responded by standing constantly and waving yellow pom-poms! Coach Brown had succeeded in getting the students to act more like the crowd at a high school game! We had four players in double figures and beat Arizona 92–79.

In a measure of payback for our triple overtime loss at Arizona

State in the middle of January we beat them 64–61 on our court. They were ranked No. 5 nationally going into the game, and it was our fifth win in a row. Cliff Pruitt, starting in place of Kenny Fields, scored 15 points. Our fans chanted until Coach Brown and the team came out of the locker room for a curtain call.

Not long after that there was another blowup between the Fields family and Coach Brown. Kenny Fields had played just nine minutes, not taking a single shot.

Kenny did not attend practice Monday or Tuesday and Coach Brown announced that he had been dismissed from the team. It was an ugly situation for UCLA and for Kenny. Coach Brown was angry and told the media that Kenny's dismissal was permanent. Neither Coach nor the quickly released "university statement" gave clear reasons for Kenny's dismissal. Although Coach arrived at his decision to kick Kenny off the team for good reasons, the abruptness of how it happened was problematic for us, and the repercussions might be felt for years to come. Letters from some of our fans, both pro and con about Kenny's dismissal, were published in the *L.A. Times*' Morning Briefing and Viewpoint sections. One letter-writer wondered why Coach Brown would kick Kenny off the team when he would soon be leaving for New Jersey.

The principal at Verbum Dei High School was Father Thomas James. I had been communicating with Father James for six years, going back to when Coach Bartow was recruiting David Greenwood and Roy Hamilton. Any problem that arose with one of the Verbum Dei kids, Father James was going to be the person I called.

Everybody trusted him and his judgment. Coach Brown had developed a good relationship with him, but I felt that my prior relationship with the Fields family going back to Kenny's high school sophomore year put me in the middle. Things had happened so quickly between Coach Brown and Kenny, the escalation left no time for diplomacy.

We were heading up north to play Cal and Stanford over the weekend. Father James called me "on behalf of the Fields family" at home Tuesday evening. He wanted to know if the damage was irreparable or if I could do anything to bridge the gap. I told him I would try to talk to Coach Brown on our trip and I would let him know when we got back. When the team gathered at UCLA to board the bus to the airport, Kenny was there to say goodbye to his teammates, an obvious attempt to reconcile with Coach Brown. We flew to San Francisco, took a bus over to Berkeley, and beat Cal 72–66.

Our new athletic director, Bob Fischer, had made the trip, and told me that he wanted to talk to me at some point over the weekend. There were many things going on around our basketball program, none of which had anything to do with our upcoming game.

We learned that someone had called Coach Brown and made threats so he would have to have police protection at the Stanford game. We would be escorted to and from the locker room by plainclothes police officers. I knew the routine. We lost to Stanford 74–72.

Back at the hotel, Coach Brown stopped by my room, and had Kevin O'Connor with him. I assumed we were going to talk about the game or our team, as we had often done after games. Or maybe we would get something to eat, which might give me an opportunity to probe his feelings on Kenny Fields. But this meeting was much different. Coach Brown told me that he had been offered the New Jersey Nets head coaching position and had not yet made up his mind on whether he would take it. He said that if he did leave, he wanted me to become the next head coach and he would support my promotion—providing that I did not get the job and immediately reinstate Kenny Fields. I was completely caught off guard. I was not shocked that Coach Brown might be going back to the NBA, but I guess I was most surprised at the timing. I didn't think anything would happen until the end of the season. As for my getting the job as head coach—now that one did surprise me! As for whether I would reinstate Kenny, I told Coach Brown that because I had not been in on the discussions when he was dismissed, I didn't know what I would do. Had I known this conversation was coming, I would have thought it through and had a better answer. He was not pleased with me or my response. When Coach left my hotel room, I thought getting his support was probably 50-50. But I respected him too much not to tell him the truth, which brought the conversation to an awkward end.

Later that evening I got a call from Bob Fischer, who asked me to come to his hotel room. Fischer told me he didn't know if Coach Brown would be staying at UCLA or leaving, but he did not want me to pursue any other coaching positions that might be offered to me. He wanted me to stay at UCLA, regardless of any other opportunities. And if Coach Brown did leave, I would be his first choice to be head coach.

I didn't allow myself to think too much about becoming UCLA's head coach because there were too many things that would have to happen before that could be a reality. First, Larry Brown would have to leave, and I wasn't 100 percent sure he was going to do that. Then, the New Jersey Nets would have to meet his demands and I was sure those would not be easy negotiations. And third, I assumed that the interest from high-profile coaches for a chance to coach at UCLA would form a line a mile long, meaning I would be only one of many candidates for the position. So I didn't allow myself to be nervous about it. Of course, all of this was to remain confidential—which was absolutely fine by me!

We returned to Los Angeles with only four conference games left in the season. We were in third place in our league behind Oregon State and Arizona State.

I called Father James and told him that the Fields family should remain optimistic, and Kenny should keep going to class. They should get people they trusted to call Coach Brown on Kenny's behalf. Coach Brown heard from many people, including Rev. Donn Moomaw, a former UCLA and NFL football player who was now the pastor of Bel Air Presbyterian Church. His church had one of the largest congregations in Southern California. (Rev. Moomaw gave the invocation at Ronald Reagan's Presidential Inauguration in 1981.) All those who spoke to Coach Brown on Kenny's behalf ultimately softened his heart. Two days later, Fields was reinstated.

We beat Oregon 98–75 with five players scoring in double

figures, and Coach Brown played Kenny toward the end of the game. We lost to Oregon State 82–76 after leading at halftime. Again, we had no answer for Steve Johnson, who scored 26 points in 30 minutes. Both Mike Sanders and Cliff Pruitt fouled out attempting to guard him. Oregon State remained undefeated with a 25–0 record.

We won our last two conference games at Washington State and at Washington to finish with a record of 20–6 overall, 13–5 in the Pac-10.

When seedings were announced for the 48-team tournament, we learned we would not play until the second round of games in Providence, Rhode Island. Our opponent turned out to be BYU, the team that had finished third in the Western Athletic Conference. BYU had advanced by beating Princeton in the first round. With that game already under their belt, BYU came out confident and ready. We never really had a chance. Danny Ainge scored 37 points and BYU led wire to wire. BYU beat us 78–55.

We were out of the tournament after just one game.

We flew home Sunday. On Monday morning, Coach Brown told me and Kevin O'Connor he was leaving to take the job with the New Jersey Nets.

Bob Fischer called me to his office to tell me that he and Chancellor Young had chosen me to succeed Coach Brown. The Chancellor wanted to meet with me, so I drove up to his residence. He told me that I had been his choice two years earlier when UCLA hired Larry Brown. I always felt that the Chancellor said that to me because he knew me and liked me, not because he didn't like Larry Brown. He told me he was thrilled that I would be the head coach at UCLA.

Monday afternoon Coach Brown called a team meeting. With everyone gathered in our locker room in Pauley Pavilion he told the team that he was leaving. Everyone started to cry, including me. Coach Brown could hardly control his emotions and struggled at times to speak. He spoke in a soft voice and tried to be stoic as he talked about the difficulty of arriving at his decision. The players had wanted to believe that stories about his departure were just rumors.

They all really did respect him and were sad to hear he was leaving. He told the players that they would be in good hands because I would be replacing him. That did soften the blow and there were a few smiles, but that was just momentary. The mood returned to very somber. Finding it even more difficult to speak, Coach Brown finished his talk and quietly left the room. Kevin and I followed him.

As sad as Coach Brown was when telling the team, it was apparent that his deal to go to New Jersey had been in place for quite some time.

Sam Gilbert called the next morning and shared some details he'd heard about Larry's contract with the Nets. He said it was a sweet deal for lots of money and the offer was on the table for quite a while. (The *Los Angeles Times* reported $800,000.) An agreement had been reached, but not signed. The Nets and Larry were waiting for our season to end before the deal was made official.

Larry Brown would prove himself to be a winner at all levels and was inducted into the Basketball Hall of Fame in 2002. He coached 10 different NBA teams and three different college teams. He considered returning to UCLA after leading the University of Kansas to the NCAA title but decided to stay at Kansas. He is the only coach to have won an NBA championship and an NCAA championship, leading the Detroit Pistons to the NBA title and the University of Kansas to the NCAA title. Wherever Coach Brown went, his teams won. All three colleges (UCLA, Kansas, and SMU) went on probation right after he left.

Coach Brown had a vision of what a good basketball team should look like, and wherever he went, his teams played that way. He won because he was unwilling to compromise his vision. My vision of what good basketball should look like came from my foundation with Coach Wooden. The belief in staying true to my vision, wherever I coached, I owe to Coach Brown.

I also learned from him how to relax and have fun when that was needed. And I learned a different sense of style. I changed more

LARRY BROWN: EXIT STAGE RIGHT

than my shirt monograms. Coach Brown loved to shop for clothes, and I would often go with him. He'd buy me a tie or a Polo shirt on a whim. I ended up with Ralph Lauren Polo shirts in every color. Because of him, I wear argyle socks to this day. I leased a BMW 320i my last year working for Coach Brown, just like the one he had. Oscar Wilde wrote: "Imitation is the sincerest form of flattery." No other UCLA coach ever reached his level of cool.

CHAPTER 19

Being Named Head Coach

The next morning I was in my office early, dressed for the press conference at which I would be presented as the new head coach. I was taking the time to organize my thoughts. The past few days had gone by so fast and so much had happened. I wanted to enjoy my introduction and I wanted to be prepared. According to one of Coach Wooden's favorite quotes: "Failure to prepare is preparing to fail." I had a pretty good idea about the questions I would be asked, so I was going over my answers in my head.

About 30 minutes before I needed to head to the Alumni Building, Sam Gilbert appeared at the door of my office. I was surprised because I didn't know he was coming. "I've got some people here who want to say hello," he said as he greeted me. In walked my mother and father! I saw my wife, Joyce, in the hallway. I hugged Mom and Joyce, who started crying and my dad, who was beaming. When I looked up, Papa Sam had disappeared as suddenly as he had appeared. I didn't need to be told that he was behind my parents' surprise trip from Denver.

My family had not yet sat down when Terry Donahue (UCLA football coach) saw the gathering through my open door and joined us. Terry shook my dad's hand and gave my mother a hug. He told them: "Get a good look at him now, because the next time you see him he ain't going to be smiling, and he ain't gonna look this young!"

When I came back from the media conference, Bob Fischer asked me to stop by his office. He told me that instead of starting me at $38,000, (which I had agreed to) I'd done such a great job with the media that my starting salary would be $40,000. I was good with the media but not that good! Angelo Mazzone would tell me later that he recommended my starting salary be the same as Larry Brown's initial salary. Angelo also told me that UCLA had been grooming me to be the head coach at UCLA for the past few years.

Newspaper coverage the next day reported that I had signed a three-year contract. That wasn't exactly correct. I had agreed to a three-year contract but I didn't actually sign it until about a year later when Mr. Fischer's secretary called to tell me she had just noticed that the contract on file did not have my signature. She suggested that I drop by and sign it. I had considered the deal done when I shook hands with Bob Fischer. My salary would go up $5,000 a year.

It didn't surprise me that we missed the little detail of the signature with all that was going on and all that would happen before next season.

As I was moving files from my old office into the larger head basketball coach's office across the hall, I experienced a very telling moment. My former teammate (JV coach) Bobby Webb had stopped by to visit and was in my old office when the phone rang. Bobby asked if I wanted him to answer it. I said, "Yeah, go ahead please." Bobby picked up the phone and said, "Coach Farmer's office." There was a pause and the next thing he said was: "Oh, he'll be right back. He's in Coach Wooden's office."

I was the fourth coach to occupy that office since Coach Wooden's retirement. Clearly, it was going to take all of us a while longer to get used to having anyone else in there. The office had not changed much over the years, although it had been painted! Some furniture had been moved, but I put that back the way it was the first time I saw it.

One of the first things I did when I sat down behind Coach Wooden's old desk was write some thank you letters to those who had come before me. I sent handwritten letters to John Thompson at Georgetown, George Raveling at Washington State, Fred Snowden at the University of Arizona, and John Chaney at Temple. If those early black coaches hadn't been successful when they were entrusted with Division I basketball positions, UCLA administrators would have had no precedents to site to those who doubted black coaches were capable of running a program.

And that opinion was definitely out there. All the coaches I thanked had prevailed despite those attitudes. They were role models for me. They were qualified, worked hard, recruited good kids, and made sure those kids went to class and graduated. All had taken over college programs that were struggling when they arrived, and all had turned them around. Thompson was the first black head coach to win an NCAA title. It was on their shoulders that I was standing.

My hiring was different. I was the first black coach to take over a program with a strong winning tradition and a current winning record. UCLA was expected to win national championships. I was hired to keep it going. Expectations could not have been higher.

I knew that, for the most part, I had the support of the UCLA administration, the alumni, and the players. I also knew that there were some who wanted to diminish my promotion and its importance in the black community by suggesting that I was hired as more or less the interim coach just to see the program through a probable probation. That was tough to hear. It also was BS and it ticked me off!

Soon after I sent my letters, I received a mailgram that I cherish. It was a rather lengthy letter from the Rev. Jesse Jackson. It was beautifully worded and he congratulated me on my appointment and the significance of it being at UCLA. Rev. Jackson was a civil rights icon, and I had admired him for many years. I had watched on TV as he marched next to the Rev. Dr. Martin Luther King and as he delivered mesmerizing speeches. The letter was flattering but it was also thought-provoking. I had the letter made into a plaque that I hung in my office as a reminder of the example I needed to set, and the people I was representing.

Late one afternoon I was in my office on the phone with the parents of an out-of-state recruit, when Wilt Chamberlain walked in wearing sweaty racquetball clothes. He had often played racquetball with Larry Brown, but now had apparently found a new partner. Wilt had talked with me a year earlier when I turned down the Cal State Fullerton job, telling me rather pointedly that opportunities for blacks to get head coaching jobs were rare. When Wilt walked into my office on this day I motioned for him to have a seat. But he didn't sit. He walked straight up to my desk, reached across it and shook my hand. Then he turned and walked out. Without saying a word, Wilt had said everything, and it meant the world to me.

I received an invitation from Hugh Hefner to attend a party at the Playboy Mansion. Something told me that I should bounce this idea off Papa Sam. He told me it was a bad idea for the UCLA coach to be partying at the Playboy Mansion. I didn't go, but I did show some close friends the very cool invitation.

Arthur Ashe called, near the end of the summer, going through Sports Information Director Marc Dellins to make his request for an interview in the proper way. Arthur had retired from tennis and was writing articles for the *Washington Post*. He was not only a world-renowned tennis player and civil rights activist, he was also a UCLA graduate. I had watched on TV when he won at Wimbledon in 1975. He set up an interview for a Saturday afternoon when he and his wife, Jeanne, would be in Los Angeles. We met in my office. In the first 30 minutes I think I asked him more questions than he asked me.

Arthur was writing an article about UCLA's special relationship with black athletes. We talked about Jackie Robinson, Kenny Washington, Rafer Johnson, Willie Naulls, and Kareem Abdul-Jabbar and the opportunities they had at UCLA when civil rights struggles were at the forefront in our society. He thought my hiring was further testimony to UCLA's forward thinking on race and opportunities. The *Washington Post* published the article on the day of my debut as UCLA's head coach.

Sports Illustrated came calling, too, for what I considered a makeup call for the article that so disappointed me when I was a senior in 1973. Now, *Sports Illustrated* was doing a story on the new head coach and they were sending—you guessed it—Curry Kirkpatrick.

The headline this time was: "Wise in the Ways of the Wizard." It was very detailed, covering my playing and (assistant) coaching

AN ARTICLE BY ARTHUR ASHE

Excerpts from an article written by Arthur Ashe and published in the *Washington Post* on November 27, 1981:

"Sometime during my mid-20s, I began to get fed up with being referred to as 'the first black player to do this' and 'the first black player to do that.' I was annoyed, although I realized such firsts were newsworthy. Somebody had to be the first.

"Tonight at UCLA's Pauley Pavilion Larry Farmer will debut as basketball coach of UCLA against Brigham Young. This is a UCLA first to be lauded.

"Farmer, a black, is eminently qualified to lead the basketball program at a university that perennially expects NCAA playoff berths.

"Farmer and I share many common experiences. We both are UCLA graduates; we both played on NCAA championship teams. (Larry lost only one game in three years while playing varsity basketball) and both of us were very much influenced by our respective coaches at UCLA—the late tennis coach and Athletic Director J.D. Morgan for me and former coach John Wooden for Farmer.

"But there is another man who Farmer admitted 'has been very helpful to me in ways Coach Wooden couldn't help.' And that is John Thompson, basketball coach at Georgetown. Thompson, too, was a black first. At Georgetown (10 years earlier).

"Perhaps a bit more cynical than Farmer, Thompson recently was asked whether he thought being black had helped him to land his star 7-foot center, Pat Ewing. Thompson intoned sternly, 'I don't know, but it's about time I got something because I'm black.'

"I was called into Morgan's office 16 years ago to talk about an offer for me to play on the Davis Cup team in the middle of the school year. Years apart UCLA coaches gave us both the same message. 'You're almost ready. Your time will certainly come. Meantime, get the fundamentals down pat.' He was right, of course. Farmer, who once got the same message from Wooden, gets his chance starting tonight."

career at UCLA. There were pictures of me playing, coaching, and even working at my desk. At the end of this article Curry acknowledged that I was unintentionally left out of his article about the team nine years earlier. He mentioned I always hoped that at some point in my life, *Sports Illustrated* might come back around.

For the first time, I ran my own basketball camp that summer. I was always impressed by how hard Coach Wooden worked at his camp and how much he worked with his campers. I would do the same.

I did not expect my choice of the team's basketball shoes to be a major issue. Every head coach decided which shoes his team wore. When Coach Brown was at UCLA, we wore PONY. It wasn't the best shoe at the time, but it was my understanding he got a pretty good deal for himself. Most coaches at high-profile basketball programs had shoe contracts. Not only would the team be provided with shoes and sportswear, but the coach was paid a salary. UCLA had worn Adidas the entire time I was a player and assistant at UCLA, so I was leaning toward Adidas. Times had changed drastically since Coach Wooden's initial shoe deal with Adidas in 1969. His deal did not involve anything being paid to him, because he didn't believe in that. But for each pair of shoes UCLA purchased, Adidas would give the school a pair free.

Allied Chemical was one of the companies making a major contribution to the 1984 Los Angeles Olympics. They provided a building on the UCLA campus that served as Olympic headquarters in L.A., and the building would be given to UCLA after the Olympic Games. During negotiations, Allied Chemical (which owned the Converse shoe company), made a proposal. They would pay UCLA an additional six-figure fee if the UCLA football and basketball teams wore Converse for the three years leading up to the Games. Terry Donahue felt as strongly about choosing his own shoe for his team as I did.

When I spoke to Chancellor Young about this proposal, I told him that the most important equipment to a basketball player was his shoes. I even joked about Coach Wooden's annual lesson on the importance of correctly tying our shoes. I knew Chancellor Young to be open minded, but I believed he was leaning toward the Allied Chemical/Converse deal. I made a proposal to AD Bob Fischer. Every shoe company had come in and offered me a shoe deal. I told Mr. Fisher that (money aside) I would have the players participate in choosing which shoe they wanted to wear.

I would request a pair of the top-of-the-line shoes from each company for each of our players to test. The players loved the idea of getting new basketball shoes every couple of weeks. Who wouldn't? But, we also told them that after they had played in the shoes, they had to be turned back in. The shoe companies were happy to have the used shoes back so they could study the patterns of wear and tear. This was especially true for the company that sent us the prototype of a shoe they had not yet put into production. This way our players weren't getting any extra benefits. For a couple of weeks they would wear Converse, then for a couple of weeks PONY, then Nike, and then Adidas. At the end of the summer, I would have each player rate the shoes, anonymously.

Bob Fischer and Chancellor Young allowed the experiment to proceed. I really did want the players to be comfortable in their shoes. I also knew if my only reason not to wear Converse was so I could get paid by another company, the idea wouldn't go over well. After each player ranked his preferences, it was unanimous. The players chose Adidas.

Toward the end of that week, we had our annual UCLA Athletic Department golf fundraiser at the Brentwood Country Club. Terry Donahue gave a speech about the upcoming football season, and I did the same about basketball. Right before the dinner started, I presented Chancellor Young with my shoe survey findings. He told me to go ahead and use Adidas. He said he might review the decision after a year, but he never did.

My Adidas salary would always be approximately equal to my UCLA salary. Sam got Adidas to throw in a $3,000 stipend for each assistant and a trip for me every year to visit European Adidas in France.

We did not lose any of the young men we had been recruiting because of this coaching change. My six years of being an assistant coach had given me a solid foundation in the recruiting community. Brad Wright (6-foot-11) was the first to sign, followed by All-American guard Nigel Miguel (6-foot-4), Gary Maloncon (6-foot-7), and Stuart Gray (7-foot-0). This was one of the best recruiting classes in the nation.

UCLA was loaded with good veteran players, too. Michael Sanders (6-foot-5) was now a senior. Mike was a coach's dream! He was a great player who was an even better person. Sanders was a tremendous offensive player (a shooter and a scorer) and was solid on defense. Through his quiet demeanor and his humble manner, he was our team leader!

I was really excited about the players on this team. There was a lot of talent. It would not be easy to stick with the philosophy I learned from Coach Wooden to use only eight players until the game was won or lost. (Five starters, and one substitute at each position.) I also knew that we might play two different styles of basketball. We could utilize a low post attack with our 7-foot centers (Stuart Gray, Brad Wright, and Mark Eaton). Or a faster tempo, spread the floor attack, with Michael Sanders or Kenny Fields playing the center position. In my mind, I could utilize both the high post offense (like the one I played in when Wicks, Rowe, and Patterson were our front line), and combine it with a low post attack (like the one I played in with Bill Walton and Jamaal Wilkes).

It was a complex endeavor that would have to be made simple so it would be easy to teach and would not confuse our players. I had the summer and the fall to play around with the X's and O's and figure out the simplest way to accomplish that goal. Our perimeter players were all proven scorers. Our big men were not. How well our centers performed in practice (scoring) would determine how involved in our offense they would be.

I also thought with our overall quickness we could have a dynamite fast break. I called Lakers Coach Pat Riley and arranged a meeting to go over the "Showtime Lakers" fast break with Magic

Johnson at point guard. I knew the UCLA fast break like the back of my hand, but I was curious how the Lakers would sometimes utilize Kareem Abdul-Jabbar in transition. Riley and I met in his office. He was gracious with his time, and showed me how the Lakers attacked in transition, and he actually asked me about the UCLA 2-2-1 press.

I had recruited Kenny Fields (6-foot-7) from the time he was in the ninth grade. He had a grown man's body when he was 17 years old and had one of the sweetest jump shots in Southern California. He needed to get tougher because in his role our team needed him to be more assertive and aggressive. I thought playing alongside Mike Sanders would be great for him, because of Mike's work ethic.

Those two outstanding offensive players with similar skill sets playing the forward positions at the same time would cause defensive nightmares for our opponents.

Darren Daye (6-foot-8) had played guard for Coach Brown. Although I was still going to let him handle the ball, especially in transition, this year's team needed him at forward. When Darren got a defensive rebound, he had the freedom to make an outlet pass to a guard and then fill a lane or dribble the ball up the court himself and assume the role of the guard in transition. Darren could both shoot from distance and score around the basket. His versatility was his biggest asset. His style of play was very similar to Scottie Pippen's. The rotation of those three players gave me many options.

Ralph Jackson (6-foot-2) was our point guard and a truly gifted player. He made everybody around him better. Ralph had the gift that all great point guards have—seeing plays develop on the court before they actually do. One of the very first conversations I had with Ralph was to explain to him how I planned to coach him. I told Ralph that when he had the ball in his hands, my job was to coach the other four players. He smiled and I reiterated to him that I had that much confidence in his decision making. He was smart and understood what I wanted from him on both offense and defense. I didn't want him looking over his shoulder when he had the ball. Ralph was a playmaker. He played more like John Stockton than Allen Iverson.

Rod Foster (6-foot-1) played the off guard position and was as fast as greased lightning! When he first got to UCLA, the coaching staff would joke about being thankful that the basketball court was marked with lines that formed boundaries so Rod would know when to turn around and run in the other direction. To go along with his great speed and quickness, he had the ability to shoot from deep range. In today's basketball, Rod would have been an excellent player on the Golden State Warriors because of his ability to make shots from so far away from the basket. Looking back, it's a shame that the 3-point shot had not been instituted yet in college basketball, because he was very good from that distance. Rod was also one of the best free throw shooters in the nation.

Michael Holton was simply our best all-around guard. He could play both point guard and the off position. I would compare him now to Derek Rose when he played for the Chicago Bulls. He was a tremendous athlete at 6-foot-4, and if given a driving lane to the basket he had absolutely no problem dunking it on anybody who might be in his way. Michael's shooting range was deadly to 18', and he was a very good passer. He was smart enough to play both guard positions well, and one of the best defenders in the nation. He played with a great deal of confidence and was a natural leader on the court and in the locker room. Holton was great in the UCLA system, but also creative enough to make plays on his own when it was necessary!

Freshman Stuart Gray was coming off a great summer. He had outplayed Patrick Ewing in the National Sports Festival in Syracuse, NY, to claim the MVP. My biggest concern was how I would protect this young 7-foot center from the inevitable, impossible comparisons to Bill Walton and Kareem Abdul-Jabbar. Stuart was going to be a terrific college player, but I was not about to let him have his confidence ruined by not living up to those unrealistic expectations. Stuart was raw offensively but was agile for a big man. He was a good defender and rebounder. He was a tough kid and you never had to ask him to play hard, because he did! His confidence offensively would fluctuate, and his self-esteem sometimes was impacted. That's not uncommon for a big man. The good news was this basketball team did not need Stuart to be a polished, consistent inside scoring threat. He was surrounded by players who could score. If he scored occasionally, off a direct pass or off an offensive rebound, that would be a plus and a part of his role on the team. He would have a year to develop offensively while rebounding and defending at the college level.

Our roster was rounded out with 7-foot-4 senior Mark Eaton, a gifted shot blocker whose game and physical play would prove to be better suited for the NBA, and senior Tony Anderson, a 6-foot-4 guard who was experienced and a complete player.

Playing time would be earned in practice. We were talented and deep. I loved this team and looked forward to teaching them the UCLA system and seeing how good they could be.

In August, while I was trying to put thoughts of possible NCAA violations out of my mind (and trying to follow Coach Wooden's advice of "Don't worry about things over which you have no control"), I got a call from Rudy Washington, an assistant coach at USC. He was giving me a heads-up, telling me that Cliff Pruitt and several other area players had played on a summer league team under an alias. It was illegal for college players to participate in organized summer leagues, and Cliff obviously knew that since he had used an alias.

This was happening on my watch, and I had control of how this incident would be handled. I acted as quickly as I could. I checked the facts and made my athletic director aware of Pruitt's situation. We self-reported the violation to the NCAA and they ruled that because Cliff had played in four illegal games, he would be ineligible for the first four games of the season.

Truthfully, I was angry with him. I took his decision to disregard the rules personally. I felt I was being tested early and needed to show everyone that I could be a disciplinarian. I needed to make a statement as I went from being an assistant coach and the players' friend to the head coach and the decision maker.

The last thing our program needed while we were already under

NCAA scrutiny was another red flag.

I received a call at the office from my old teammate Jamaal Wilkes, who was now the starting small forward for the L.A. Lakers. He told me that the Lakers owner, Dr. Jerry Buss, wanted to meet me. I was flattered and excited.

A date and time was selected, and Jamaal insisted on picking me up at UCLA so the two of us could drive together to the Forum. Jamaal owned a brown Mercedes-Benz sedan, a very nice car befitting an NBA star.

He picked me up in front of the J.D. Morgan Center. As we were chatting and getting caught up, Jamaal's attention turned to a car that was stalled in a precarious position. The cars in front of us were slowing but driving around the stalled vehicle. The gentleman at the wheel was dressed in a business suit. He was alone in the car and had his door partially open, hazard lights flashing, and was obviously trying to figure out how to get his car out of the road.

Jamaal slowed and pulled to the shoulder of the road slightly behind the disabled vehicle. As he was opening the driver side door, Jamaal said, "Let's get this guy out of the way." He approached the car from the left; I approached from the right. The motorist did a double take at these two very tall black men approaching his car. It took just a second before he realized that this was not going to be a carjacking. His smile appeared the moment he recognized Jamaal Wilkes of the Lakers. He glanced over at me and continued to smile as I saw that he recognized me as the new head coach at UCLA. I sensed that he was a basketball fan!

Jamaal directed him to get back in his car and steer, while we pushed him out of the flow of traffic. This guy could not stop smiling, and it seemed he couldn't believe what was actually happening. I mean, what was more significant? That he was getting assistance in his time of need from two good Samaritans in L.A. traffic? Or whether anyone would ever believe who he said pushed his car to the side of the road?

As soon as we got him safely out of traffic, Jamaal and I walked directly back to the Benz to get ourselves out of harm's way. We drove off with the motorist still smiling and thanking us.

Once we arrived at the Forum, and after a rather lengthy wait in the outer office, we met with Dr. Buss in his private office. I remember it being rather dimly lit, and it reminded me of the kind of decor you might see in New Orleans. He was genuinely a nice man, and I was happy to get to meet him. It was a very casual conversation, and he asked many questions. He made me feel right at home. He ended our meeting by extending an invitation for me to be his guest for dinner and a Lakers game in the very near future.

A week or so later, I was parking my car with a VIP pass and heading into the famous fabulous Forum Club to have dinner with Dr. Buss. As I entered the Club, I was greeted by aides to Dr. Buss who, in typical L.A. tradition, arrived fashionably late. There were about eight other guests having dinner at his table in his private dining room. Two who I recognized immediately were June Lockhart of the TV shows *Lassie* and *Lost in Space,* and George Peppard, a motion picture star who was in the timeless classic *Breakfast at Tiffany's.* He would later star in the hit TV show *The A-Team.* There also was an up-and-coming prizefighter, who I didn't know but would later see fight in person as the headliner on a fight card at the Forum. It was all very impressive!

After dinner, I was led into the arena and introduced to radio legend Chick Hearn, who was warming up his voice for the Lakers broadcast. We recorded an interview to be used before the game began. I was then led down to courtside to be introduced. I arrived as the teams came out of the locker room to warm up.

When pregame activities ended, I was told to walk to center court, acknowledge the crowd in all four directions, and then walk back to the sideline. When the public address announcer called my name, I walked to center court and started to wave. As I completed my 360-degree turn, I looked at the Lakers bench. My eyes and attention were immediately drawn to Kareem Abdul-Jabbar and Jamaal Wilkes. Sure, I was aware of James Worthy and Jim Brewer, my old roommate from my brief stay with the Cleveland Cavaliers, and of course Magic Johnson and Norm Nixon, the Lakers starting guards. But my focus was on my two fellow Bruins. Jamaal was standing and clapping, along with everyone else in the arena, and he was smiling at me. When I looked at Kareem he gave me a nod of approval. The expectations on the UCLA program and its head coach are extraordinary. It felt good to have the support of two who loomed so large in UCLA history.

Classes at UCLA had already begun, and with the start of practice right around the corner, preparation for the season began in earnest.

My coaching staff (Kevin O'Connor and Craig Impelman) and I spent two days off-campus hunkered down in a hotel room to plan our strategy for the season. This is standard procedure for most staffs and it's a great way to get mentally and emotionally focused. I had personally planned our first week of practice. I loved planning practice. Day by day, minute by minute, and drill by drill. While I was an assistant, I kept every daily practice plan in a three-ring binder. I had three goals for this team's practices—to get our players in great shape, fundamentally sound, and playing as a team, just as Coach Wooden had taught me.

I also had copies made of several years of Coach Wooden's practice plans, which Gary Cunningham had kept when he was an assistant. I studied the practice plans from the first years that Kareem Abdul-Jabbar and Bill Walton were on the varsity. I used those practice plans like reference books. I could track exactly which drills were directed toward the centers as well as how much time was spent on each drill. I thought that would help me with the development of freshmen Stuart Gray and Brad Wright.

When I left my office with my practice plan on a 3 × 5 card to head down to Pauley Pavilion to run my very first practice, I was nervous and excited. I remember thinking that if I ever made this walk and I wasn't excited, it would be time for me to leave.

We walked into the upper level at Pauley and looked down at the court, happy to see that all of the players had arrived early and were out there shooting in their new practice gear. They were ready. But there, in the middle of my team, was Wilt Chamberlain! He had

joined in the fun and was laughing and joking with the players while
throwing up a few shots of his own. This would've been great except
that his participation was against NCAA rules. I stopped, turned to
Kevin and Craig, and asked, with a smile, which of them would vol-
unteer to go down and tell Wilt to get his big behind off the court.
Kevin and Craig flipped a coin. Kevin lost and headed down. Craig
and I waited up top. O'Connor was talking to Wilt and occasionally
looking up and pointing at me. Finally, Wilt looked up at me and
waved, then picked up his stuff and headed toward the exit. In the
coaches' locker room I asked Kevin how it went. He said: "It went
fine, Coach. I told Wilt that I had no problem with him being out
there with the team, but that you had ordered me to tell him that he
should leave." It took a second or two for that to register but it had
us all laughing.

Starting practice was great but another not-so-pleasant memorable experience was awaiting me before the start of the season.
Now that I was the head basketball coach, I was included in the
prestigious group that traveled to NCAA headquarters in Kansas
City to be informed of the allegations against us. I went with Chancellor Charles Young, Vice Chancellor Elwin Svenson, Athletic Director Bob Fischer, Assistant Athletic Director Angelo Mazzone,
and faculty representative Douglas Hobbs for the meeting on, as
Fischer described it, "Friday the 13th."

We sat behind tables arranged in a "U" shape so that we were
actually facing NCAA officials and members of the NCAA Infrac-
tions Committee as the list of allegations was presented. There were
30 or 40 items on the list, detailing incidents that had occurred up
to 10 years earlier. Three had my name attached to them, but I knew
I could clear up the obvious misunderstandings on those.

We were given six weeks to respond. By the end of the meeting, it was clear that some of the allegations could not be easily explained away.

I was advised to retain legal counsel to help me write my responses. Sam Gilbert introduced me to Alan Rothenberg, who
served as legal counsel for the Los Angeles Lakers when they were

owned by Jack Kent Cooke, and later served as the president of the United States Soccer Federation. The responses he wrote for me were accepted by the NCAA. I was cleared of any wrongdoing.

Other responses were not accepted. It would be almost a month—after the start of our season—before we knew the NCAA's ruling on sanctions.

I went into my first season as head coach fearing the worst but hoping for the best.

CHAPTER 20

Year One:
Probation, Pressure, Perseverance

Our season opener was a game at Pauley Pavilion against Brigham Young University. BYU was coached by Frank Arnold, the former UCLA assistant who replaced Denny Crum on Coach Wooden's staff. We were both familiar with what the other coach was going to try to do. Coach Arnold's team had eliminated us from the NCAA tournament the year before, expediting Larry Brown's exit to the NBA. BYU no longer had Danny Ainge but the frontline players were all back from the lineup that had beaten us 78–55. They were very good.

Good enough to spoil my debut as the coach at UCLA by beating us 79–75.

After the game, as I shook hands with Coach Arnold, he said to me, "You'll be fine, Coach. You're going to have a great year. Let me know if there's anything I can do for you." Coach Bartow, too, had lost his first game as the UCLA head coach. But that was on the road, to Indiana University in St. Louis. He survived it, and I knew I would. But I was extremely disappointed.

We played Pepperdine the next night and managed to eke out a seven-point win. Coach Jim Harrick, the head coach at Pepperdine, was a dear friend, but we needed to win a home game, and I was happy to get that one.

The next weekend we traveled to New Jersey to play Rutgers before going on to South Bend to play Notre Dame. We lost by three points to Rutgers, a team that had struggled to beat Fairleigh Dickinson and had lost to Princeton. On paper, it looked like a bad loss. No one on the West Coast knew how good Rutgers and its star player, Roy Hinson, really were. Rutgers would go on to win 20 games that season. Hinson would be a first round NBA draft choice.

Larry Brown was in attendance and asked if he could talk to the team after the game. The guys still loved Coach Brown, and I thought he might be able to lift their spirits. After his talk, he pulled me aside to ask how I was doing.

The backdrop of our conversation was at times awkward for me because word was out that we would be going on probation and a couple of the violations occurred during his tenure. A story in the *Los Angeles Times* that morning had reported that UCLA had been informed of sanctions and "sources" were saying it would be a two-year probation including being banned from the NCAA tournament after this season. It was national news. There was no escaping the subject.

On the front page of the *Los Angeles Times* Sports section the next day Coach Brown was quoted as saying: "I have nothing to be ashamed of in the way I ran the program, and the people who were in charge know that." The story about our game against Rutgers was inside the section. On another inside page, in the "Newswire," Notre Dame Coach Digger Phelps was quoted calling for stiffer penalties for violating NCAA rules, including four-year probation not only for the school but also for the players involved if a recruiting rule was violated.

Digger made his comments in a scheduled conference call with college basketball writers and columnists, knowing that his opinions would be published nationally—on the day before UCLA played at Notre Dame.

Saturday, as the UCLA players were being introduced, Coach Phelps led the student body in taking out car keys and shaking them. His clever way of mentioning our pending probation on national TV.

Rod Foster had a very sore ankle from a sprain, so I moved Michael Holton into the starting lineup with Ralph Jackson. We were ahead by three points at halftime, but we hit them with a Bruin Blitz in the second half, blowing the game wide open. We pressed Notre

Dame to try to speed up the tempo, especially as our lead started to grow. When Notre Dame broke our press, instead of trying to attack and score, Digger had his team set up in the half-court and run a very deliberate offense. When you have a 20-point lead and the other team is slowing things down and taking time off the clock they are, in effect, running your delay game for you. So I stayed in the press, even though I had substituted out all of our starters and cleared our bench.

Late in the second half, while I was standing up directing my team, I saw that Coach Phelps was saying something to me—and he was absolutely furious! We were up by almost 30 points. Digger yelled: "SO, YOU GONNA STAY IN THE PRESS?" Given that they weren't turning the ball over, I hadn't really thought twice about remaining in the press. I was a first-year head coach (whose team was 1–2) trying to win a game. I wasn't trying to run up the score. When he brought it to my attention, I immediately got the team out of the press.

We won by a final score of 75–49, making it seem like an easy win. But winning in South Bend was never easy, as I knew from losing there with four different UCLA head coaches. This was a huge win!

When Digger and I shook hands at the end of the game I tried to apologize for the press but he blew me off and snarled, "You did what you had to do!"

In seats behind our bench were Bobby Webb and Pete Trgovich, two former UCLA teammates. I stopped to hug both of them.

That moment was shown live on national TV, prompting NBC's Al McGuire (former Marquette coach) to say that I was back in South Bend with no support, with nobody from the administration there to answer any tough questions about UCLA possibly going on probation. He said that was unfair to me.

From that point on, there was always a member of the administration traveling with the team.

Dick Enberg, NBC's play-by-play announcer for this game, had also been the play-by-play announcer when I played my first game in South Bend as a sophomore in 1970. On his game boards for that day he wrote a very nice message to me, saying that I had represented the university well and exuded class as both a player and as a coach. He signed the message and gave me the game boards in the post-game press conference. Some of the reporters who were in the room thought it was pretty cool. I had that framed and hung in my office. Years later when I went to work for ESPN and CBS as a broadcaster, I used the way he formatted his boards as a template for mine.

On Sunday we traveled back to Los Angeles, giving me a week before our next game on Saturday, December 12 against Boston University. I needed the week to deal with the fallout around the official release of violations and penalties that I knew would be out on Wednesday, December 9.

I had time to meet with the team and give them all the details before the news was made public. We would not be allowed to play in the NCAA tournament. I remember looking around the room and telling them that we already knew the day our season was going to end. The only thing we could control was how we played from now until that day. We could either make the most of every game we played and show the nation how good we really were, or we could snivel and feel sorry for ourselves. I told them that absolutely nobody outside of this locker room was going to feel sorry for UCLA! Certainly none of our opponents. The choice was ours.

I volunteered to deliver the university's letter to Sam Gilbert, which was one of the toughest things I have ever done. UCLA had a mandate to "disassociate" with a "representative of the athletic interest."

The letter essentially blamed Sam for a portion of the NCAA penalties. It requested that he stay away from the program and the players to eliminate any further problems with the NCAA. I was in the meeting with the administration when the letter was discussed. It was written by lawyers, and in their vernacular. I told both Chancellor Young and Bob Fischer that I did not want the letter mailed to Sam or sent by a currier. I told them I would take the letter to him personally. I thought it might somewhat soften the blow. It did not.

Sam and Rose and I had sat around their kitchen table many times. It was kind of my place in the house, the place we always wound up sitting when there was something I needed to talk about. It was amazing to me that in this vast, beautiful home, we always gravitated to the kitchen table. I sat in my usual spot facing the den; Sam in the chair nearest the kitchen, which would have been considered the head of the table, and Rose across from me. As I handed Sam the letter, I started to explain to him that I thought this was a bunch of BS. The investigation went back 10 years. It had been an exhaustive process, just to come up with a scapegoat, and that was Sam. He was a smart man and he knew this was coming. Handing him the letter was merely a formality. He spoke in his quiet way about the many people (not just athletes) that he had helped over the years. He would need to reconsider, from now on, how he went about trying to help others. I've seen this very tough-minded, strong, and sophisticated man in many situations, but this was one of the saddest moments.

As the conversation seemed to end itself, I kissed him on the top of his bald head, hugged Rose, and quietly let myself out. On December 9, 1981, UCLA was, officially, hit with probation for violations of NCAA rules. From the original list of about 25 allegations, UCLA was found guilty of nine. As expected, the cars that had been in the news were an issue. It was determined that players received deals on the purchase of their cars, that the prices they paid were lower than the price someone else might have paid for the same vehicles. The NCAA also determined that some players had rented apartments for lower than the market rate and one player had not put down a deposit.

I was told that the investigators also interviewed young men we had recruited, focusing on the ones who chose to go elsewhere. The players were asked about their visits to UCLA and about whether they had been given anything improper. One prized recruit, a highly sought-after center, told the investigators that all he was given was a UCLA T-shirt. He later explained that he thought a T-shirt was so insignificant he was answering "no" to whether he had been given anything. The T-shirt, which was purchased by an assistant coach at the bookstore, was No. 6 on the list of violations. There was an institutional violation that turned out to be a bookkeeping error that affected some basketball players and some football players. Several players had been allowed to keep the full amount awarded to them by the Basic Education Opportunity Grant. The BEOG, now known as a Pell Grant, is a federal student aid program granting funds to students of lower income that can be used for any cost of education, including living expenses. The amount of the award is determined by the tax returns of the student's parents. The NCAA put a cap on how much BEOG money an athlete could receive above and beyond his scholarship. The NCAA has since changed that rule so students who qualify for the grant are allowed to keep it all, which makes sense, but back then it was a violation.

By the letter of the law, UCLA was guilty of the violations. By the spirit of the law—to keep coaches from having bidding wars to entice athletes into signing—these were not major violations.

The news leaks about the sanctions proved true. UCLA was put on a two-year probation, with the first year banning us from participating in the NCAA tournament. On Saturday, December 12, we beat Boston University 77–43.

DePaul was, once again, very good and very talented. They had Terry Cummings, Bernard Randolph, Walter Downing, Tyrone Corbin, and Teddy Grubbs. They were ranked No. 7 in the country and came in with a 5–0 record. They led at halftime but we put together a solid second half behind Kenny Fields' 24 points and Mike Sanders' 17 points and won the game 87–75. It was another big win for us. DePaul would go undefeated until losing in the tournament.

Louisiana State University Coach Dale Brown had big plans for our next game, which would be played in the Superdome. Coach Brown thought that with the proper promotion, we might break the attendance record set by the Houston vs. UCLA "Game of the Century" in the Astrodome in 1968. That game had 52,693 fans in

attendance. About an hour before the game we heard that LSU personnel were actually on Bourbon Street telling people they could go
to the game for $1. LSU was able to attract only 28,880 fans to the
Superdome, but at the time it was the fifth-largest crowd in NCAA
basketball history. We beat LSU 83–76, with five players in double
figures. In my view, any time you get five players scoring in double
figures, your offense is operating efficiently.

Our last game before we started conference play was at home
against Maryland. This team, coached by Lefty Driesell, played
in the ACC and had a strong national reputation. The game was
scheduled for national television at the last moment. This Maryland team wasn't nearly as talented as the ones a few years earlier
when people were calling them the UCLA of the East. Every time
Maryland missed a shot, we turned it into a fast break. When we
played up-tempo, we played at our best. Our winning score against
Maryland was 90–57.

The *Los Angeles Times* sports editor, Bill Dwyre, wrote: "There
had been those among UCLA backers who felt that the recent penalties handed down by the NCAA against the Bruins, penalties that
include keeping them out of this season's postseason competition,
weren't that severe since this team was struggling so badly anyway.
Well, after Tuesday night's rout that featured quickness, sharp passing, and a devastating fast break . . . there will be many feeling much
worse about the NCAA action. For this night, at least—this night
and the DePaul game, certainly—the Bruins looked like the Bruins
of old."

We opened Pac-10 play at Washington State. Coach George
Raveling knew that playing slow down basketball and milking the
clock would be the best strategy to neutralize our fast break. It was
a close game all the way and at the end of regulation the score was
43–43. The game went three overtimes before we ultimately lost
due to missed free throws and turnovers.

We headed to the University of Washington, hoping to get a
split out of the trip. Coach Marv Harshman's Washington Huskies
had just beaten USC by one point. I played only seven players in the

game, and Mike Sanders struggled to score for the second game in a row. He had six points at Washington State; eight at Washington. We lost at Washington 56–50.

I had originally told the team that when we got back to Los Angeles we would take the day off. We didn't play USC until Saturday. But I was angry so when we got back to campus we had a two-and-a-half hour practice. No sooner had practice ended than I realized that I had probably handled losing both games in Washington the wrong way. The team was tired and had every excuse to feel sorry for itself. No matter how much I didn't want to let it be our mindset, no matter how many times I said publicly that having no postseason awaiting us was not affecting our performance, there was no denying how we all felt.

So the following day, instead of going to my weekly morning press conference, I decided it was more important to smooth things over with the players. As each player came to our offices to meet with Craig Impelman and get their class schedules, I met with each of them just to let them know that I cared about them and my anger was meant to motivate and not punish them. I sent Kevin O'Connor to the press conference.

I had stood in at these media breakfasts for Bartow, Cunningham, and Brown prior to becoming the head coach, but the timing here made it look like I didn't want to answer for the losses. It wasn't the reason, but it seemed so to the L.A. media and Bob Fisher.

USC was up next at the Sports Arena.

The Beverly Hills Rotary Club had a huge luncheon in advance of the UCLA-USC game Saturday to recognize both programs. The Rotarians invited the teams, bands, and cheerleaders. It was a very nice luncheon in Century City, culminating with USC Coach Stan Morrison and I both speaking about our teams and the rivalry. I had come up with the idea to talk with Stan about playing USC Friday and Saturday, back-to-back. That's how it was done in 1969–70, my freshman year. So while sitting on the dais with Coach Morrison, I started to talk to him about how great that weekend was and how we practically shut down Los Angeles while sports fans all over

Southern California focused on just our two schools. I was selling this idea to Stan. The festivities that these Rotarians were showering us with helped get him moving in that direction. He said we would revisit this subject after the season, and I felt pretty good about my chances of pulling it off.

We then got the crap beat out of us at USC 86–71. It had been 20 years since USC had beaten UCLA by 15 points, since 1961 to be exact. UCLA had not had an 0–3 start in the conference in 36 years, not since 1946. One USC starter (Jacque Hill) was asked after our game what he would do if he were a basketball player at UCLA. Hill paused, then he laughed and said, "Transfer."

When I was alone with my thoughts I could admit that it was hard on the team to be constantly bombarded with negativity over probation. The taunts coming from the fans at Washington, Washington State, and USC were personal. Even though we pretended not to hear them, we did. I sure as hell did! And it was different now. When Digger Phelps and the fans at Notre Dame shook car keys at us, probation was expected but not yet a reality. Now we were on probation and playing conference games that did not hold the usual importance for seeding into the NCAA tournament.

After the USC loss I went back in the locker room where my postgame speech to the team was sporadically laced with profanity. That was rare, but I wanted the players to know that I was angry. I knew if they sensed for a moment that I didn't care anymore, then they had permission to do the same, and I wasn't going to let that happen. I was not going to make excuses for them and let the season go to hell.

The most critical game in our season would be the next one, and that was at home against Arizona. If we lost that game, my fear was the season would be lost. Arizona Coach Fred Snowden was my friend and one of my role models. He was an elegant man and a sharp dresser. He was smart and cunning. Snowden was a trailblazer and someone I looked up to. Arizona was in last place, and there were some academic issues with the basketball program. Coach Snowden had announced that he was stepping down as coach and going into administration at the end of the season. I was going to love and respect Coach Snowden, before and after the game, but during the game we were both going to try to beat the heck out of the other. His players played hard for him despite his lame duck status, which was no surprise to me. I expected the hard-fought game and I was happy to get the 65–56 victory.

Stuart Gray had 12 points and 11 rebounds against Arizona. Certainly this was a game that he could build on and maintain his confidence.

We then beat Arizona State 75–59. We could not have played the two last-place teams at a better time, because we needed a confidence boost. I knew the team had not quit playing for me, because we were still having really good practices. Symptoms of quitting or not caring show up in practice before they show up in games. We had a successful road trip up to the San Francisco Bay area, beating Stanford in a low-scoring game 42–34 and then blowing out Cal 83–56 in a more up-tempo affair. In the second half of the Cal game we shot 65 percent, and had two of the old school Bruin Blitzes (a 10–0 run and a 17–0 run) when the game was on the line. The schedule was very favorable to us at that point with our next four games at Pauley.

Coach Ralph Miller's Oregon State team was once again one of the teams to beat in our conference. Oregon State came into Pauley Pavilion with a record of 14–2 overall and 7–0 in the conference. They were leading the Pac-10. They were excellent defensively and were holding Pac-10 opponents to just 47 points per game. Their best player, Charlie Sitton, was a young man I recruited to UCLA. He reminded me of my former UCLA teammate David Meyers, who was a first team All-American and a first round NBA draft choice. Their other forward was AC Green. Both Kenny Fields and Michael Sanders played terrific games and scored 54 points between the two of them. Mike had been ineffective for about six games, mostly because opponents focused their defense on him. It was great to see him come out of that slump. We beat OSU 74–68 and then handled Oregon 84–61.

We had won six conference games in a row.

The *L.A. Times* chose this time to print a major story on Sam Gilbert. The story on Sam dwarfed the article about how we had jumped on Oregon State, opening the game with a 20-point lead. The article stated that the nine violations that UCLA was found guilty of were only the tip of the iceberg. And then it went on to interview several people to add substance to that claim. It was by far the most negative article that was written about the probation, before or after it was official. It wasn't like we needed a reminder that we weren't going to be allowed to play in the postseason! The article went to great lengths to show that Sam and I had a close relationship. As if that were ever a secret or in question. There was little to be gained by further punishing the team and Sam Gilbert. But the hatred by some aimed at the UCLA program would continue, and there were several follow-up articles leading up to our rematch with USC.

The USC game was really important on several fronts. They had just lost to Oregon State, and now they were in second place in the Pac-10, one game ahead of us. Before losing to OSU they had won seven in a row. That streak had started when they beat us a month earlier.

This was a payback game; the pride of the city was at stake. This was a real rivalry. Getting swept and living with that fact all summer was not an option! During warmups, one of the USC players left their layup line and ran up to me to offer an apology while extending his hand. I shook his hand but I really didn't understand the gesture. He was back in the layup line when it dawned on me that this was Jacque Hill, the young man who made the "transfer" comment after our last game.

This was a classic USC vs. UCLA basketball game. Packed house, loud fans, reputations at stake. It was like a bareknuckle fistfight, with a little trash talking and showmanship thrown in. But at halftime, the Trojans were winning the fight 31–24. USC was kicking our behinds in the hustle areas of the game—loose balls and rebounding. That was my halftime message to the team. I didn't want us to get "out-toughed" by the Trojans, especially in rebounding! Although we shot 65 percent in the second half, we still found ourselves trailing by six points with five minutes to play. Mike Sanders hit a couple of huge baskets to right the ship and we were able to win 69–66.

Two days after beating USC, we played Notre Dame on a Sunday afternoon in a nationally televised game. The stage couldn't have been better set for another Notre Dame win in Pauley Pavilion, because we were clearly still riding high from having beaten USC. I knew Digger Phelps would have a special game plan coming to L.A. after accusing me of running up the score on his court. I expected him to play a very slow game. Coach Phelps had used that strategy against UCLA going back to when I was a player. I expected him to spread the court, run time off the clock, and just lull us to sleep before looking to score.

If you don't practice playing like that, it's not easy to do. Coach Phelps was good at teaching that style and he knew that it had worked against UCLA in the past when he felt like his team was overmatched. I'm sure he anticipated that we would have a USC hangover. We were flat, and our fans were flat as well. We had a three-point lead when John Paxson caught an inbound pass, took about three dribbles, and shot it from half-court, swishing it through just before the halftime buzzer. The stall strategy was working, and we led by just one point. At halftime I did a lot of yelling as I let the team know we were embarrassing ourselves on national TV. In the second half both teams would score 17 points to keep it a one-point game and set up an exciting conclusion.

There were some smart coaching moves from both benches late in the game. Coach Phelps started double-teaming Mike Sanders (who finished with 20 points), effectively forcing him to pass the ball. Sanders was providing most of our offense and they needed to neutralize him. Notre Dame then fouled Darren Daye, who missed the front end of a one-and-one. Notre Dame dribbled to half-court and at Digger's instruction, called a timeout with 14 seconds on the clock. They were behind 48–47 and were going to run a play to get the last shot.

Right at the beginning of the timeout, even before our players had reached our bench, Assistant Coach Kevin O'Connor sprinted over to me and alerted me to the fact that we still had two fouls to give before Notre Dame would shoot free throws. The game had been played at such a slow pace we had not been fouling. So I instructed our team to let John Paxson catch the ball (I figured that's who Digger wanted to get the last shot) and as he started to initiate action, to foul him. That would force Notre Dame to take the ball out of bounds again, with less time to run a play. That defensive strategy worked perfectly and now only seven seconds remained. The next time Notre Dame tried to inbound the ball, I told Michael Holton not to let John Paxson catch it, and he didn't. Ron Rowan, a Notre Dame freshman, wound up receiving the ball, turning it over and then fouling Kenny Fields. Kenny could have ended the game by making two free throws, but he missed the front end of a one-and-one. Notre Dame got the rebound and gave the ball to Paxson, who launched a half-court shot at the buzzer. We had seen him swish a similar shot to beat the halftime buzzer. This time the ball hit the front of the rim.

We had an ugly but crowd-pleasing 48–47 victory. I had my second straight win over Notre Dame and Digger Phelps thanks to a big assist from my staff.

We next traveled to Arizona to play the two desert schools, Arizona and Arizona State, who were still bringing up the rear of the Pac-10 standings. We trailed Arizona by nine points at the half but came back for an 88–73 victory. Darren Daye scored 10 straight points during a second-half run and led us in scoring with 18 points. We never trailed in the game at Arizona State and I was able to play everybody who made the trip. We won 72–60. Darren again led us in scoring. UCLA moved into third place in the conference behind Oregon State and Washington.

UCLA had beaten Cal 45 straight times. It took Michael Holton's superb play in overtime to make it 46. We managed a 70–65 victory with Holton scoring five of our seven points in the extra five minutes. The Stanford game wasn't nearly as competitive. We were flat at the beginning of the game, which I attributed to a quirk in our schedule. We played Cal Friday night and Stanford Saturday afternoon. Still, we blew them out 79–53.

Our last road trip of the season was to the state of Oregon. And I had to tell Mark Eaton that he wasn't making the trip.

In a move designed to save athletic departments money, the Pac-10 conference had put a restriction on the number of players you could take on the road. Prior to this new rule, if you were on the UCLA varsity, you traveled. It was up to the coach and the athletic director how many players traveled. This new limitation meant I was going to be forced to leave one player home. We had four conference road trips this season—to the state of Washington, the Bay Area, Arizona, and Oregon. So I had a very difficult decision to make about which scholarship player was not going to make those trips. I decided instead of punishing one player, and that's how I saw it to leave a scholarship player at home, that our last four players on the roster would each miss one road trip, and travel on the other three. It was a decision that I hated to make, but I had no choice. The last four guys on the roster were Mark Eaton, Dean Sears, Brad Wright, and Gary Maloncon. Making the decision even more difficult was the fact that both Mark and Dean were seniors. Each game was very precious to them. I also did not want to leave Brad Wright or Gary Maloncon at home for all four road trips, because I didn't want to lose them. Brad worked hard every day and his best basketball was ahead of him. Gary was a warrior and had a terrific upside. So by leaving each one at home for one road trip, at least I could take them on the other three. I knew they would be crushed on many levels and probably hate me for leaving them at home. I thought it would be best for them, and the team overall, if we did it that way.

Telling each player that he would miss a road trip was very difficult, but without a doubt telling Mark Eaton that he was not going to travel was the hardest. Mark was a great kid, and although I wasn't playing him very much, he never complained and continued to work hard every day in practice. I decided to leave him at home for the Oregon and Oregon State games in late February. Both teams were smaller and played at a fast pace. Because of his size I figured he would be least likely to be given an opportunity to play there, so he would miss that road trip. I told Mark after practice in the coaches' locker room privately that I was going to be leaving him at home. He was obviously crushed and stormed out. He didn't swear, act disrespectful, or take a swing at me. He simply got up and left. I later got a hand-written letter from Mark. In it he explained to me how disappointed he was in being left at home, and how unfair he thought that decision was because he was a senior. I initially read it in my office. Later, I took it home and read it again. The second time I read it, it brought me to tears. I really and truly did understand how he felt. I kept that letter in my office desk drawer to serve as a reminder that every tough decision I had to make impacted young men's lives. A head coach makes difficult decisions; that's what you sign up for. I knew I could always live with myself if I made the hard choices for the right reasons. Mark's letter touched my heart and served a valuable purpose. I have kept that letter to this day.

Our first stop was at Oregon State against a team with an over-all record of 20-3 and a league-leading record of 13–1. Their one conference loss was to us, and they were looking to avenge it. They were ranked No. 4 in the nation, and their students were camping out in tents around the arena the night before the game to get the best seats. Oregon State beat us the next day, convincingly, 72–58.

At Oregon it took Rod Foster scoring 35 points, including 22 in the second half, to help us finally pull away and win 88–66. Rod was spectacular. He was already leading the nation in free throw percentage (96 percent) and had made 32 in a row. When he missed one in the Oregon game it caught us all off guard. The final stats showed that he made 11 of 12 shots from the field and 13 of 14 free throws. It was one of the most incredible individual performances I've ever seen.

Our last two games of the season were at home against Washington and Washington State. As chaotic and emotional as the season had been, there was a certain sadness realizing that it was now coming to an end.

I should have known we were not yet in the clear. There was time for one more unnecessary distraction.

UCLA teams had always stayed in hotels the night before games, including home games. Coach Wooden started the practice not only to get the players thinking about the game but to be sure everyone got a good night's sleep. Curfew was at 10 P.M. Ducky Drake (the former track coach and our longtime trainer who was 78 at this time) stayed at the hotel to oversee check in and bed check. The coach always stayed at the hotel with the team. When I went to my room, all was well.

At 8 A.M. Ducky knocked on my door. When he walked in I could see he was not in a good mood. He had a very deep voice and at times like this he spoke in a slow, measured manner. He said, "Farmer, I've got some bad news for you. Darren Daye snuck out of the hotel last night and I caught him. I don't know what you want to do, but there it is!" I was stunned. I asked Ducky if there was any way he was mistaken. No chance. Ducky explained that he had overheard Darren talking about leaving the hotel after bed check. So Ducky made a second check on Darren about an hour after his initial check. Ducky found Darren's roommate, Michael Holton, in his bed, but there was no one in Darren's bed. Ducky then did what he had always done in these situations. He took off his shoes, climbed into Darren's bed, and went to sleep. This way Ducky didn't lose any sleep and he would know exactly when Darren got back.

Of course, word spread quickly through the team about what had happened. After the pregame meal, I told Darren that I was angry but had not yet decided what consequences he would face. We were about to play one of our toughest games all season and now one of our best players had put me in this no-win situation. I let him suit up for the game. He sat on the bench the full 40 minutes wondering when I would put him in. Every time it seemed we needed Darren on the court, I would call on Tony Anderson, who played 26 minutes. The game went down to the wire and we won 68–67. There is no doubt in my mind that the game would have been a much easier one to win if I had played Darren. It took Ralph Jackson, a 63 percent free throw shooter over the course of the year, making four in a row in the last minute of the game to help seal the victory.

I spoke with Coach Wooden a few days later about how I had handled the situation because I was bothered by it. Coach reassured me that punishing Darren was appropriate and necessary. Not only for Darren, but for the sake of the team. He did, however, tell me that I might have been a little bit heavy-handed. He didn't use those exact words. He said he would not have started Darren and he may or may not have played him in the first half, but he would have played Darren at some point in the game. By sitting him out the whole game, I was in fact punishing the team by giving us less of an opportunity to win. Coach Wooden was right, and that made me feel even worse.

Our last game of the year was against Washington State. I thought about starting all the seniors, but there was just too much at stake not to finish out this year with a win. I was always conscious of not ever letting the players think that because of the probation each game or the season in its totality didn't mean anything. Starting the seniors might be seen as putting sentimentality above giving our best effort and it might just be enough of an emotional lapse to cost us the game.

I started the lineup I thought gave us the best chance to win and we did win 57–54. Our seniors were honored in the usual way. The ceremony on Senior Night was always emotional for me and now, as a head coach, I was fighting back tears.

Mike Sanders scored 11 points in his last game as a Bruin. He had played for three different head coaches and had always given us his best effort. His last season was ending too early. I would miss Dean Sears, Mark Eaton, and Tony Anderson, too. They were all great people and I knew they would go on to do wonderful things in their lives. Mark Eaton would become an NBA star, and one of the all-time great shot blockers.

We finished second in the Pac-10 with a record of 14–4. That's nothing that would make the most ardent UCLA fan happy, except we started in last place. We won 20 games for the 16th straight year, which also was expected. We finished with a record of 21–6. To do that, after starting the season 6–5, we had to win 15 of our last 16 games. I was most proud of the strong finish because it confirmed our character. Despite being on probation, none of our players gave up on the season.

CHAPTER 21

Wheeling and Dealing

The offseason began way too early. It was the first time in all my years at UCLA that the NCAA tournament bracket was announced, and I had no personal stake in it. I'd be watching the first round on television.

But first, everything about my first season had to be analyzed and evaluated by the fans and the media, both local and national. The *Los Angeles Times* called its critique my "report card." I don't remember a postseason report card for any other UCLA coach, and it seemed condescending to me. At least I passed and coaches I respected made encouraging comments and even defended me. The article concluded: "So Farmer had a good year, did a good job, still has some to learn . . . And he's coming back."

Among the items on my list of things to do in preparation for coming back were the schedule adjustments I wanted to negotiate. Following up on the conversation I had with USC Coach Stan Morrison at the Rotary Club event, I met him for lunch over near the USC campus. I enjoyed spending time with him, because he was genuinely a nice guy and a terrific coach. He agreed to return to the back-to-back USC vs. UCLA games right away. We would both go back to our athletic directors and make it happen. I was so excited about Stan's agreeing to my proposal, I bought lunch.

I also explained to my athletic director, Bob Fischer, that I was not happy about enabling Digger Phelps to recruit in Southern California by playing Notre Dame every year home-and-home. Phelps would go into the homes of top recruits in our backyard and brag about the UCLA series. He was able to promise them a trip home every season so their friends and family could see them play in

Pauley Pavilion. I understood that to eliminate a game with Notre Dame we would have to schedule another game of equal importance. I had in mind a nationally renowned program and coach that would not result in a loss of TV revenue: the University of Louisville coached by Denny Crum.

Louisville had just made it to the Final Four, losing to Georgetown in the semi-finals. I had a chance to visit with Denny a short time later at a basketball coaches' clinic where we were both guest speakers.

I told him I wanted to start a UCLA vs. Louisville game every year. Since he was a part of the UCLA basketball family, a regular season game between the two universities would be an instant hit on both campuses. It would certainly be a game that would attract a national television contract. Denny agreed on the spot.

When I brought it up to Bob Fischer, he too thought it was a great idea. Scheduling at UCLA was done at the administrative level, with the head coach having only a little input into the nonconference games we played. Mr. Fischer was looking to add a game to our schedule for the upcoming season, but was looking for a much easier opponent, which is what he thought I would want. He was thrilled that I wanted to add another premiere game.

Mr. Fischer said he would immediately go to work scheduling the game and getting it on national TV. He said he also would give some thought to changing the Notre Dame series and we would revisit that. The Louisville deal was done quickly. We would play Louisville at UCLA in the upcoming season.

Recruiting never really ends but because we had signed four players the year before—centers Stuart Gray and Brad Wright, power forward Gary Maloncon, and guard Nigel Miguel—there would not be as much to do on the recruiting front as in some years.

I did have some personal business to handle. My wife, Joyce, had earned a PhD and was developing her career, so in some eyes we were viewed as the perfect UCLA couple. We were both UCLA graduates. She had been a Song Girl, was well-known, smart, and great-looking. I was a basketball player-turned-coach. Alumni and

FIRST-TERM REPORT CARD

About a week after our season ended the *Los Angeles Times* published an article by Richard Hoffer, the reporter who had covered UCLA all season. He mixed his observations with opinions from several coaches. The headline called it "Farmer's First-Term Report Card."

I was annoyed to be "graded" after my first year. I knew none of my predecessors were subjected to having their performances graded in this manner. However, most in my inner circle thought the report was pretty positive.

Hoffer started off in a light-hearted way, saying, "A pretty good coach, went 21–6, about right for first-year men at UCLA. Second in the Pacific-10 at 14–4. About right but no record. Great dresser, maybe better than Larry Brown, possible record, NCAA. Had no nervous breakdowns before the press, ties first-year record, NCAA, set by Cunningham."

Then it became more serious.

The article said: "The ol' record is still a pretty good standard for job evaluation. Farmer's was 21–6, without a postseason tournament. Not too many UCLA coaches have done better in such a short season. Wooden went 22–7 his first year. Gene Bartow went 28–4, Gary Cunningham 25–3 and Larry Brown 22–10. The latter three had the luxury of the NCAA Tournament to pad the record: Farmer didn't.

"Of Farmer's losses . . . one was by four points to Brigham Young, another by three to Rutgers, one to Washington State in triple overtime. Only Washington, USC, and Oregon State beat Farmer with any decisiveness.

"Of his victories, one was over DePaul, another over Oregon State. Not too many coaches, rookie or veteran, beat either of those teams this year. . . .

"Aside from the internal commotion created by a radical change in coaching style and the addition of even more talent to a talent-rich team, there was UCLA's NCAA probation and a series of articles in the *Times* detailing Farmer's close personal relationship with Sam Gilbert, the man identified in some of the NCAA allegations of wrongdoing. Consider Farmer's record in light of such trying circumstances."

The coaches who were quoted did seem to consider the circumstances.

Washington State Coach George Raveling said: "I think he inherited a very difficult situation for a first-year coach. Most first-year coaches end up with teams of little talent. But he had one with maybe too much. And expectations, especially at UCLA, tend to be unrealistic. Not only was that thrust on his shoulders . . . along comes the probation. . . .

"Follow that up with the Sam Gilbert situation, the Cliff Pruitt transfer—I think it was miraculous he could keep the ship afloat."

Coach John Wooden explained why having too much talent can be a problem. Wooden said: "It's quite difficult, a situation like that. Who do you play? How long do you play them? He had good talent that wasn't starting. That was the toughest part of my job; it bothered me for years. But I think Larry coped with it well."

Legendary Coach Pete Newell said: "He never got pushed around by the talent, never compromised by trying to accommodate everybody. He believed in an eight-man squad and stuck with it. He believed in certain players and stuck with them. When you become a head coach, you can't vacillate. You want your own identity, what you're comfortable with. If you stick with it, right or wrong, that's a strength."

Newell acknowledged: "(Farmer) has a lot to learn. He's 31. Wooden was a better coach at 45 than at 35. Better at 55. Pretty good later on, too. We all had a lot to learn."

But Newell's opinion was encouraging: "As a first-year coach, he showed a lot of strength. When you consider the probation, the very poor start in league play, he comes out as a fine leader. UCLA has a strong coach and strong person."

fans had essentially watched us grow up in the Bruin family. Behind the scenes, however, there were problems growing between the two of us. Our individual ambitions and focus on careers had caused us to grow apart. The process of ending our seven-year marriage began during my first season as head coach and was finalized after the season.

I rented a two-bedroom condominium in North Hollywood. My mom came from Denver to help me shop for furniture and settle in. For some reason that I could not fathom, she lined the kitchen drawers and cabinets with shelf paper. It seemed like a waste of time to me, but she insisted. Mom was in Los Angeles for about five days and went with me when I spoke at the Verbum Dei High School athletic banquet. Father James introduced her before he introduced me. That was a first for her and she really enjoyed it.

My younger brother, Aubrey, had graduated from the University of Colorado with a communications degree in radio and TV. He had been planning to move to Los Angeles to pursue a career in sound engineering. The timing was right, so he moved in with me.

I wanted to send my parents on another vacation. They had really enjoyed their seven-day trip to Hawaii right after I was named head coach. My parents' vacation was my first big expenditure with my new salary. I turned to Vicki Serrianni (VJ) for her expertise. VJ had been the basketball secretary at UCLA during the Gene Bartow years but had left to run her own travel agency.

My family had never been able to afford a vacation. Besides, my parents were always working. I remember staying with relatives in Denver so they could attend a funeral when someone in my dad's family died. That could hardly be called a vacation. They drove to Arkansas, stayed two days, and drove home. For their second vacation I suggested the Caribbean. Several destinations were discussed, but the conversation always came back to Hawaii. Pearl Harbor was of interest to my dad because of his time in the military during World War II. Also, my father's all-time favorite Christmas album was Bing Crosby's *White Christmas*. He enjoyed singing "Mele Kalikimaka," a song about Christmas in Hawaii, which is a nice thought when there's a foot of snow in Denver.

This time I sent them for two weeks. And instead of having them stay in a hotel, I rented them a condominium. They loved it. And I was glad that I could do this for the parents who had sacrificed so much for me.

Changes had been occurring in the athletic department, changes that went beyond remodeling the building and renaming it the J.D. Morgan Center.

For years, J.D. Morgan had run the UCLA athletic department as if it were a separate entity from the UCLA campus and administration. Winning, national visibility, and generating revenue gave Mr. Morgan the power to operate with more independence than other programs on campus. It was just accepted that there were different rules and expectations for operating athletics. When Mr. Morgan retired and his longtime assistant, Bob Fischer, was made the interim athletic director, we all expected business as usual. That changed when Chancellor Young assigned Vice Chancellor Elwin Svenson to serve as his "liaison" to monitor athletics. Fischer would report directly to Svenson, even after the "interim" was removed from his title.

Vice Chancellor Svenson seemed to enjoy being vicariously involved in athletics. He became very visible during Larry Brown's tenure at UCLA, and his role continued to grow. When the basketball program was hit with NCAA probation, it gave Chancellor Young the opportunity to put the administration in full control of the athletic department's day-to-day operations.

Our offices were moved into a row of trailers while the athletic department building was remodeled. From my trailer office I would see Svenson walk from the administration building to Fischer's office almost every day to be updated on what appeared to be just about everything. It was extremely awkward and I'm sure deflating for Fischer to operate this way, but he was nearing retirement. He could ride it out.

An important item of business during the offseason was renewing our contract with Adidas. Fischer assured me that Chancellor

Young was fine with the basketball team wearing Adidas for another season. Once I got the go-ahead, I spoke with the Adidas representative in America who was responsible for setting up my international trip. My contact in Europe would be Bill Sweek, a former UCLA basketball player who lived in France. Sweek had played at UCLA on the Kareem Abdul-Jabbar teams.

The trip was set. I would fly to Paris and Bill would pick me up. We would spend a couple of days in Paris, and then head off to Strasbourg, where Adidas had turned an old hunting lodge next to one of their Adidas factories into accommodations for its guests. Sam Gilbert would join us there for just three days. I used my second round-trip ticket to fly him over.

I had already let Sam know what I wanted him to accomplish with this contract. One of the perks that Sam put in some NBA players' contracts was the use of an automobile. He would tell the team that he wanted them to lease an automobile for the player, usually for three years. At the end of the contract, the player would have the option of getting another car leased by the team or buying that three-year-old car from the club for $1. Sam would make that a part of the contract only at the player's request. I requested that he try to get that same deal for me with Adidas. Sam thought it was an interesting idea. He was always up for a challenge that involved his ability to negotiate.

When I arrived at Charles de Gaulle airport it was 8 P.M. local time. Bill Sweek took me directly to one of his favorite nightclubs to meet some of his friends. Even though I had been traveling all day, I was up for some Paris nightlife. Bill took me to a beautiful discotheque that was packed to the rafters. Bill's friends were four Parisian women, and he started ordering champagne by the bottle. When Bill decided to go to a different club, I reminded him that I needed to check in to my hotel. At the elegant old hotel Bill had arranged for me, everyone piled out of Bill's car and went into the lobby. I said I needed to go to my room to call my mother and let her know I had arrived safely. The ladies all burst into laughter and started speaking in French. Bill told me the ladies wondered how old I was if I needed to get permission from my mother—who is in America—to go out for the evening. I let them laugh. My mother was getting a call regardless.

Bill and I arrived in Strasbourg a day later. The Adidas factory was about a 15-minute drive out in the countryside in a small village. Some of the roads were paved, some were dirt, but they were all surrounded by farmland. The village had cobblestone streets, old cars, tractors, horse-drawn wagons, and the lodge, which was old and beautiful. Sam was scheduled to land in Paris that morning and then by various means of transportation arrive in Strasbourg. Bill told me that Adidas would be providing Sam with an automobile to drive while we were in France.

After dinner the three of us sat down and Sam laid out his outline for my second-year Adidas contract. When Sam brought up the automobile, Bill seemed OK with the idea. He wasn't as enthusiastic as I would have liked, and Bill mentioned that the American division of Adidas might have to enlist the European side to chip in on the automobile's purchase. He said he would look into that, and Sam was very optimistic.

The next day Sam and I walked around the small village and he had fun speaking in French and sometimes German to the locals. The town of Strasbourg is on the border between France and Germany and had changed hands many times—most recently when the Nazis occupied it during World War II. Later, Bill took us to the Adidas factory.

Bill had to go back to Paris but he arranged for us to have dinner that evening at a very fancy restaurant in Strasbourg. Bill had other guests at the lodge who were going to that same restaurant, so they rode with us. We had plenty of room in the Mercedes that Adidas had provided.

It was the first time I had been in the company of Curry Kirkpatrick, the renowned *Sports Illustrated* writer, when he wasn't writing a story about UCLA or me. Curry was there with his wife, Maryanne, and his six-month-old daughter, Chelsea. Curry had been in the country to cover the French Open, but now they were simply vacationing. What a small world! Both of us at the same quaint lodge as a guest of a former UCLA basketball player.

In the course of conversation I discovered that Maryanne also was from Denver. She had been a teacher at Smiley Junior High School and remembered that I was one of her students! Wow! What a really small world! She was introduced to Curry by Larry Brown when he was coaching the Denver Rockets. There were UCLA connections everywhere.

The restaurant was amazing. It was like sitting in a forest. We were facing a wall of glass with a view of trees, beautiful landscaping, and more trees. After the sun went down we noticed restaurant staff moving through the foliage with flashlights. Sam asked our server what they were doing. He told us, "Escargot." Apparently, my appetizer was quite fresh.

Before we could get back on the road the weather took a dramatic turn for the worse, and a thunderstorm made visibility on the dark country roads almost impossible. On our drive back to the lodge the windshield wipers couldn't keep up with the rain, which caused Sam to miss a turn. The car went into a shallow ditch and rolled over on its side. Sam wasn't wearing a seat belt so he was thrown on top of me in the front seat. It was too dark to see where everyone was in the backseat, but I remember the baby crying. It was scary for all of us. Fortunately, there was enough room for us to open the passenger side doors and crawl out. Once everyone was standing in the road and we had confirmed that we were all sound, we walked a short way to a farmhouse, and we were given a ride back to the lodge. We were all soaked, and a little shaken up, but there were no real injuries.

The next morning, Sam enlisted the help of one of the local farmers, who used a tractor to pull the car out of the ditch. We drove to Paris and made our flight home. The worst part of the ordeal was the angry lecture from Sam's wife, who blamed me for putting Sam in harm's way on the other side of the world. We got word a few weeks later that Adidas had agreed to all aspects of the contract and that between the two entities of Adidas (American and European), they would make the car deal work. Sam was proud of his negotiating skills, and I was ecstatic. All in all, it was a successful trip.

CHAPTER 22

Year Two: Playing the Toughest Schedule and Winning the Pac-10

Historically, UCLA had been accused of playing an easy nonconference schedule. When I played for Coach Wooden, a lot of basketball experts complained that our schedule was weighted with home games and inferior opponents. And other than Notre Dame, Loyola, or DePaul, we never consistently went on the road to play other ranked opponents. There was some truth to that, because everybody wanted to play against UCLA, largely making it our choice. I remember teams coming to campus for practice the day before the game and parking their team bus in front of the student union so the players could go into the bookstore and buy UCLA T-shirts. Opposing coaches would point out the UCLA game on their schedule to recruits, using our game as the "crown jewel" event of their season. So home games were easy to schedule. And not all our opponents were inferior. Some of Coach Wooden's teams just made them look that way.

No one could say that about the 1982–83 schedule. That year's schedule was ranked among the most difficult in the country. Iowa Coach Lute Olson said UCLA wasn't ducking anybody, and Maryland Coach Lefty Driesell called our schedule the hardest in the country. Five of our first eight games were nationally televised, and two others were televised regionally. In a world in which ESPN had just come into existence, having nationally televised games was huge. I had a veteran team, and I felt we were up to the challenge.

Speaking to our booster groups before the season, I sensed an air of excitement about the schedule. There were no further NCAA penalties, so postseason play was once again in our sights. When the season actually rolled around and I was reminded that our first three games were on the road against BYU, DePaul, and Notre Dame, I did wonder what in the heck I had gotten myself into! That schedule looked more exciting when it was three months away than when it was three days away.

We opened the season at BYU on Friday, the day after Thanksgiving. We had a light and quick workout early Thanksgiving morning before our flight to Salt Lake City, on which the airline served us a turkey lunch. I told the players that we had ordered a very nice Thanksgiving dinner for them at the hotel in Provo. I remember telling the team that this was what it was like to play in the pros— away from your family and traveling on holidays. I personally was excited about another shot at BYU.

The Marriott Center held 23,000 fans and there were no empty seats. The game was a battle. BYU played zone defense to neutralize our quickness, but it left Rod Foster open. He scored 28 points. With 24 seconds left we were ahead 82–80 with Michael Holton shooting free throws. The crowd was going absolutely crazy trying to distract Michael, but he made both free throws. We won 85–82.

When I shook hands with Coach Arnold at the end of the game I said, "Your kids played a great game, Coach. If I can ever do anything to help you, just let me know." I'd been waiting a year to say that to him. I really didn't know what it meant just as I didn't know why he had said it to me after beating me in last year's season opener.

A week later we were in Chicago to play DePaul. They were coming off a 26–2 season, and one of those two losses was to us. They had been tough to beat for quite a while, having won 80 out of 84 regular season games. Gone were NBA players Mark Aguirre and the previous year's star, Terry Cummings. But DePaul had won 27 straight games at home in the Rosemont Horizon, and this game was going to be tough. They were expecting 15,000 fans, but because of flooding in the Chicago area, we played in front of a noisy and enthusiastic crowd of 13,500. DePaul wanted to play tough, half-court basketball. They played a physical game, screening inside and getting the ball as close to the basket as they possibly could. As simple as that sounds it was very difficult to guard and they were often playing 10 feet to 12 feet from the basket. UCLA, on the other hand, loved to spread the floor to let our offense generate open shots. When DePaul missed, we ran our fast break, took advantage of our speed, and got high percentage shots. When they got us in the half-court, they were physical and played in the three-second area. The score was tied with about one second left in the game and DePaul had the ball out of bounds under their own basket. They had just enough time to make the inbound pass, catch, and shoot the ball. The ball was on the opposite end of the floor. (Teams always like to have the offense in front of their bench in the second half, making it easier to communicate.)

I was up screaming for our guys to get ready to defend this inbounds play because Walter Downing, DePaul's 6-foot-9 center, was looking confused. I could tell they were setting up the inbounds play to lob the ball right over the top toward the basket, without our defender being ready. It's an old playground trick. They did surprise our guys with the pass, but the ball was poorly thrown toward the basket, and the ball bounced harmlessly off the rim. We dodged a bullet and would win in overtime 73–70. Darren Daye was unstoppable in the first half and finished the game with 23 points and 10 rebounds.

Our game in South Bend was as close as our first two. With 27 seconds left, John Paxson was shooting two free throws. He made the first and I called a timeout hoping to ice him. But he stepped up to the line and made his second, putting us down by one point. Notre Dame had been playing man-to-man defense throughout most of the game, and they had spent the last 10 minutes of the game playing tough man-to-man. So I called another timeout to go over what play I wanted to run against their man-to-man and when I wanted to start the action so we would have time for one shot and maybe an offensive rebound. The last thing I told Ralph Jackson was not to be afraid to penetrate their defense, because I was sure they were in their huddle talking about not fouling. When we inbounded the ball, Notre Dame immediately went from showing a man-to-man defense into a zone. Digger figured correctly that I would have spent the majority of my time talking about what to run against a man defense, and he cleverly switched to another defense. The play that I had planned was now moot. Having guards with experience really helped in this situation. Michael Holton identified the change in defense and calmly called for a zone set, passed the ball, and cut to the basket, drawing a defender. Ralph, remembering what I had told him about Notre Dame probably playing soft, took the pass from Holton, shot-faked and drove to the basket, shooting a finger roll over the last defender. The shot bounced up off the rim and into the basket to give us a 65–64 victory.

Ralph Jackson finished with 14 points. John Paxson was magnificent for Notre Dame, scoring 26 points, but it wasn't enough.

It was at halftime of this game that I saw my career flash before my eyes. After the team had headed for the court, I stepped back into the locker room and was shocked to find my assistant coach, Craig Impelman, with both hands on the collar of Kenny Fields' warm-up jacket, pinning Kenny up against the wall, like he was choking him during a fight. I almost passed out. Craig said, "It's all right, Coach. It's all right. I'll explain!" Still, I asked, "What in the hell is going on?" Again Craig said, "I've got this Coach. I'll explain to you on the court." Craig had not let go of Kenny, who was looking embarrassed and not saying anything. So whatever was going on didn't have Kenny too upset.

I walked back to the court, thinking "I'm going to kill my assistant coach, and then get sued by Kenny Fields' parents for allowing this abuse." When Craig and Kenny came out of the locker room, Kenny jogged onto the court and Craig walked straight to me and sat down. I'm grinding my teeth in anticipation of what he's about to say to me before I strangle him. Impelman explained that Kenny's dad had told him that Kenny could lose his focus at halftime, so he asked Craig to shake him up a little bit to get his juices flowing. Kenny's dad said he used to do it at halftime of Kenny's high school games. Craig admitted he might've taken this a little bit more literally than Kenny's dad had intended. Craig assured me he would be better at it next time. The last thing I told Craig on the subject was if he and Kenny were going to do that, they better never again let anybody see it, especially me.

I felt better after Craig explained, and I felt even better heading back to Los Angeles with a record of 3–0.

We beat San Jose State 94–71 before facing a big challenge from Coach Lute Olson's No. 6-ranked Iowa Hawkeyes. Iowa was the preseason favorite to win the Big Ten. They came into our game with a record of 6–0. Iowa had 6-foot-11 forwards (twin towers) Greg Stokes and Michael Payne. We were now ranked No. 3 in the nation, and this game would be shown on NBC nationally. It was a hard-fought game but we were able to pull away in the last 90 seconds for a final score of 75–66. Kenny Fields scored 21 points and Darren Daye added 20.

LSU was returning our road game from the year before when we played in the Superdome and they tried to gather an all-time record crowd. Now LSU would get a taste of what it was like to play in front of 12,000 UCLA fans. Make that 10,000 fans. It was our last home game before the Christmas break, so a lot of the students had already left campus and it seemed some of our fans were already waiting for Santa Claus. We were up by 10 points with just over eight minutes to play when Stuart Gray and LSU's Howard Carter got into a little physical exchange (initiated by Stuart) and both were ejected. I was proud of Stuart. He was a good kid but he wasn't about to be bullied.

LSU Coach Dale Brown took exception to their leading scorer being thrown out, saying his guy was averaging 18 points a game and our guy hadn't scored a single point in a month, so they were losing much more. Stuart had scored more than a single point during the month of December, but that physical exchange might have been Stuart's best score of the night. With Carter gone, we had one less high-scoring Tiger to worry about. We beat LSU 82–68.

Undefeated after playing six games of this demanding schedule, we faced another ranked team on the road three days later.

Maryland Coach Lefty Driesell said he had been looking forward to this game for a year, ever since we blew them out 90–57 in Pauley Pavilion. Driesell had decided to play at a slow tempo after that game. They beat North Carolina and several other ACC opponents with that slow game. Driesell called the UCLA loss one of the worst defeats in his coaching career. He went on to say that he had been preaching revenge to his players all week leading up to our game on their court. We had heard stories about some of Lefty's tactics. For example, it was not beyond him to have the heat turned up in the visiting team's locker room, making the players uncomfortable during their halftime rest. The theory was players in that hot locker room would continue to sweat and would tire in the second half. Kevin O'Connor went into our locker room first to let us know if the locker room was hot, and it was. We had the team sit down in the hallway outside of the locker room and that's where I gave my halftime talk. We started the second half lethargically anyway and we got behind right away. We were playing catch-up in front of their sellout crowd of more than 14,500 people. We took Maryland to double overtime before we lost our first game of the season 80–79.

After the game Lefty voiced his opinion that we were, without question, the No. 1 team in the country, playing the toughest schedule of any of the ranked teams. I learned a valuable lesson—never schedule a road game right before Christmas break. Sometimes your kids get in the holiday spirit before that final horn goes off. We traveled back to Los Angeles on December 24.

Three days after Christmas we played our last big nonconference game before opening Pac-10 play.

We had Coach Denny Crum's University of Louisville team coming to Pauley Pavilion with eight of 10 players back from the team that had played in the Final Four the year before. They were absolutely loaded with talent. I had recruited one of Louisville's starting forwards, freshman Billy Thompson. They had terrific guards, Lancaster Gordon and Milt Wagner. And to top it off, they had two brothers, Rodney and Scooter McRae, completing their front line. Denny and I both taught Coach Wooden's system, so we ran versions of the same offense.

Denny Crum was my friend, but in one of my press interviews leading up to the game, I misspoke and made it seem that I had an issue with him. It was my fault because of my word usage. When asked about my relationship with Coach Crum I said he takes credit for everything I have accomplished at UCLA. I meant to say he should get credit because he took a chance on me when he recruited me to UCLA and I learned a lot from him when he was an assistant coach. Taking credit for someone else's success is entirely different.

On game day, before the teams were even on the floor for warmups, Denny and I sat in the stands visiting and getting caught up. A photographer came over and took pictures, and then one of the cameramen from CBS saw us sitting there having a conversation and filmed a sound bite. It was later said that we must have patched up our differences.

The fact is we never had any differences.

When the jump ball went up there were 10 players on the floor who would be drafted and spend some time on NBA rosters. This was a high-level college game. Louisville immediately jumped out on us and were just kicking our behinds! I called a couple timeouts in an attempt to stop the bleeding. At one point in the first half we were down 15 points. They were coming at us with a combination of fast breaks, good defense, flashy passes—you name it, they did it to us. At halftime we were still down by 15 points. We made several attempts to get back in the game, but midway through the second half we were down 10 points again.

It was in the second half of this game that Stuart Gray came to life and showed the nation how good he really was. He played well in the first half, doing a lot of the little things that don't show up on the score sheet. When he picked up his fourth foul, I was forced to take him out. With just under four minutes to play, when we were down by four points and I felt the game slipping away, I put him back in.

Louisville went into their delay offense and spread the floor, more than willing to take time off the clock and finish the game at the free throw line. They were waiting for us to start gambling or intentionally fouling. But a couple of key turnovers sparked our last run. Stuart would score all 14 of his points in the second half, including two dunks that came on a run when we took the lead. UCLA won 76–72. Our students rushed the floor when the horn went off and surrounded Stuart in a show of their appreciation. I could not have been more proud of him. The fans' show of appreciation was overdue.

There was absolutely no doubt that playing the tough nonconference schedule had prepared us for anything we would face in our conference. It was worth the risk.

The University of Arizona had a new coach, Ben Lindsey. He was replacing Fred Snowden and his team was going through a difficult transition. They had a record of 2–6 when we opened conference play in Tucson. We played horribly and were lucky to get out of there with a 92–87 victory.

We went over to Arizona State, where they also had a new head coach: Bob Weinhauer, who had come to Scottsdale from the University of Pennsylvania. His two assistants were Doug Collins, formerly a star with the Philadelphia 76ers, and Henry Bibby, my former teammate and another former NBA player. This was a very good staff. Not only were they going to be tough to play, but they were also going to be extremely tough to recruit against. Rod Foster scored 30 points, including the winning basket, to put us up by one point with 15 seconds left. We escaped ASU with an 87–86 victory.

One thing was clear. We were getting everybody's "A" game! Back at Pauley Pavilion we took a big lead against Oregon and I was able to play a couple of the players that didn't often get an opportunity. Brad Wright took complete advantage of his 11 minutes, scoring 16 points while going 8-for-8 from the field.

Oregon State, the team that had won our conference three years in a row, had four starters back. I knew our players would be up for this game, and they were. We made 13 of our first 15 shots, shot 77 percent from the floor in the first half, and 66 percent for the game. We maintained a 20-point lead throughout the game and won 99–77. Coach Wooden always tried to avoid emotional highs and lows during the course of the season. He believed in keeping his teams, mentally, somewhere in the middle. I can't say that the players were even keel coming off that victory, having a record of 11–1, and being recognized as the No. 1 team in the country.

So, yes, it did occur to me that we might have a letdown when we went to Berkeley to play Cal, a team UCLA had beaten 46 games in a row. I did not want my name attached to the game that broke that winning streak. We had the better team. All we had to do was play our brand of basketball, and we would be fine.

Michael Pitts and Mike Chavez were starters on the University of California team. UCLA had offered both of them scholarships. They could be expected to do a little extra to beat us. We managed to beat Cal 68–63 after scoring on a couple of designed lob pass plays against their 2-3 zone defense late in a very close game.

Stanford also played a zone defense. Their head coach, Dr. Tom Davis, loved to play a full-court (1-2-1-1) press, and then play a 1-2-2 half-court zone defense. The way we attacked an odd man front zone (1-3-1) or (1-2-2) was to overload the baseline—put two big men on the baseline, one on either side of the basket—and have a shooter (like Rod Foster) moving from one corner to the other on the baseline. I told Rod days before the game that if he wanted to score 30 points, just concentrate on shooting from both corners during that week of practice. On game day, Rod wanted to get up some extra shots, so Craig Impelman took him by taxi to Maples Pavilion to put up some shots from those very spots. Rod was dialed in when the game started and scored 31 points. We beat Stanford 101–87.

Two very good non-league opponents were up next. We played Alabama and Notre Dame in nationally televised games. The Notre Dame game was on Super Bowl Sunday, but we could not look past Alabama, which had been ranked as high as No. 5 nationally and had blown out Patrick Ewing and Georgetown 94–73 earlier in the season.

I was in a coaching staff meeting with Kevin and Craig on

Wednesday morning when the basketball secretary buzzed me and told me that Digger Phelps was on the phone for me. Ordinarily, she would not interrupt meetings, but this one sounded urgent. When I picked up the phone I truly did start off the conversation in a very pleasant way, because I did, deep down, like and respect Coach Phelps. The conversation quickly turned negative. He wanted to know what was going on with his team not being able to practice in Pauley Pavilion on Saturday. Kevin O'Connor, who could hear Digger yelling through the phone even though he was sitting on the opposite side of my desk, quickly answered the question. Kenny Rogers was putting on a concert in Pauley Pavilion on Saturday, with all proceeds being donated to the UCLA General Fund. Kevin is telling me (as I'm listening to Digger) that Notre Dame basketball was notified both with a phone call and a follow-up letter early in the year that both UCLA and Notre Dame would be practicing in the Men's Gym the night before our game. Kevin had given Notre Dame a choice of practice times. Apparently, Coach Phelps had not received that information until just then. He was really upset! I told him that I was sorry about the situation, but we had no control over it. We would not be practicing in Pauley Pavilion, either. Well, that wasn't a good enough answer and he cut the conversation short. It ended with Coach Phelps saying to me, "Don't you F#@K it up against Alabama, because we want your ASS!" And then he slammed the phone down. He had called me, cursed at me, and hung up on me, so now I was pissed off.

We played a horrible game against Alabama and trailed the entire game. We were down 16 in the second half before a furious comeback tied the game with 35 seconds left. I took a timeout. I told the team that our defense was going to win the game for us, because it had been our defense that had enabled us to dig out of a hole. We had an idea of what Alabama was going to run to try to get the last shot, so I did spend some time describing how they would look to score on us. I told the team to play smart and not to foul. "No fouls" was the last thing I said.

Alabama was taking time off the clock and getting organized

to run a play for one last shot. We did a good job of defending their initial action, and they appeared to be a little bit out of sync. We denied the ball back to their point guard, so they passed the ball out toward half-court and would have to hurry their last play. Rod Foster got confused and played as if we were still behind, as if he had to prevent the shot at any cost. With 10 seconds left he committed an intentional foul. There was a gasp from the crowd of 12,500 people in Pauley Pavilion. The Alabama team was stunned and took a few seconds before they reacted to having a chance to go ahead without running a play. I think it was the sound that the crowd made that drew Rod's attention to the scoreboard and the clock. I'll never forget the look on his face when he realized what he had done. Alabama made both free throws. I called a play to try to get a shot off now that we are down two points. We ran the play in transition and Rod got a pretty good look but missed. We lost 69–67.

After I shook hands with Alabama Coach Wimp Sanderson, I immediately went to Rod and put my arm around him. I told him that anybody could have made that mistake, and we would never have been that close had it not been for his play throughout the game. I told him he had won—would win—more games than he would ever lose for UCLA. In postgame interviews reporters were actually kind when they asked about Rod's foul.

We played Notre Dame on Super Bowl Sunday. And, of course, Digger came out playing a slow tempo. Notre Dame was in no hurry to shoot. With John Paxson playing point guard, they were always going to get a quality shot. They don't panic when the ball is in his hands, especially in a close game. It was a one-point game at halftime.

But it was our point guard, Ralph Jackson, who was the hero of this game. Besides guarding Paxson (who scored 18 points), Ralph played good defense at the end of the game, got a key rebound, and made the game-clinching free throws in our 59–53 victory.

At the end of the game, it is customary that the two head coaches walk down the sideline, meet at half-court, and shake hands. They then shake hands with the assistant coaches and maybe even the players from the opposing team. But I was still angry over the phone call at the beginning of the week. When the game ended, I walked directly toward the center circle, heading for our locker room and completely avoiding him. Coach Phelps yelled at me, "What's wrong, you don't shake hands anymore?" I looked back at him as my assistants strategically positioned themselves between me and him and ever so gently guided me towards the locker room. I yelled at him, "Digger, you're too much!"

That's the only time in my coaching career that I refused to shake the opposing coach's hand after a game. I had, of course, shared the telephone conversation with Bob Fischer. Little did Coach Phelps know that hanging up on me was all the ammunition I needed to convince Bob Fischer that, going forward, we should schedule only one game a year with Notre Dame, as in 1967 when the series started. We would end the 10-year run of home-and-home scheduling that started in 1972.

Next we played Washington State, who came into Pauley Pavilion undefeated in Pac-10 play (7–0) and having never won on the UCLA campus. They had played hard and had given us many close games, but Coach Raveling's teams continued to be denied getting that signature win at UCLA. We had a record of 6–0 in conference play, so this game was for the lead. The game went to overtime, but we won 89–87. We had less trouble beating Washington 84–65. We got great contributions from the guys coming off the bench, specifically Gary Maloncon, who came in and did a good job defensively against Detlef Schrempf (future NBA star) and scored 10 points on 5-of-6 shooting.

We traveled to Oregon and won 67–56.

At this point we were undefeated in the Pac-10 and had an overall record of 17–2.

Our national ranking had slipped from No. 1 to No. 7 after the Alabama loss, but we were playing with a great deal of confidence and working well together as a team.

At Oregon State we were expecting a hard-fought game that would go down to the wire. Instead, we had two key injuries, made adjustments, trailed the whole way, and lost 69–64.

Just 25 seconds into the contest, A.C. Green fell and rolled into the side of Stuart Gray's leg. Stuart went down, and Ducky reported that it might be a partially torn ligament. About 10 minutes into the game, Kenny Fields reached for a loose ball and heard a pop in his shoulder. Ducky judged that to be a partially dislocated shoulder. Ducky put him in a sling and applied an ice pack. So we're down two starters and we haven't even reached halftime. I was coaching this game while worrying about the health and status of two key players. I was really drilling down on the officials to make sure that they kept the game under control, and I wound up getting hit with a technical foul that I didn't deserve. We managed to play a close second half but never took the lead.

I was reminded after the Oregon State game about how our league opponents felt about UCLA and our dominance through the years. When we played Oregon State in Los Angeles, one of Coach Ralph Miller's players was sick, and Charlie Sitton had just come back from minor knee surgery. When asked after this game about our injuries, Miller responded: "Turnabout is fair play." I believe the team finally realized that beating UCLA was a big deal again. We were going to bring out everyone's best game and no one was going to feel sorry for us.

We would find out later that Stuart's ligament was strained, so he would be out for three to four weeks. Kenny's shoulder was partially separated, and we were told that he might need just a week.

Stanford and Cal were coming to Pauley Pavilion. Kenny was able to practice but I held him out of contact early in the week. There was a chance he could play, but we definitely would not have Stuart back in time for these games, so I decided to start Brad Wright at center. He had a good week of practice and earned it. Gary Maloncon would come off the bench. We got solid play from that position and beat both Cal and Stanford. Our winning streak against Cal went to 47 games.

The time had come for our back-to-back extravaganza with USC. We would play them at Pauley Pavilion on Thursday and at the Sports Arena on Saturday, just as we did back in 1969, my freshman year. Although back then, we didn't have a day of rest in between, since we played Friday and Saturday. That whole weekend was about UCLA-USC basketball. I truly believed that playing them back-to-back would give us our best chance of sweeping, which is why I wanted to do it in the first place.

That was why I went to work on convincing Coach Stan Morrison that it would be a good idea the year before. In 1969 the varsity split—each team winning on the other team's home court. But that same weekend, my freshman team won both games. Thirteen years later, I thought we dialed up a little of the same magic. For the previous three years we had split the series with USC. It had become more of a competitive rivalry because of USC's improvement. Coming into this game, UCLA had a record of 11–1 in Pac-10 play; USC 9–3. We spanked USC 77–60 in Pauley in front of a packed house. I knew our guys would be fired up to play USC, and with that short turnaround, USC wouldn't have a lot of time to regroup before we played them again. Time to mentally recover had become the key to why we kept splitting the series. One team would win the first game and three or four weeks later, after the loser had time to regroup, we would play again—resulting in a split series. But not this time. Shaking a 17-point loss in just two days would not be easy.

The second game was much closer. I did remind the team how it felt leaving the Sports Arena the year before. Despite hitting the Trojans with a 16–0 Bruin Blitz in the first half, we could never really shake them. USC would cut the lead to just two points with just over a minute to play. That was when Ralph Jackson, who had not been shooting free throws well, made two in a row to give us the cushion we would need to beat the Trojans 71–64 and complete the sweep.

When Stuart hurt his knee and could not play or practice, I decided it was best for us to go back to running the high post offense. There would still be plenty of opportunities for our guards to score, but there would be a few more opportunities for our forwards. It wouldn't take a lot of re-teaching. Kenny and Darren continued to thrive on the court, and the high post offense was only going to give them a few more quick looks.

We traveled to the state of Washington with an opportunity to clinch the Pac-10 championship by winning both games. We beat Washington 90–66 in one of our best games on the road.

We headed to Pullman to play Washington State knowing it would be a difficult game. They had played us to overtime in Los Angeles, and we had beaten them by only two points. This rematch would also be extremely close and go down to the wire.

Toward the end of the game, on a lob pass play, Kenny caught the ball well above the rim and as he attempted to lay the ball in, a player from WSU stepped underneath him, knocking him to the floor. The rule as I understood it (and as it read) was that the offensive player should be allowed to land, and Kenny was not allowed to land before contact was made. The officials completely screwed up the call. I didn't get a technical foul (I probably should have) because I didn't want to hurt our chances of winning. With the score tied at 68 apiece, they got the last shot. I believed their game clock operator gave them a little bit of extra time to get their shot off when the horn should have been sounding. They had time to tip the ball in at the buzzer to win.

Their fans stormed the court. One of their backboards cracked because of a fan swinging on the rim. The team cut down their own nets! There was a picture the next day in one of the Pullman newspapers showing Bryan Pollard (who had tipped in the winning basket) with a net around his neck holding a broken rim in his hand.

It was the same as it had been the year before when we lost at Washington State under unusual circumstances and their fans rushed the court. Coach Raveling got away with switching a free throw shooter in a clutch moment of the game. I was up screaming at the referees about the call and didn't notice that Raveling put a guy at the line that was a much better free throw shooter than the one who had been fouled. The referees didn't catch it, either. None of us caught it until I watched the game film. And some people had the notion that beating UCLA wasn't that big a deal anymore? Wrong! My comments to the media at this game's conclusion did not include complaining about the refereeing, but it wasn't very good.

A lot of basketball experts were quick to point out Stuart Gray's weaknesses, but many of his strengths—including defensive rebounding—were never fully appreciated. Those strengths were obvious to me and our team. We might still have been out-rebounded by Washington State, but they would not have gotten 19 offensive rebounds if Stuart had been able to play. Nonetheless, we lost 70–68. Rod Foster led us in scoring with 26 points, shooting an amazing 13 of 17 from the floor.

We returned to Los Angeles for our last two conference games. The University of Arizona had suffered through a difficult season, winning just one game. There were already rumors about first-year coach Ben Lindsey getting fired. We beat them 111–56. Our 53-point winning margin ranks 10th all-time in the UCLA record book.

The conference championship was undecided going into the last day of competition. Washington State was favored to beat Washington that afternoon, and they were just one game behind us in the race for the championship. If Washington State did win, we would need to beat Arizona State to win the title or a share of the title. But Washington upset Washington State by one point. So we knew that win or lose against Arizona State, we were conference champions. Athletic Director Bob Fischer approached me before the game and asked if I thought the team should be introduced in its usual way or if we should let the fans know that we were the Pac-10 champions. Fischer asked me this right before the game started, and my initial thought was to not change anything up and just to have the introductions be as they have always been. I thought about what we had gone through last year with probation. The "rattling of the car keys," the catcalls on the road, and the newspaper articles that not only embarrassed but humiliated our team and our program. I sensed that Mr. Fischer wanted our team to be introduced as champions, and I agreed. So after Don Sawyer introduced Arizona State, he started our introductions by saying, "And now, your Pac-10 champion UCLA Bruins!"! Our fans erupted. The standing ovation was longer than usual. Now everybody in the building knew we were already the Pac-10 champions.

And I knew at that moment I had made a mistake in having our team introduced that way. Byron Scott went off in the game, scoring 25 points in Arizona State's 78–76 victory. I know introductions had nothing to do with guarding him or with our team making shots. But if I had to do over again, I would not have had our team introduced as conference champions.

Whether it was a letdown at the beginning of the game because the players knew we were already conference champions or because it was our last home game (Senior Day) and our players thought we would win, we were not ready to play.

Saying goodbye in Pauley Pavilion to Rod Foster, Michael Holton, and Darren Daye was not easy. When they came in as freshmen we finished fourth in the Pac-10 and made it to the NCAA championship

RINGS AND WATCHES

Shortly after the season ended I met with Bob Fischer about recognizing the team's Pac-10 championship. I thought it would be nice to get watches for each of the players with "Pac-10 Champions 1983" on the face. He let me present my case before he said that UCLA gave rings and watches for national championships, not conference championships. He didn't say it in a nasty way, just very matter-of-fact.

After that I called Sam Gilbert, Maylee Wang, and Keith Sinclair. I shared my talk with Mr. Fischer and asked if they would be willing to contribute to the purchase of watches. I was not looking to put UCLA back on probation, so Rolexes were out of the question. The three of them worked out the details and a couple of weeks later, the simple watches had been produced. The watches were more symbolic than functional. My watch stopped working after two years. It remains in my safety deposit box, along with my three NCAA championship rings and three NCAA championship watches. I am proud of all of them.

Michael Holton was our team captain when we won the Pac-10 title. He was a study in outstanding character. He was not a game. Their sophomore year we finished third in the conference and were eliminated in the first round of the NCAA tournament. Then their head coach (Larry Brown) left to go to the pros. Their junior year we were on probation but finished second in the conference. And now their senior year, finally, they were Pac-10 champions.

We finished the regular season with an overall record of 23–5 and a conference record of 15–3. Now we would wait to see where the NCAA tournament committee would send us.

Our loss to ASU knocked us down from a No. 1 seed team in the West Regional to a No. 2 seed. We would play in Boise, Idaho, against the winner of the Utah vs. Illinois game. Utah became our opponent by beating Illinois in a very competitive game 52–49.

Utah's coach, Jerry Pimm, was well-known and respected in our profession. I had known him for years and considered him a friend.

---

starter his senior year and that could not have been easy for him, but he never let it affect him on the court or in the locker room. He would have been our team leader regardless of whether he was captain because his teammates held him in such esteem. His senior year, he had his highest shooting percentage (54.7 percent) and averaged the most points (8.3) and assists (2.8) of his four years. Michael played for the Phoenix Suns, the Chicago Bulls, the Portland Trailblazers, and the Charlotte Hornets. In 2001, he became head coach at the University of Portland.

Almost 20 years after we won the conference championship, I got a call from Michael. He had talked to all the guys on that 1983 team and they agreed that we should each have a championship ring. The conference title was still important to them. Michael had designed a ring and worked out the cost. I was thrilled but not surprised. He wanted my approval. He was asking several of us to contribute a little extra for the players who might have a difficulty paying for their rings, which I happily did. Of all the rings I received throughout my playing and coaching career, it was the 1983 conference championship ring I wore to my UCLA Hall of Fame induction ceremony.

I also knew from experience that Utah would have a slight advantage having played an NCAA tournament game already and worked through some of the nervousness that accompanied the first tournament game. Back in 1980, Larry Brown's first year, we played Old Dominion in the first round and beat them before facing the No. 1 overall seed, DePaul. We were loose. DePaul came out tight and a little flat, and we beat them. Our seniors hadn't played in the NCAA tournament since our "one and done" game two years earlier (Larry Brown's last season) against Danny Ainge and BYU. But we had the better team, and we had played so many tough opponents (both nonconference and conference) throughout the course of the season that I felt we were prepared for anything.

We started off the Utah game not quite in sync and showing some nerves. Although we led 34–32 at halftime, we started the second half much like the first. We shot just 30 percent from the floor. For the season, we were shooting 53 percent as a team (one of the nation's best). Utah, on the other hand, was loose and really played like they were not only inspired, but had nothing to lose.

The longer the game went on the more confident they got.

I remember needing a basket late in the second half and calling out the double down play in the offense for Michael Holton to get a shot. As the play was developing, Michael's route was to cut underneath the basket, wait for the center and forward to come together, and set a double screen for him to run off the baseline and look for the shot. Michael, in an effort to score a little bit quicker, did not run his route properly and consequently did not get the clean shot I was hoping that he would. I remember saying to Michael, "You've got to go all the way underneath the basket and come off the screens shoulder to shoulder!" The look he had on his face showed more concern over the score of the game than the execution of the play. I never thought it was too late to teach, but this was something Michael had learned years ago. The seriousness of the moment impacted his execution.

It was at times like this that your execution needed to be at its best. I'd never seen that look on his face before, and I realized we were in big trouble.

We lost the game to Utah 67–61. Neither Darren (who made only four of nine free throws) or Rod (who made only 4 of 12 from the floor) played well offensively. We always needed one of those two to pick up the slack if the team was struggling, because we could always count on Kenny Fields to score. Kenny scored 18 points but did not shoot a very high percentage (7 of 16) and that put us behind the eight ball.

After the game, I heard just about every reason for our team's poor performance and subsequently getting upset in the NCAA tournament. Things from "a pregame meal belch" or "we should have gone to Boise earlier" to being cocky and looking ahead to playing the winner of the UNLV and North Carolina State game. None of those were factors, in my view. We played poorly at the wrong time and got beat.

CHAPTER 23

The Changing of the Guard

When we returned to Los Angeles, the weight of having lost our opening game in the NCAA tournament was overwhelming. I closed my office door and was "unavailable" for a couple days before taking on the issues of the offseason.

Bob Fischer had undergone triple bypass heart surgery in late March, and ultimately, he resigned June 9, 1983. Mr. Fischer had been a part of UCLA athletics from the day I stepped on campus as a freshman, and I literally grew up with him being in the athletic department. His departure hit me very hard.

It was bad news not only for me personally, but it also hurt the program.

The next day, Peter Dalis was named our new Athletic Director. I knew little about him, and his hiring made me uneasy. I was not alone in that feeling. Football coach Terry Donahue and I had lunch together later that week off campus and shared what we had learned about Dalis. Dalis had not come up through the ranks in the athletics department, but through the recreation department at UCLA.

I had heard that he had a social relationship with ex-UCLA basketball greats Mahdi Abdul-Rahman (Walt Hazzard) and Jack Hirsch. Our biggest fear was that Dalis would operate the athletic department at the direction of the UCLA administration, through Vice Chancellor Elwin Svenson, who was the "liaison" between athletics and the university. There was a trust and a comfort level with Bob Fischer. Now, with Dalis, we worried that he would be more of a company man than a director of athletics who put our programs first. Terry and I agreed that we would watch each other's backs and keep each other posted.

A top priority during the offseason was recruiting forwards. I needed to replace Darren Daye and ultimately, the following year, Kenny Fields. We had already signed Reggie Miller, and we had Gary Maloncon and Nigel Miguel returning. Nigel and Reggie could be either big guards or small forwards in our system. Bringing in one more forward would be good; two more would be perfect!

Leading our list were two Southern California players—John Williams (6-foot-8) out of Crenshaw High School and Chris Sandle (6-foot-7) from Long Beach Poly High School. I was poised to offer them both scholarships and sign them on the spot if they accepted. There was also a terrific forward out of Colorado named Craig Jackson (6-foot-8) from Montebello High School in Denver. Not only was he a good player but had the reputation of being an outstanding student. Basketball pundits in Denver said Jackson reminded them of me.

I received word in the early summer through Peter Dalis that Chancellor Young would not allow us to sign John Williams or Chris Sandle. He named them specifically. This was an absolute first! In all my years as an assistant coach at UCLA, the chancellor's office had never gotten involved in our recruiting or our admissions. I was familiar enough with UCLA entrance requirements that I could look at a young man's transcript and tell whether he was going to have the necessary academic requirements to even be considered for "special action" admittance into UCLA. If he did not, I wouldn't even send the transcript to the admissions department to be evaluated. I could not make that call on these two prospects because we had yet to request transcripts. We always requested transcripts in the fall. I had been told two of the most visible players in Southern California were off-limits to me before their senior years even started.

Both players would be asked to name the schools they were considering. When they didn't say UCLA, people would want to know why. No doubt I would be pressed to explain why we were not recruiting two of the best players in Los Angeles.

Somehow the chancellor had been given the word that those two might be problematic academically. Dalis apparently had offered no pushback to the chancellor's office, even though I would have expected my Athletic Director to offer counter points and at least suggest waiting for transcripts. He had merely passed the information along to me.

All of this was a byproduct of what had happened with football player Billy Don Jackson.

The problem was not that a tremendous former UCLA football player from Sherman, Texas, had entered a no-contest plea to voluntary manslaughter in the stabbing death of a drug dealer. The problem was that a story in the *Los Angeles Times* on March 27, 1982 included damning comments made by Prosecutor Marsh Goldman at the sentencing hearing. Jackson's sentence included a condition that he take remedial instruction to "increase his ability to read and write."

The *Times* quoted Goldman: "My God, they brought this kid to one of the top universities in the country and it takes a court order for him to properly learn to read and write."

The prosecutor called the one-year sentence "just." Goldman said: "After all, Billy Don Jackson is himself a victim—a victim of the shoddy system we call intercollegiate athletics. Hopefully, somebody in college sports will learn something from this tragedy." The university was embarrassed, and the fallout meant tightening the academic screws on every sport, including men's basketball. Obviously, UCLA's administrators and faculty wanted to protect the university from the slightest chance such an event ever occurred again, and I agreed.

The basketball staff did a great job of screening recruits. We did not pursue any prospect who would not be capable of handling the academic requirements and, eventually, getting a degree. Once recruits signed and were in school, we surrounded our players with enough academic guidance and support to maximize opportunities for learning and graduating.

Dalis' response was that we just needed to expand our recruiting list. He said there were enough good players out there and UCLA should be able to find them, which demonstrated how naïve he was about big-time college recruiting. Good high school players went to the mid-major programs in Southern California. The great players went to UCLA. Every UCLA head basketball coach, including Coach Wooden, had teams that were 90 percent great local talent. A longer list of good players was not the answer. I wasn't shocked by his proposed solution because, after all, he was new to Division I athletics.

Word eventually started to circulate that UCLA was not recruiting two of Southern California's best players, so I decided it would be in our best interest to give the public appearance of recruiting both Williams and Sandle. I thought it would look better if I got out-recruited as opposed to looking disinterested. I would watch them play all summer as if I were actively recruiting them. I didn't expect the chancellor to change his mind, but somewhere deep down inside, I was hoping he might and I wanted to be ready. I would make in-home visits in the fall and do everything except ultimately sign them to the letter of intent. There was certainly no guarantee that either of them would choose UCLA, anyway.

That fall we requested both players' transcripts and learned both would have been "special action" candidates. They met NCAA eligibility standards and barring any missteps during their senior years, we would have been able to work with them. Nothing out of the ordinary. The basketball program had proven over the last decade that our "special action" recruits had graduated from UCLA.

We made visits to the homes of both John Williams and Chris Sandle. We prepared and delivered terrific in-home presentations for two recruits we weren't going to be allowed to sign. John Williams would ultimately sign with Coach Dale Brown and LSU. Chris Sandle signed with Arizona State and stayed there for two years before transferring to the University of Texas at El Paso (UTEP).

One thing was certain: my approach to recruiting was going to have to change drastically.

There would be more star players I would not be able to recruit if our academic standards were going to become more like Ivy League standards. And the kids we couldn't get into school would be playing against us for other schools, maybe even a rival school close by or a school in our conference.

Kenny Fields followed fellow UCLA Bruins Marques Johnson and David Greenwood in being named Pac-10 Player of the Year. It was a well-earned recognition. After the season, I met with Kenny and his family about rumors he was considering entering his name into the NBA draft and leaving school early. Exploring his options after such a great year was the natural thing to do, so I had no issue with that. But when I met with the family, they told me that indirect information from NBA scouts and executives had convinced them it was best for Kenny to stay at UCLA for his senior year. Obviously, I was very happy with their decision.

It was around this time that I started hearing talk about changing my coaching staff. Over breakfast with Sam and Rose one Sunday morning, Sam brought up his feeling that perhaps I needed more help on the bench. He had nothing against Craig Impelman or Kevin O'Connor, but felt I needed more aggressive and more knowledgeable assistants working behind the scenes on my behalf. It was Sam who first mentioned to me Mahdi Abdul-Rahman (Walt Hazzard) and Jack Hirsch. It was typical Sam, being protective and looking out for me. He knew that because of our relationship I would listen to him. He did not have enough influence over me to force me to make a decision against my own judgment, but he had enough to get me thinking about it. I trusted him. Hazzard had coached at Compton Junior College in 1980. In 1982, he was hired as the head coach of Chapman College, a Division II program in Orange, California. Coach Hazzard had maintained a friendship through the years with Sam, and I knew Sam well enough to know that if Sam was talking to me about this, he and Hazzard had talked about it.

I first met Hazzard when I was a player at UCLA. He was still playing in the NBA in the early '70s and would often play basketball in the summer games in the old Men's Gym. He was a legendary figure and great player at UCLA, and along with Gail Goodrich provided Coach Wooden with his first national championship. He was a larger-than-life figure, and just being around him, watching him play or talking about the old days at UCLA, mesmerized me.

Hazzard had started to become more visible around UCLA in 1975 (after retiring from the NBA) when Coach Bartow was hired. Like many former players, he told Bartow he would do anything he could to help the program. Jack Hirsch also was a member of Wooden's first national championship team, and he and Hazzard were best friends. Their friendship carried over into their professional relationship, with Jack assisting Hazzard at both Compton Junior College and at Chapman College. Jack seemed like a nice enough guy. I had heard he was from a very wealthy family. We were friendly, but I certainly got to know Hazzard much better than I did Hirsch. I admired Hazzard. However, I was satisfied with my current coaching staff. I trusted and respected both Craig and Kevin and barring one of them leaving to take another coaching position, I did not intend to make changes.

I had lunch one day shortly after the season ended with my friend Maylee Wang. She was constantly on me about taking better care of myself. She was a member of a paddle tennis club located on the beach near Santa Monica and she had gotten me out to play several times. Maylee was the first to bring to my attention that I was getting bald spots, telling me she could see them from her seats behind the bench at Pauley Pavilion. When I got a hand mirror so I could see the back of my head, I did see a couple small bald spots. I called Kami Parsee, the gentleman who operated a salon in Westwood, hoping he would say he nicked me. But he said he had noticed the spots and assumed I was aware of them. He thought it was probably stress but suggested I might talk to my doctor. After I contacted my doctor, who referred me to a dermatologist, it was confirmed that my hair loss was due to stress. I was 32 years old and my hair was falling out. I had aged. I looked older and my face was a little bit more drawn. Maylee made me promise to take a vacation, something that I hadn't done since being hired as head coach at UCLA. I promised her that I would take some time off.

I had my basketball camp in Thousand Oaks at Cal State Lutheran college in July. It was run at the same place under the same management group (Sports World) that ran Coach Wooden's basketball camp. I worked hard every day, but everything was already in place and the camp ran like clockwork. I did a handful of camps for my old friend Kelly Warner's Northwest basketball camps, and I managed to work in a couple of fishing trips (as a part of my deal with Kelly.) I also accepted an opportunity from Adidas to return to France and speak at one of their European coaches' clinics in Nantes near the west coast of France. I would spend three days at the clinic and four days vacationing in Paris. I would return for five days in Denver with my folks. That would be my two-week vacation.

While in Denver, I decided to hang out with my favorite cousin, Robert Jenkins, who had been like an older brother to me. His nickname when we were kids was Dovey, from a song in the mid-50s called "Lovey-Dovey." My Aunt Letha (his mother) gave him that name. As an adult, and a member of a black motorcycle club called the Sons of Darkness, his nickname was "The Cuz." The Sons of Darkness had chapters all over the United States. They would have massive rides or gatherings a couple times a year.

My parents loved him but they had worried, since I was a child, that my rather rambunctious cousin might be a bad influence on me. He wasn't.

Dovey always had flashy, tailor-made clothes that I would borrow for school dances and other special occasions. I would stop by his apartment so he could get me properly dressed up! I would literally walk into his apartment with my shoes, socks, belt, and underwear. The rest was up to him. My classmates thought I had really cleaned up my act my senior year, that I was a sharp dresser, but it was all my cousin's doing!

On this particular day, we got into one of his "hot rods." He had worked on this car to make it unbelievably fast. He didn't hesitate to show me. Around lunchtime he took me to the headquarters of his motorcycle club to introduce me to the some of the members. I was a little nervous, because I really didn't know anything about motorcycle clubs, other than the stereotypical view. There were beautiful Harley Davidsons parked at the clubhouse. My cousin put on his denim vest, which had several patches on it, each signifying an achievement or a milestone, and of course his nickname on the back. When we walked into the club there were about 20 bikers there, playing cards or dominoes or just hanging out. I walk in wearing a Ralph Lauren polo shirt, Bermuda shorts, and low-cut Adidas tennis shoes. My casual appearance made me even more self-conscious. The first person he introduced me to was the president of the club. My cousin, who had never really said that he was impressed by my new title of head coach, introduced me to the president of the motorcycle club by saying, "This is my cousin, the head coach at UCLA!" Not my name, just that. I shook the president's hand, and later teased my cousin about my new name, "head coach." He introduced me to one of his other riding buddies named "Doodoo." Not wanting to really know how he got that nickname, I didn't ask. Doodoo was a soft-spoken, articulate, older fellow. He was a basketball fan and had followed my playing career. I was there for about 45 minutes, and most of the time it was just three of us visiting. My cousin did eventually introduce me to everyone in the clubhouse, and he reverted to calling me Larry Farmer. It was refreshing (after a while) that most of them had no idea who or what I was, other than The Cuz's real cousin! There were some real characters in the clubhouse. Some were physically intimidating, but all of them friendly toward this outsider. As we left to head back to my parents' house, I did wonder if Coach Wooden had ever been invited to a motorcycle club to hang out with a biker named after you-know-what.

Also during this summer before my second season as head coach at UCLA, I accepted an invitation from Kansas State Coach Jack Hartman to spend a week in Colorado Springs as one of his assistant coaches at a tryout camp. Coach Hartman would select the 1983 Pan American team from approximately 50 elite college players. Some of the notable players there were Michael Jordan, Charles Barkley, Karl Malone, Patrick Ewing, and Chris Mullins. Karl was very young and a freshman in college. He was also very quiet and shy.

My parents drove up most days from Denver to be at the camp at the Air Force Academy. During periods of inactivity, Karl would often go over to sit and talk to my mother and father, and they became quite fond of him.

Charles Barkley was an amazing talent. He was slightly overweight, but a big-time athlete who could jump out of the gym. He was turning heads with his play, but during the course of the tryout camp had rubbed a few of the assistant coaches the wrong way with his behavior and attitude. It was in a morning coaches' meeting that Hartman said Charles's attitude was probably going to hurt his chances of making the team. I volunteered to pull the young man aside and talk to him.

I asked Charles to my dorm room and we talked for half an hour. I wanted him to know what was being said about him. His behavior was distracting from who he really was as a person and how incredibly talented he was. I tried to emphasize to him that he should allow people to judge him by what he really was, not only by the way he acted. He could not have been nicer and more polite. He thanked me for talking to him as he left the room.

I didn't see Charles again until 1991, when he was a star for the Philadelphia 76ers. I was an assistant coach on Don Nelson's staff with the Golden State Warriors and we had just beaten Philly at home. Shortly after the game, Charles wandered into our locker room to talk to Tim Hardaway just as I was leaving the locker room. Before I could remind him of who I was, he gave me a hug and told Hardaway that I had once been a big influence in his life. That made me feel very good about our conversation those many years earlier.

At the tryout camp players were divided into six teams. Every evening, each of the six coaches there to assist Hartman would coach one of the teams in a scrimmage. The last night of camp, I got to coach the team that Michael Jordan was on. This team was undefeated, as was the team we would scrimmage that night, so in a sense this was for the camp championship. Because it was the last night of competition, there were enough spectators to make it feel like a game.

From the start, Michael was playing very well on both ends of the floor. He was scoring at will, and we got out to an early lead.

We couldn't have been more than five minutes into the game when Jordan looked over at me and motioned that he was tired and wanted me to substitute him out. Colorado Springs is more than a mile above sea level, so the air is very thin. That is the reason for training there. He did need rest, but I needed him to score one more time so I pretended I didn't see him tugging on his jersey. I wonder if Coach Dean Smith ever did that? He scored on the next possession and I immediately called for a sub.

We had a two-point lead late in the game when the other coach called a timeout to "ice" our free throw shooter. I went over scenarios for what to do if the free throws were made or missed. When I finished, Jordan added, politely, "Either way, we still have the lead, so we just need to get a stop!" He was right, and it was the one little nugget I hadn't emphasized. It gave insight into how high his basketball IQ was. We made the free throws, won the game, and I walked away not realizing that I would one day be able to say I had coached one of the greatest players in the history of the game for 40 minutes.

As the summer came to an end, the J.D. Morgan Athletic Center was finally completely remodeled, and we were able to move out of those dreadful trailers. The building had been practically gutted, and although it sat on the same footprint, it was a completely different building on the inside. My assistant coaches did not have offices, but just desks in cubicles. Gone were the days when an assistant coach could pull a player into his office to watch film or have a private conversation about how school was going or anything that might be concerning. There was no privacy. My office was huge and had a door. It was on the first floor, not the second, which would take me some time to get used to. Most of the furniture from Coach Wooden's office had been replaced.

Shortly after we all moved in, Joe and Russ stopped by to check out my new digs. I had worked with these two guys as a groundskeeper when I first arrived on campus. They could not have been more proud that the freshman they let sneak into the gym to shoot was now the head coach. It was no mystery to me who was keeping my little office refrigerator stocked with beer. I knew who had keys!

CHAPTER 24

Recruiting Reggie Miller

Now that everyone knows Reggie Miller as one of the greatest players ever in the history of the National Basketball Association, he loves to embarrass me by saying that I didn't really want him when he was a phenom at Riverside Poly High School and I was the head coach at UCLA.

Reggie found a great audience for that story when he happened upon me having breakfast with a group of high school coaches when we were all in Houston for the Final Four in 2016. Bollingbrook High School Coach Rob Brost heard Reggie's version that day and he continues to tease me about it.

According to Reggie, I really wanted Antoine Joubert, a 6-foot-5 shooter from Detroit who was named 1983 Mr. Basketball for the state of Michigan. Joubert also was a McDonald's All-American. The way Reggie tells it, I didn't start recruiting him until after Joubert committed to the University of Michigan.

Not true!

I admit that I was a step slow in pursuing Reggie Miller, even though my staff was on him early, because I actually had Reggie Williams at the top of my wish list. I didn't turn my full attention to Reggie Miller until Reggie Williams started leaning toward Georgetown.

Here is the whole truth.

We needed a small forward and had been recruiting that position all year. For each position we recruited, we kept a depth chart that went five men deep. My No. 1 recruit was 6-foot-7 forward Reggie Williams from Dunbar High School in Baltimore. I'd seen him play in the summer several times, and he made an official visit to UCLA. He was a prototypical high post forward (shoot, pass, rebound), who would fit perfectly in the system we were running.

I had also received a call earlier in the year from former UCLA teammate Curtis Rowe, who was starting for the Detroit Pistons. Curtis told me about a young man who was lighting up Detroit and the state of Michigan named Antoine Joubert. After several positive phone conversations, I flew to Detroit to make a home visit to Antoine and his family. I stopped by Curtis' house and spent time with his family before my visit. Curtis had already talked to Joubert's coach and was instrumental in helping set up the visit. I was diligent about following up on any player recommended to us by former UCLA players. After all, it was Mahdi Abdul-Rahman (Walt Hazzard) who told us about Michael Sanders. That one worked out exceptionally well for UCLA. It seemed only natural to me. Who better to recognize someone good enough to play at UCLA than somebody who played at UCLA himself? My evaluation of Joubert was that he was a scoring guard. My home visit with Antoine was cordial, but just OK. I got the impression that he was probably going to stay closer to home, which he did.

UCLA had guards. We had already signed Montel Hatcher, a guard from Santa Monica High School. Montel was a terrific shooter, and an amazing athlete. He was also a McDonald's All-American. But he was required to redshirt his freshman year. We had recruited a guard out of Oregon named David Immel. David was the Player of the Year in the state of Oregon and had been heavily recruited by both the University of Oregon and Oregon State. David's father, Jerrold Immel, was a television music composer, and had written the theme tunes for popular serials like *Dallas* and *Knox Landing*. David had grown up in Southern California before relocating to Oregon as a teenager. So recruiting him out of the state of Oregon was not as difficult as it otherwise might have been. David was a high-level shooter, further making the need for a guard unnecessary. Lastly, we had Corey Gaines out of Saint Bernard High School in Southern California. He was a 6-foot-3 combo guard, who reminded me a lot of Michael Holton with his ability to play defense, his athleticism, and his high basketball IQ.

Two other players on our list were Tom Sheehey from New York and Reggie Miller from Riverside, California. Kevin O'Connor would be the lead recruiter on Sheehey, who was 6-foot-9. We actively recruited Tom, and he was one of our early priorities. He was selected as a first team *Parade* magazine All-American and signed with the University of Virginia in the spring.

Craig Impelman had seen Reggie Miller play as a sophomore in the "Slam and Jam" summer league in Los Angeles, and thought he was a terrific player who was going to be an outstanding prospect. A year later, Craig received a call from Coach Jim Harrick, then-head coach at Pepperdine, telling him he thought Reggie Miller was the best player in the state, and UCLA needed to be recruiting him. Craig told Harrick that he did know Reggie was terrific, but we were already locked into several small forwards. Harrick convinced Impelman that regardless of who we were looking at, we needed to be recruiting Reggie Miller. Craig went out to watch him play again toward the end of his senior season, and Reggie was amazing in the game, so Craig thought I needed to see him play right away.

The first time I saw Miller play, he must have gone for 40 points. He was making shots from just about everywhere on the court. He scored more points the second time I saw him than he did the first time, and made it look easier! Ultimately, the only two players that I wanted were Reggie Williams or Reggie Miller in that order. I would be happy with either one.

Reggie Williams was being recruited heavily by Georgetown Coach John Thompson. It became increasingly apparent that Arizona State, with Henry Bibby and Doug Collins on the staff, were doing an equally good job of recruiting Reggie Miller.

By the time I realized Georgetown was in the lead on Reggie Williams and we moved Reggie Miller up to our No. 1 spot, we were behind. That was a mistake on my part. But Craig had done a good job of staying in touch with Reggie and his family, and that kept us in the ballgame. Reggie told Craig that UCLA was one of five schools he was considering.

I thought we had a very good in-home visit with Reggie and his family. However, the more we encouraged Reggie to commit to UCLA, the more we feared we were behind Arizona State.

Reggie made quite an impression on us when he made his official campus visit, starting with the drive from Riverside to Westwood. He was a lot of fun and fully relaxed in the car with the UCLA head coach and both assistant coaches. I asked him what kind of music he liked to listen to and he told me he loved Prince and Michael Jackson. He was not shy about taking over control of the car stereo to find the stations he liked listening to. He even sang along. It was while he was surfing radio stations that I noticed the fingernail polish on both of his pinkie fingers. No judgment from me and no comment.

I asked Reggie if he could dance as well as sing. He told us he could moonwalk. So when we arrived at campus and got out of the car, we encouraged him to show us his moonwalk, and he did! He performed Michael Jackson's moonwalk in the parking lot perfectly. He was almost as a good a dancer as he was a shooter!

I thought Reggie had a terrific weekend recruiting visit and thought we were in very good shape to get him to commit to UCLA. But he had also visited Arizona State and had a great time on their campus. Henry Bibby was not only a former teammate but a good friend of mine, and he was personable, charming, and a relentless recruiter. Between Henry and Doug Collins, they had many NBA experiences to share with an interested Reggie, and I'm sure that heightened Arizona State's appeal. As a matter of fact, Henry had gone from winning a national championship at UCLA in 1972 to winning an NBA championship with the New York Knicks in 1973.

Both of Arizona State's assistant coaches could relate to young men and had done a great job recruiting Reggie. The situation got so troubling we requested a second home visit with the Miller family. They agreed. We went back in and I did a more intense presentation. I had done that only one other time, and that was when there was a coaching change. We needed to introduce Larry Brown and the new member of our staff. We did it this time because I sensed we were behind.

Once again, I thought the visit went well. As we were leaving the house, the Miller family told us that Reggie would probably be making his decision that weekend. His sister, Cheryl Miller, the great women's basketball star who was playing for the University of Southern California, would be coming home for the weekend and they would talk about Reggie's decision as a family. I remember telling the Millers that Reggie was our No. 1 priority, and if he chose UCLA, he would get his degree and have a great basketball career. I also mentioned to Mr. and Mrs. Miller that they could drive to USC and watch Cheryl play, jump on the 10 freeway to the 405 freeway, and be at UCLA in 25 minutes to watch Reggie play in person later that same evening.

That was my best and last sales pitch to the family, and I didn't know if that was going to be good enough. What I did know was if UCLA didn't get Reggie Miller, it would have been my fault for not making him my No. 1 recruit from the start.

A few days later we got the news from Reggie and his family that he was going to sign a letter of intent to play for UCLA. We were thrilled, and it remains one of those recruiting stories where you get the young man in the end, but it's not because of anything you did right at the beginning.

We made a great comeback to get Reggie Miller to UCLA and the rest, as they say, is history.

Reggie Miller had a great freshman year for me, shooting 51 percent and stepping up to make a difference for us in a couple of Pac-10 games. He also made some amazing shots that foretold of the great times ahead for him.

One memorable shot began with Reggie driving to the basketball and going up for the layup. When the shot was contested, he floated to the other side of the basket and reversed it. His momentum took him out of bounds. Reggie was so pleased with that reverse layup that while the action moved to the other end of the floor, he took a moment to moonwalk on the baseline.

None of us saw it during the game because we were following the action. But later that night Craig called to say he saw Reggie's fancy footwork on the videotape. What? We don't dance on the court at UCLA. Certainly not an "end zone" celebration. I told Craig he needed to call Reggie to his office and explain to him the UCLA way.

Coach Wooden had threatened to bench me for a reverse layup many years earlier—calling it a "Globetrotter play"—and I didn't even dance! So Craig met with Reggie and told him that moves like that would get him benched. After the meeting Craig reported to me that Reggie defended his dancing by explaining that those moments got him psyched up. Craig told Reggie he understood, but it still was not how we did things at UCLA.

Not wanting to send Reggie away on such a sour note, Craig asked Reggie if he could teach him how to moonwalk. That perked Reggie up and he got right to it in Craig's office. Craig's moonwalk still needed some work at the end of the lesson, so Reggie told him to practice by putting both hands on his refrigerator and sliding his feet.

The last time I asked Craig to demonstrate his moonwalk he moved his feet but didn't go anywhere. I'm not sure Craig understood about the refrigerator.

The 1983 recruiting class worked out quite well for us. It worked out well for Georgetown, too. Reggie Williams helped Georgetown win the national championship in 1984 playing alongside Patrick Ewing. In his senior year at Georgetown, he became a consensus first team All-American. Reggie Miller scored 2,095 points at UCLA, making him the third all-time leading scorer in UCLA history. His No. 31 jersey is retired at UCLA. He was drafted in the first round by the Indiana Pacers and was a five-time NBA all-star, scoring 25,279 points, making him the 14th all-time leading scorer in NBA history. His No. 31 jersey was retired by the Pacers. He won a Gold Medal in the 1996 Olympic Games in Atlanta and was inducted into the Basketball Hall of Fame in 2012.

CHAPTER 25

Year Three: Breaking the Two-Year Trend

The 1983–84 basketball schedule was more like the schedules of old. With our more traditional schedule we would play seven of our first eight nonconference opponents at Pauley Pavilion, leaving our home court only to play at Notre Dame.

I wasn't aware of it at the time, but some of our fans were not happy with the toning down of the pre-conference schedule. Their unhappiness was reflected in attendance at some of the games.

We opened the season with a win over Idaho State, then beat Long Beach State. After playing well in the opener, we were flat in the second game. They played a zone defense that forced us to play with more patience and at times to rely on the outside shot. Late in the first half, and again late in the second half, freshman Reggie Miller came in and hit four key shots. It was obvious he would have no problem taking big shots at critical times.

For the first time since 1971, our game at South Bend would be the only game of the season against Notre Dame. Digger Phelps complained vigorously to the L.A. media about the change in the series. He made it clear it was my decision, not his, to drop one of the games. He even threw in a dig suggesting that I did not always run my own program when he said this one was my decision—not Sam Gilbert's or anyone else's.

He followed that up with a compliment, stating that he had coached against five UCLA basketball coaches, and I was doing a good job. He said the three toughest jobs in America were Notre Dame football coach, UCLA basketball coach, and the President of the United States.

Notre Dame had its customary student pep rally at the same

time as our practice the night before the game, close enough for us to hear the noise. And Coach Phelps came into our practice, unannounced, "to make sure that everything was OK." But this time Phelps was different, noticeably more subdued. He said to me, "Larry, we've got to figure out a way to rekindle our two-game-a-year series. College basketball deserves it!"

Digger knew exactly what I had done and why I had done it. But he was not about to apologize, so our brief conversation was nothing more than small talk.

I was looking forward to the game the next day, and so was our team. Another sellout crowd welcomed us to the Athletic and Convocation Center. We were tight in the first half and played at a subpar level, but so did Notre Dame, so I was thrilled to have a 32–21 halftime lead. Kenny Fields got in foul trouble, which forced me to play zone in the second half, which worked well for us. Stuart Gray, who had worked on his free throw shooting all summer, made four big free throws down the stretch and we left South Bend with a 51–47 victory.

My record against Coach Phelps went to 5–0. Four of those games, including this one, were close. I had often imagined, as a young assistant coach, what it would be like as a head coach facing Digger down the stretch with the game yet to be decided. It was a chess match that he played well.

It was, to me, a major achievement that I never lost to Digger Phelps. Every other UCLA coach who faced Digger lost to him at least once, and remember, the record 88-game winning streak that spanned three seasons ended with a loss at Notre Dame at the hands of Digger Phelps.

The sweet feeling of victory lasted only until the next weekend, when we played the University of New Mexico. Coach Gary Colson was an old friend and a terrific coach. We had a little over 8,000 fans in Pauley Pavilion for this game, prompting Coach Colson to say that folks needed to get behind me and this team. Colson was so emotional about his 65–60 win that he actually cried after the game, calling it the biggest win of his coaching career.

One thing was clear, this UCLA team was not good enough to play poorly either on offense or defense for stretches at a time and expect to win. One element could not carry the other. Our margin for error would be that slim. For one of the few times in my coaching career, I brought the entire team in before the start of practice to watch film. I wanted each player to see his mistakes so that he could make corrections.

We played Memphis State next, with All-American forward Keith Lee, a future NBA standout. Memphis State was ranked No. 6 in the country and would be a formidable foe. We had 12,500 fans in the stands, and the game was on national television. I had been starting a front line of Stuart Gray, Kenny Fields, and Nigel Miguel. Nigel was a terrific defender and an outstanding athlete. I saw him as a similar version with his versatility to Darren Daye. The problem was we weren't getting enough scoring out of that position, and going into the Memphis State game, I decided to change my starting lineup and put Gary Maloncon at the other position.

In our back court we were starting Ralph Jackson and Montel Hatcher. By moving Gary Maloncon into the starting lineup, I was able to put him (defensively) on Memphis State center Derrick Phillips, which allowed me to match up Stuart Gray on forward Keith Lee. I thought Stuart's size and his physical play would bother Lee, and it did. We held Lee scoreless (0–3) in the first half, which had never happened to Lee before. Lee picked up his third foul before the half ended. We led by 15 at the half and opened it up to 20 on our way to a 65–51 victory.

The press labeled us schizophrenic, noting how poorly we played against unranked New Mexico and how we rose to the occasion against a much better Memphis State team.

Two days later we played Howard University, an HBCU (Historically Black Colleges and Universities) team from Washington, D.C. that had won its conference a year earlier with a record of 11–0. Howard came into our game with a record of 3–4. Still, I was shocked when the game drew only 5,300 fans—a record for the worst attendance for a UCLA game in Pauley Pavilion. Many of our students already had left for Christmas break, but I had never seen anything like this.

We played Howard December 19 and I feared that the crowd for our game against St. Mary's on December 22 might be even worse. We drew a little bit better (5,800 fans) and those who did come were treated to a preview of what Reggie Miller would do in his incredible career. Reggie played 13 minutes and scored 11 points. Many of those points came late in the game, enabling us to keep the lead and ultimately win 63–54.

Reggie was not getting more playing time because we were not getting the defensive play from him that we needed. We had plenty of players who could shoot, but we were consistently scoring in the 60's, which was a red flag for me. It meant that the teams we were playing were able to control the tempo. We were playing too many grind-it-out games instead of playing at a fast pace and running our fast break, either through our press creating turnovers or good half-court defense and rebounding.

Right after the Christmas break we beat BYU 82–73, before opening the conference season at home against Arizona State. Before the start of the game, some of their players were talking trash, rubbing it in about having upset us the year before. We had won the conference title despite the two-point loss because, on the same day, second-place Washington State also lost, allowing some to say that we backed in. Backed in, dove in, all in, I didn't care. I didn't see this as a revenge game, but apparently I was all by myself in that thinking. We beat them 79–57 then flew to Tucson to face the University of Arizona.

Lute Olson had left Iowa and was in his first year as coach at Arizona. We had a horrible shooting game, with only one player able to score in double figures. I remember looking at the score sheet and not believing we won having shot so poorly. Kenny Fields made just 3 of 10 field goals. Arizona had a freshman named Steve Kerr who showed great promise, scoring 10 points in the game. Zone defenses were forcing us to shoot from the outside, but our talented shooters were not making open shots. We beat Arizona 61–58 thanks to a terrific game from Ralph Jackson, who led us with 18 points.

We returned home to play Stanford, which had an overall record of 11–3 but was 0–2 in the Pac-10. We were 9–1 overall with a
conference record of 3–0, but we certainly were not playing consistently. As a coach you wonder if your players are paying any attention to your opponents' records and letting that affect whether they
are up to play or taking the opponent for granted.

My first two years as head coach I was always concerned about
the games right before and right after nationally televised games.
Now I also worried about an opponent's lack of success.

If the team was not staying focused and playing at its best at all
times, that, without question, was my responsibility. I knew that.

We struggled to beat Stanford 71–66. Despite still recovering
from the flu, Kenny scored 19 points. Reggie Miller played 27 minutes and had 12 points, hitting six of nine from the field. Reggie's
ability to score, and our team's inconsistent shooting, was making
him more valuable.

Disaster awaited us at the University of Oregon. We had not lost
to Oregon in seven years, dating back to 1977. We went into the
game with a record of 10–1, ranked No. 6 in the nation. Oregon had
changed coaches again, going from Dick Harter to Jim Haney and
now to Coach Don Munson. This time we were done in by a combination of uninspired play and terrible shooting. The Oregon fans
celebrated their 62–51 victory by storming the court. Oregon center
Blair Rasmussen likened the fans' reaction to what he had seen when
we lost at the buzzer the previous season at Washington State.

We headed home to play the University of California in what
suddenly felt to me like a dangerous game. We hadn't lost to Cal in
23 years, which meant we had a 49–game winning streak. If ever we
were ripe to have that streak come to an end, it was now.

Fortunately, we beat Cal 76–54, and I was able to empty the
bench. Jeff Dunlap and Curtis Knight got a chance to play for the
first time all year. In a lighthearted moment, our students were
chanting for our trainer, Ducky Drake, to report to the scorers' table.

Because of our loss at Oregon, our ranking had dropped to

No. 9.

In our return game at Louisville, before 16,600 fans in Freedom Hall and a national television audience, the Cardinals were seeking revenge. They jumped out to a 24–4 lead and never looked back. Louisville made 18 of its first 24 shots. At the end we were able to make the score look respectable, but we still lost 86–78. I thought we played well in getting ourselves back in the game, but we essentially had gotten blown out by a really good team. I was hoping there were lessons to be learned from this game.

This was, indeed, a difficult stretch, as we went home to play USC and then DePaul. Sweeping USC in 1983 was very satisfying, and I had tried, in the spring, to get Stan Morrison to agree to doing another back-to-back game weekend. Before I could get the proposal on out of my mouth, Coach Morrison respectfully declined. We had only 10,000 fans show up for our crosstown rivalry game. In typical UCLA-USC fashion the game was close throughout and we wound up having to win it in overtime. The final score was 75–69. Going back to my first year as head coach, we had beaten USC four games in a row.

My good friends Esther and Keith "Bubba" Sinclair could not make it to the USC game because Esther was at Cedars-Sinai Medical Center in labor with their first child. I had promised to stop by the hospital after the game to check on the two of them, which by then should have been three of them. With the overtime and all my postgame duties, I didn't get to the hospital until after 11 P.M., but they were kind enough to extend visiting hours for me. Esther was not quite ready to deliver, but she was extremely uncomfortable and not happy with Keith having visitors. The right thing to do was give her a quick kiss on the cheek and ask for a call when the baby was born. But, of course, Keith wanted to hear about the game. I tried to give a quick summary but one of Esther's doctors was interested in hearing more. Before long we had two doctors and a nurse in Esther's room listening to me talk about the game. Keith moved us into the hallway. A few more hospital workers joined us. Esther was in labor in an empty room. After about five minutes she got out of

the bed, walked out into the hallway, and demanded that all attention be redirected back to her. Everyone but Esther thought it was
absolutely hysterical. Kevin Sinclair would come into the world at a
wonderful time, just after an overtime victory over USC.

DePaul had a record of 15–0 and was ranked No. 2 in the nation, so we expected a big challenge. What we did not expect was
DePaul to jump all over us and beat us 84–68—the second-largest
margin of defeat in the history of Pauley Pavilion. UCLA had lost at
home to Oregon by 20 points seven years earlier in Coach Bartow's
first season.

The embarrassing loss had me wondering if I should have saved
my show of respect for Coach Ray Meyer until after the game. Coach
Meyer had already announced that he would be retiring after the
season. In tribute to him and the great rivalry, I planned something
special for the last time he coached against UCLA. I had bought
a UCLA letterman jacket for him and had his name embroidered
on the back. Before the start of the game, when Coach Meyer was
introduced, our public address announcer honored the man and his
career. I presented the UCLA jacket, shook his hand, and gave him
a hug. Our crowd gave him a rousing standing ovation.

I inspired another standing ovation for Coach Meyer many
years later, when I was coach of Loyola University of Chicago.
To kick off every basketball season, the media had a dinner at
Lawry's, the prime rib restaurant in downtown Chicago near the
Miracle Mile. The head coaches from Northwestern University,
Loyola, DePaul, and the University of Illinois Chicago would share
a terrific meal and give a preview of the upcoming season. In 1999,
before my first season at Loyola, Coach Ray Meyer was at the event
as a guest of DePaul. Coach Meyer was not moving around as well
but he was still as kind and jovial as he was back in 1984 when he was
kicking my behind. When it was my turn to get up and speak about
my Loyola Ramblers, I told the story of giving Coach Meyer a retirement gift on the night he gave me misery. As I was telling the story
to this group of over 100 people, Coach Meyer smiled and nodded.
When I finished telling the story, everyone in the restaurant gave

him a standing ovation. The look on his face told me that honoring him as I had was the right thing to do.

The DePaul game was nationally televised but we had a very small crowd. When you can't fill up Pauley Pavilion for the USC game, you know you're not going to get a packed house for DePaul. We weren't having any problem attracting fans on the road, but the Bruin faithful weren't coming out as they had in the past.

We obviously did not play well against DePaul. Media coverage was ugly. Coach Meyer said after the game that DePaul always got up for the "better teams like UCLA." The *L.A. Times* reporter scoffed at that, writing, "Better teams? Surely, he wasn't talking about the UCLA team that fell flat on its prat before the 10,264 fans at Pauley Pavilion . . ." As head coach, my teams had beaten DePaul two of the three times we played. But this game was by far the most one-sided. I took my lumps.

Putting the DePaul loss behind us, we headed to The Palouse and beat Washington State 73–59. It felt good to shake hands with George Raveling and walk off the court and not have their players and fans swinging from rims and cutting down their own nets. That was the good news.

The bad news was we were on our way to face a University of Washington team that was solidly in first place in our conference. Washington had just dismantled USC 79–47. Detlef Schrempf, a spectacular player from Germany, fit perfectly into what Coach Marv Harshman was running. Also, 7-foot Christian Welp, another German player, was skilled and could shoot. It would take three overtimes and a bad call on Kenny Fields to help seal Washington's victory.

Kenny had scored 26 points when he fouled out with almost four minutes left in the final overtime. I certainly had noticed that Washington had four players with four fouls each in the first overtime, and not one of them drew another foul over the extra two periods. I went after official Charlie Range, who made the call on Kenny. I came close to getting a technical foul, but we still had a chance to win at that point so I restrained myself. When the game finally ended, and we had lost, 89–81, I very uncharacteristically told the media about what I felt was poor officiating. Charlie Range was a good official but he had a bad game and it cost us a key player down the stretch. We may have lost, anyway, but we will never know. That three-overtime loss was crushing.

Our record was 13–5 as we traveled home to play Oregon and Oregon State. There had already been a news report about my job being in jeopardy. My original contract had been for three years. After we won the conference championship, I was given a one-year extension, meaning that I had one more year after this one. I had asked that the university not announce the contract extension, because I really didn't want anyone to feel stuck with me. So the bottom line was, if UCLA decided to get rid of me, they would owe me for just one more year.

Athletic Director Peter Dalis was asked about my job security, and he said that he had heard the rumblings and had seen the letters and articles in the papers, but he had talked to no one about replacing me. He did mention that he and I had talked earlier and had agreed to talk again at the end of the year.

With the heat clearly on me, and just having lost to DePaul at home (splitting in the state of Washington was not always a bad thing), we came home and lost to both Oregon schools. We lost to the University of Oregon in overtime 87–83 after one of their players hit a miracle shot at the buzzer in regulation time. We then lost to OSU 72–63. I was told in the press conference afterwards that never in the history of UCLA had the school lost three home games in a row.

After setting records throughout my playing career I was now, too often, on the wrong side of margins and streaks.

The last time I saw the atmosphere around the basketball program at UCLA this negative was when Gene Bartow was coach. There was no getting around it. There were plenty of people wanting me gone. But there were also those who had watched what I had done in my first two years and were still solidly behind me. I was being encouraged to keep a positive attitude and not give up.

Once again, the Cal game presented more pressure than a normal conference game. We had beaten Cal 49 times in a row but no doubt they had noticed we were in the midst of a three-game losing streak. That had to make for great speeches in the Cal locker room. They were motivated, and they hit us with something that we hadn't seen all season—a small lineup. Cal started three 6-foot-1 guards—Butch Hays, Kevin Johnson, and Chris Washington. They spread the floor and tried to use those small, quick guards to attack us one-on-one. They would have been difficult to guard if they had played a normal lineup, but spreading the floor gave us problems.

Initially, I decided that we would back off their guards and give them a large cushion so they couldn't drive past us to the basket. This strategy wasn't working. We were giving them too many mid-range shots. And they were making them. The game slowed down to a crawl, and Cal completely controlled the tempo. They led by as many as eight points early in the second half.

I decided to go with Kevin O'Connor's suggestion that we pressure up and force them to play, invite them to attack the basket. Both Kenny and Stuart were good shot blockers and shot changers. If we got them to shoot, and they missed, we might be able to counter with our fast break. UCLA would take a two-point lead, but Cal freshman Kevin Johnson hit a shot with under a minute to play to send the game into overtime. Luckily, Montel Hatcher made 7-of-9 free throws in the overtime to help us get a 70–62 win.

We played Stanford in front of a sellout crowd of 7,550 screaming fans and lost to a team that, according to Coach Tom Davis, played its best game of the season. When they won 75–64 their fans flooded onto the floor, chanting "N. I. T! N. I. T!" When I first heard the fans chanting I thought they were taunting us about where we were headed! But after watching their fans jump up and down and hug players, it seemed clear to me that the NIT was Stanford's goal.

Both Kenny and Ralph complained to the media afterwards about what they felt was poor officiating. Stanford shot 37 free throws, making 29. We shot just 14, making 10.

The end of our season was going from bad to worse.

Back in Los Angeles we lost to USC 80–72, ending our four-game winning streak against the Trojans. Then we lost to Arizona State 76–67 in Tempe. It was our second three-game losing streak of the season. We had lost six of our last seven games.

In Santa Monica, just off Wilshire Boulevard and Ohio Street, was St. Sebastian Catholic Church. I would go there from time to time when I was stressed and needed comfort. I'm not Catholic, nor did I ever attend a service there, but the doors to the church were usually open. I could sit in the back to think and pray. It was a beautiful church, and it had brought me tranquility dating back to my playing days. I'd gone there at the start of this season to ask the Lord for courage, strength, good health, and a successful season. I returned to the church the morning after we got back from ASU seeking guidance and a strengthening of my faith. I usually would go in the afternoon when there were no parishioners to disturb. To my surprise, when I arrived at the church, the front doors were locked! Was the Lord angry with me, too?

It brought to mind the words of the great Satchel Paige, "Don't pray when it rains if you don't pray when the sun shines." Perhaps if I had come here to thank the Lord when we started the season 10–1, the door would not be locked now.

I walked around to the side of the building to see if I might find another door or a priest, who would probably ask me if I needed help, which would certainly give me a few minutes to open up and get some concerns off my chest. I was heading back to the front of the church to try knocking on the door when I saw a police cruiser slowing down. The officer gave me a good once over but continued on his way, slowly. I smiled and waved but got no response. I could see the headlines: "UCLA coach arrested for attempted church break in!"

At my weekly press conference the next morning, it was obvious that my job security would be a topic. Any time the heat is on a UCLA coach, the media comes out in force. The room was packed with reporters from newspapers, radio stations, and TV stations. This was the largest crowd of media for one of these breakfast meetings I had ever seen during my tenure as head coach.

I tried to lighten the mood by sharing my story about the church. To my relief, the folks in the room laughed. I might've even said something about the Good Lord wanting a refund on his UCLA season ticket. Even though the ice was broken, questions about the team losing and my job security had to be asked. I did hope maybe some in the media would write what I had to say about not giving up. Maybe even mention that I maintained a sense of humor. I stayed direct and positive, saying I would continue to do my job and get the team back on track.

After the press conference, one of the reporters I knew pretty well came up to me to tell me he thought it was one my best presentations. He asked if I was open to a suggestion. I said of course I was. It was about how I was pronouncing the word "police." He acknowledged that I was saying "POLE-lease" because that's what I had heard all my life in the black community. He pointed out that it sounded wrong to my white audience—and on this day, as usual, I was the only person of color in the room. He said "pull-LEASE" would sound better. I sensed no racial bias from him. I believed he had the best of intentions. Historically, the use of black dialect had social implications and was often used to judge level of education and intelligence. Still, the dialect was part of our heritage. It was a touchy subject. In my position I was expected to do a lot of public speaking and I hoped to one day do some work in television, so I wanted to continue to be viewed as well-spoken. I remembered how impressed I had been when Floyd Little spoke so eloquently at my high school. So I made a conscious effort to say "pull-LEASE" from that day forward. I actually preferred hearing that observation as opposed to hearing that I didn't talk like I was black, or I didn't sound like I was African American when I spoke in public. The latter never happened at a press conference, but it was something that I did hear throughout my 44-year career. That never really sat well with me!

When the stories from the press conference made the news and the sports shows, I got several calls and letters from fans who sent me invitations to their churches saying that their doors would never be locked.

I had a private meeting with Athletic Director Peter Dalis around that same time. It was the dreaded "vote of confidence meeting" that you have when your feet and ankles are tied, the point of the sword is in your back, and you are standing at the edge of the plank. It was an impromptu meeting and Dalis really did try to be positive in his support of how hard he thought I was working. Dalis' tone changed when he mentioned that he had heard I was considering making changes to my coaching staff. He said that the names Hazzard and Hirsch were mentioned. I told him I'd heard the same rumors, but changing my assistants was the last thing on my mind at the moment. I could tell that caught him off guard, because his body language changed, and so did the conversation. He went back to his business-like tone and kept the conversation on topic, which was his faith and confidence in me. He reassured me that my job was not in jeopardy, and we would sit down at the end of the year to go over this season and what we needed to do in moving forward. He wished me luck with our upcoming game.

The circumstances in which I found myself (team losing, program struggling) did leave me open to listening to advice from people who cared about me. Sam Gilbert was promoting a change of my staff and preferred both Hazzard and Hirsch to Kevin and Craig. He felt my assistants might ultimately cost me my job. Fred Slaughter, my former attorney and good friend, was a UCLA teammate of Coach Hazzard on the 1964 national championship team. Fred heard that Hazzard was interested in coming back to UCLA as an assistant. Slaughter said that he'd been encouraging Hazzard all along to get into coaching after he retired from playing. He thought it was something I should consider. Two of my own former teammates, Bob Webb and Larry Hollyfield, heard the rumors and asked me if the rumors were true. All separate conversations happening at different times, but it did signal a chorus that was being sung behind the scenes.

So, I called Coach Hazzard to set up a meeting. Hazzard said he and Jack would love to meet with me, but I told him I wanted it to be just the two of us. We met one evening at The Apple Pan, one of Coach Wooden's favorite restaurants. We spent some time getting caught up before we turned to his interest in possibly becoming an assistant at UCLA. He said he thought he and Jack could really be a benefit to me. Get us back to winning! We all grew up and played in the same winning basketball system and shared a similar philosophy. Coach Hazzard rarely talked about himself alone. I had to press that question directly, asking about his interest in joining my staff by himself, and he quickly let me know that he and Jack were team, a package deal, and that if they both didn't come, then he wouldn't come! That surprised me. Coach Hazzard was obviously very loyal to Jack Hirsch.

I was loyal to my assistants, too. I asked Coach Hazzard what he was looking for in terms of a salary. That's when the conversation became most enlightening. He told me not to worry about his salary; it had already been discussed. He said that to reassure me, but it set off alarm bells. The only person with the authority to settle the issue of salary was my Athletic Director, who apparently was negotiating with assistants for my staff without including me in the conversation.

The rumors that had been circulating about Hazzard and Hirsch joining the coaching staff included details about how long Dalis had been close with Hazzard and Hirsch. There were stories about them being poker buddies. I had kept that information in the category of hearsay, not really knowing if that was true. This further led me to believe that behind the scenes there were deals being made that I knew nothing about.

This was proof that potential changes in my staff were not just hearsay—as Dalis had told me in our "vote of confidence" meeting.

When Coach Hazzard and I parted I told him I would be in touch when the season ended.

Talk about Hazzard and Hirsch joining my staff was so insistent that Dalis was forced to deny, publicly, that there was any pressure on me to make changes. Whatever had been going on behind the scenes was leaking out, and I believed Dalis was right in the middle of it.

Both Ralph and Kenny spoke to the media about how important the upcoming Washington game was for them. They felt that our team changed when we lost at Washington in triple overtime. Clearly our confidence and subsequently our record suffered after that game, and we lost six of our next seven games.

This time we blew out Washington 73–59 playing the best 40 minutes of basketball we had played in quite a while. We had just under 7,000 fans at the game. We followed that up by beating Washington State 83–64. We had 4,800 fans show up for the WSU game, but they were as loud and as raucous as a crowd double the size.

Once again the team seemed refocused, playing with renewed vigor and energy. It wasn't so much that we won those two games, but how we won them that convinced me they still believed in me and what I was trying to get them to do. They were not just going through the motions. We were still working hard and playing as a team.

UCLA's 1964 national championship team was honored with an emotional tribute before our Washington State game. The recognition marked the 20th anniversary of that title, and Hazzard and Hirsch were stars on that team. After the game they both came into our locker room to congratulate the team. Their locker room visit did not escape the *L.A. Times.* The article mentioned, of course, the rumors they would be joining my staff.

Our last home game was against the University of Arizona. It was Senior Day, the last home game for Ralph Jackson and Kenny Fields. We beat Arizona 68–60 in front of 7,400 fans. I handled this Senior Day as always, like most folks handle weddings. I cried. Ralph and Kenny had been through so much and had given so much to the university and the basketball program. I was very proud of both of them.

Our last game was at Oregon State. We played an outstanding game, a tight game, but lost 70–65. Kenny had a career high 28 points, playing against A.C. Green, the 1984 Pac-10 Player of the

Year. Ralph Jackson scored 21 points in front of the sellout crowd at Gill Coliseum.

We played our best four games at the end of the year and we all wanted to keep that momentum going in the postseason. But we finished fourth in the Pac-10, so we were at the mercy of the NCAA selection committee.

We had finished fourth in the league in Coach Brown's first year and were one of the last teams picked to get in the tournament. But our league, overall, was not as strong this year as it was then.

Getting in would definitely be a longshot.

CHAPTER 26

The Final Days:
March 11, 1984 to March 27, 1984

We would find out on Selection Sunday, March 11, whether we were included in the NCAA tournament.

Our seniors, Ralph and Kenny, had both indicated publicly that they would be open to an NIT invitation. When I was asked about the NCAA tournament, or the NIT, I let the media know that Athletic Director Pete Dalis had informed me that accepting or declining an invitation to the NIT would be an administrative decision.

When the NCAA pairings were announced on TV, we were not included in the NCAA tournament bracket.

Peter Dalis promptly announced that we would be declining our invitation to the NIT, and our immediate snubbing of that invitation was not well-received, particularly with our players. Both Kenny and Ralph expressed their disappointment. Brad Wright said publicly that the administration should have let the players vote.

The press picked up on the angle that UCLA was looking down its nose at the NIT tournament.

I had been contacted by our assistant sports information director Sunday morning about going to the office for a quick press conference after the NCAA tournament teams were announced. When we were excluded, I had nothing more to say about not making it to the tournament for the first time since 1966 (or 1983 if you count not being included because of probation.) I had nothing new to say about my job status. I knew of no politically correct answer for why we snubbed the NIT. I was not happy about it, and since I was not included in the decision process, my words would not have followed the company line. I passed on the press conference.

On Tuesday, March 13, Dalis came out with a press release stating that UCLA had declined the NIT invitation to 1. Allow our players to refocus on their studies, and 2. Allow the coaching staff to get a head start in recruiting. Neither of those reasons floated, and because they were an afterthought, hastily put together, and issued to defend against the backlash UCLA was experiencing on the nightly sports news, they weren't well-received. Most of the collegiate basketball world gave us a thumbs down. I'm sure some of the diehard UCLA fans were in agreement with not going to the NIT, but they were quiet and certainly in the minority. The decision to turn down the NIT invitation hurt our image (in basketball circles) as a sign of elitism, and it hurt us in recruiting.

Craig McMillan, a highly recruited shooting guard from Cloverdale, California, said at the time that it caused him to second-guess UCLA. He told me when we were both coaching in Kuwait years later, that turning down the NIT was being used against us by other recruiters.

We had finished the season playing very well, particularly in our last four games. The mood of the team seemed upbeat. Throughout all our trials and tribulations, we were playing our best basketball. When teams don't make the NCAA tournament and go to the NIT, it is important to know how your players feel about it. If the players aren't excited about playing in the postseason, the NIT could be a disaster, leading to another embarrassing loss to a team that you would certainly be expected to beat. I knew that our team was disappointed that we didn't go to the NCAA tournament, but they really did not want the season to end, and all seemed to be on board to play in the NIT. That put my mind at ease because I was confident I would get their best effort. I also had confidence that we would continue to play as we had in our final games. I would take my chances against whoever we might be paired against in the NIT. But Dalis turned it down, so that was no longer an issue, or choice.

Only two teams from the Pac-10 were invited to the NCAA tournament—the University of Washington and Oregon State. We had split with both of those teams, including the three-overtime loss at Washington.

Just as UCLA had some decisions to make about whether they wanted to honor the one remaining year on my contract or buy it out, I had to decide if I wanted to stay.

You learn a lot when you work at UCLA under three different head coaches. For a variety of reasons, including pressure, each had decided to walk away after just two years. That pressure was usually saturated with unfair scrutiny and expectations. Even with a 15–3 start, I spent the season looking at a sparsely filled arena and listening to speculation about whether UCLA or its fans wanted me to stay. Going 2–8 the rest of the way understandably made it worse. Based on what had been written and said about me during my third year, I somehow had become more inexperienced than I was in my first two years and was guilty of not winning the big games or beating the teams we were expected to thrash by big enough margins. I was getting second-guessed by many basketball experts who also said I wasn't getting enough help from my coaching staff. I thought back to the year before (1982–83) when we played the most difficult schedule in the country. My inexperience or winning big games (on national television) didn't come up. I was in no way perfect, and I certainly made plenty of mistakes. In truth, I was inexperienced— which was no secret. But winning makes everything okay and losing brings out the stench of criticism. I thought back to my first year (1981–82), when there were those who felt I was hired only because UCLA was going on probation and they couldn't get anybody of stature to take the job under that cloud. In the probation year we started off 6–5, and then won 15 of our next 16 games. I wasn't given the keys to the city, nor did I expect that, but apparently none of that mattered and the experience that I had gained those first two years had apparently been forgotten.

Oddly, no one asked me if I wanted to stay. It was just assumed that I did.

I was concerned that I had reached the point of not enjoying the walk from my office into Pauley Pavilion for practice. I knew, deep down, what that meant. I now fully understood what Bartow and Cunningham meant when they both said they weren't having fun anymore. I remember joking when I was hired that my goal was to last longer than the three previous coaches who had each stayed only two seasons. I had just finished my third season.

I was made aware of a couple of schools asking UCLA for permission to talk to me about their coaching vacancies. Dalis told them that once my situation at UCLA had been discussed and worked out, any subsequent conversations would be up to me.

I talked to Bob Fischer about my situation. I trusted him and, after all, he was the Athletic Director that hired me. I told him that I was really unhappy and this last year had taken an emotional toll on me. Mr. Fischer told me that looking at my body of work over my first three years, I had done a good job. He said he thought I had earned the year UCLA would owe me and I should not quit under any circumstances—I should let them fire me, because they would have to finish paying my contract. When he said that, we both laughed. I thanked him for his honesty, and I really did appreciate what amounted to his vote of confidence.

Every time Athletic Director Peter Dalis was asked about my job status (which started about midway through my third year) he would answer by saying that he had not talked to anybody about my job, and I was still the coach at UCLA. We would sit down and talk about the program at the end of the year. Well, that wasn't exactly true. While he might not have been interviewing prospects for replacing me as head coach, he had certainly had conversations about replacing my assistants. So whenever I heard his neutrality and denials, I grew more untrusting.

On Wednesday, March 14, Dalis released a statement to the media announcing that I would definitely be back for next season; there would be no coaching change. That was his announcement, not mine.

Saturday, March 17 was a day devoted to talking with my brother Aubrey and calling Denver to speak to my mom and dad. Did I want to stay or did I want to go? My wounds from the season were still open. That evening I told my mom and dad, and my brother, who was sitting next to me, that I was going to resign. I told my family that I would talk to Sam and Rose Sunday morning. I knew it would be a difficult conversation because Sam would try to talk me out of leaving.

It had been a week since we lost at Oregon State but it seemed like a month had gone by. I called Sam and told him I wanted to stop by Sunday. He was happy to hear from me and, as always, was more than welcoming, telling me he was going to make me a huge Jewish "soul food" breakfast.

I didn't realize until afterwards, when things were all said and done, that Sam had been feverishly working behind the scenes to make the change in my assistant coaches. He was even "leaking" to the media that this was what I should do.

While the season was still underway, Sam had invited Craig Impelman to dinner at a restaurant in the San Fernando Valley. When Craig arrived, Peter Dalis was also there. Craig said Sam was his usual warm and charming self as Sam tried to convince him that he needed to resign in order to help me. Craig said Dalis looked uncomfortable and just sat there and nodded in agreement with everything Sam said.

When Craig told me about the dinner meeting with Sam, I wasn't surprised. It was like Sam to tell Craig what he should do to help me. And it was like Craig to tell Sam he would resign only if that was what I wanted.

But no one told me that Dalis was there, too, until I talked with Craig about it while writing this book more than 35 years later. It wasn't, really, that both Sam and Dalis wanted my assistant coaches gone. More correctly, both Sam and Dalis wanted Hazzard and Hirsch on my staff, which meant that my assistants had to go.

They wanted the same thing but for different reasons. Sam wanted me to get what he perceived to be more help to win and stay as coach at UCLA. Dalis wanted coaches that he personally knew and liked. It's not unusual for a new athletic director to want to bring in his own coaches, but it's usually head coaches.

Sunday morning, March 18, I drove out to Sam's. After breakfast

I explained why I was going to resign. With each point I made, Sam made a counterpoint. If this were a boxing match, the referees would have called it a draw. Sam and I agreed on only two things. First, that Sam would help me draft my letter of resignation. Sam believed it could be written so as not to alienate those at the university who supported me, most important of those being Chancellor Young. Sam and I talked through each point of the letter and I wrote it by hand. Second, I should not resign before having a conversation with Chancellor Young, and not with Pete Dalis. I agreed. I had a great relationship with Chancellor Young. If I could make him see how seriously recruiting would be hurt if we, in the basketball program, were not allowed to continue to make careful, responsible use of "special action" admissions, I thought he might ease up on the new restrictions.

Monday morning, March 19, I went back through the many academic files from my time as an assistant coach and I put together a list of players who had graduated in four years after being admitted to UCLA through special action. I had the names of 15 players. The first name on the list was mine! I listed the player, his major, and his overall GPA at the time of graduation. I had it typed up. It was a very impressive list, including All-Americans and first round NBA draft choices. All were people of good character who made UCLA proud. I needed for Chancellor Young to understand that I was not asking to recruit prospects who could not succeed at UCLA and I wanted him to see how much amazing talent we would not have had if current standards had applied then.

I called the chancellor's office and requested a meeting, which his secretary set for Wednesday evening, after business hours.

Monday evening, I went to see Joyce, my ex-wife, and asked her to type my hand-written letter of resignation. The visit gave me a chance to tell her why I was leaving after three years. She was still closely following the team and was surprised that I had arrived at this decision. She primarily just listened. She agreed with Sam that I could win enough to keep my job, but after hearing my reasons she understood. Joyce dated my letter of resignation March 21. I had what I needed for my meeting and I had all day Tuesday to prepare my presentation.

Wednesday, March 21, I drove to the chancellor's residence. I wasn't nervous at all. I was looking forward to laying out a case. If I could get him to reconsider how we evaluated our prospects' academic abilities, I would not resign. I would stay for my last year and fight it out. I was capable of winning at UCLA. I had shown that. I could still bring in a great recruiting class that would reflect UCLA standards. I had done it before. I still loved UCLA. I would stay and finish the last year on my contract, provided I could recruit competitively.

When I arrived at the chancellor's residence, I was dressed in a sport coat and tie. I was greeted at the front door by Chancellor Young. But to my surprise, Vice Chancellor Elwin Swenson and Peter Dalis were also there. I was completely taken back. I was immediately on the defensive. I had planned to talk openly and honestly with Chancellor Young. With two other people there that I didn't fully trust, that approach was out. I felt I had been ambushed. I seemed to be at a decided disadvantage, three against one.

I had my list of graduating players in my briefcase and my letter of resignation in my jacket pocket.

We all sat down in what I would describe as the library. The pleasantries didn't last long before the chancellor asked me what I had on my mind. I began by telling him that for the last decade, the basketball program had been unique in its approach to academics. Gary Cunningham was Coach Wooden's academic advisor, and I had stepped into the role for all three of the head coaches that followed Coach Wooden. Cunningham had handled academics when I was a "special action" student, and I learned how to do it from him. I talked about personally getting transcripts early from high school guidance counselors' offices. I knew many of the guidance counselors and principals at schools we frequently recruited—Crenshaw, Verbum Dei, Santa Monica, Inglewood, Long Beach, Poly, and so on. We looked, in depth, at a young man's personal background and his academic history, learning more than we could from the grades on his transcript. Ultimately the transcript would be evaluated by UCLA. The vice chancellor made a positive comment about what I was saying, which was a bit of a distraction but supportive.

I talked about how I, too, had one of my assistants in the role of academic support who also had attended UCLA. I told him we monitored our players' class attendance and progress. I told him that, unlike some programs that work only to keep players eligible, we made sure players were making progress toward degrees. When I got to the part about how successful we had been, I pulled out the list of players who had graduated. I knew the chancellor would recognize every name. But after glancing at it, he handed it to the vice chancellor and then cut me off. The chancellor seemed irritated, because the points I was making were in contradiction to his current position. The chancellor then went on what might best be described as a filibuster, talking about everything from the unfair perception and negative press regarding UCLA academics, to the outstanding professors and the superior curriculum offered at UCLA. All true. But it had nothing to do with why I was meeting with him. My presentation was derailed. I had completely lost control of my message.

The vice chancellor looked quickly at the list, and then handed it to Dalis. He looked at it closely for quite some time before setting it on the coffee table. When it was finally my turn to speak again, I knew I would have only one good shot at this. I said I thought that basketball had demonstrated the ability to choose athletes who were able to succeed in the classroom. I reiterated that everybody on the list I had presented was admitted through "special action." When I rehearsed that part of my presentation, the chancellor would have been able to look back at the list, which would have been in his hand. Except now it wasn't.

The chancellor said he wasn't going to change his stance on who we could recruit at this time, but we would revisit it maybe a year or two later. I was the only one who chuckled. I pointed out that I had only one year left on my contract. I wasn't being a smart ass, or disrespectful, I was trying to let him know that he would have to make that decision now to affect my ability to recruit.

At that point the chancellor stood up, looked at Dalis, and said, "Let's add two years to Larry's contract." He looked at me and said, "If we add two that will give you three years, right?" Dalis answered that it would. The chancellor added, "You know, Larry, you were my choice when we hired Larry Brown and you are my choice now. You can handle it. You can get it done. Let's see how things go and we can talk about this again next year."

With that, the meeting was over.

I had not gone there seeking an extension on my contract. I went seeking a return to reasonable academic requirements. If I couldn't get that, I was going to resign. I walked out having accomplished neither. Extending my contract completely threw me off.

Chancellor Young must have assumed, like everyone else, that my priority was my job security.

If the whole scenario hadn't been so crazy, it was almost comical. Now I had more to think about. I planned to think about it for a few days before, once again, making a decision.

I called my parents and told them about the meeting. Then I called Sam who was, of course, thrilled with the contract extension.

The next day, Thursday, March 22, Chancellor Young was at a large breakfast gathering on campus. There were reporters there who were in town covering the NCAA Western Regional. In an impromptu question and answer, he was asked about my job status. Without thinking twice, Chancellor Young announced that my job was not only secure but I'd been given a two-year contract extension.

Word of that spread like wildfire, and everybody's phone started to blow up. Our sports information director was forced to arrange a press conference to make the announcement official. I left my office to avoid answering questions. I didn't return until the next day, just in time for the press conference. I tried to put on a good face and answer questions appropriately, but my heart wasn't in it. One writer asked if I was surprised by the contract extension. I wanted to answer him by saying "you don't know the half of it" but I didn't. I simply answered questions appropriately, but I was still considering resigning.

I kept picturing what recruiting would look like going forward. I was not comfortable with the pressure from those who wanted me to fire two hard-working assistants and replace them with two assistants who were best friends. I had never worked with either one of them, so how could I know if I could trust them? Did I really need to change both assistants, or should I change just one? Most important, I clearly did not have the support of the athletic director, who was my boss.

I wasn't the only one thinking that way. A month later, April 17, 1984, the *Los Angeles Herald-Examiner* wrote, "Even though Farmer obviously had the support and confidence of the chancellor, he knew by then—for certain—that Dalis and Svenson were not behind him. Furthermore, he knew that he would have to work with at least one new assistant (Hazzard) with close ties to Dalis. One source put it this way: 'He would have needed a knife to fight off Hazzard and Hirsch, a gun to protect himself from Dalis.'"

My brother and I did the math on how much money I would make if I stayed at UCLA for the next three years. With the salary increase, the TV and radio package, my shoe deal, and my basketball camp, I would make about a half-million dollars. That amount of money over three years doesn't seem like much now, especially compared to what coaches are paid today, but it was a lot of money to walk away from in 1984. But money was never the issue.

Having all that extra time to weigh my options probably was the Lord's way of making sure I knew I was right to resign. In the final analysis, I was right back where I was two weeks earlier.

If I went along with being told who I could recruit, who my assistants should be, and whether we'd go to the NIT with no input from me, what's next?

Tuesday morning, March 27, I phoned Dalis and told him I needed to talk with him but I didn't want to do it on campus. I asked him to meet me at the Holiday Inn in Westwood. The lobby wasn't busy but we moved into the empty lounge. I told Dalis that after carefully considering the circumstances I had decided to resign my position as basketball coach at UCLA. I handed him the letter of resignation. He had a blank expression on his face, and it never changed. He took the letter, we shook hands, and I left.

Marc Dellins, UCLA's sports information director, would later tell me what the next phone call from Dalis was like. Dalis told him that he needed to arrange a press conference regarding Larry Farmer's job status, and Dellins' response was, "I thought we already did that."

One of the first things Dalis pointed out to Dellins was the date on my resignation letter. I hadn't bothered to change it. It was dated March 21. It didn't take Sherlock Holmes to figure out that I hadn't just arrived at my decision to leave.

News of my resignation spread quickly. I stayed as far from my phone as I could. Many of my friends and teammates didn't call, but just drove out to my apartment. It was quite an impromptu get-together.

Tuesday evening, March 27, we watched the TV news reports announcing that Dalis had hired Hazzard. I was getting as many calls about how quickly the vacancy had been filled as I was about why I had quit with a winning record and a three-year contract.

It had taken J.D. Morgan almost a month after Gary Cunningham quit to hire Larry Brown. Mr. Morgan interviewed several coaches, including me, before he arrived at his decision. The fact that a few hours after I quit, without even waiting to see if other very qualified coaches might show an interest, Dalis had his man. Replacing me was just that easy.

Reality gave credibility to my fear of what life might have been like if I had stayed as head coach, fired my assistants, and hired Hazzard and Hirsch. The term "dead man walking" comes to mind. You certainly don't want to have a job as difficult as being the UCLA head basketball coach while worrying that your boss wants somebody else to have your job.

On Thursday, March 29, Jim Hill, from KCBS in Los Angeles, interviewed me. Jim presented the interview fairly, but in his comments wrapping up the segment, he said: "Larry Farmer was a very confused young man."

I was not a confused young man. Dalis and Chancellor Young had made a series of announcements before I had made my decision. I should not have agreed to the press conference before I was ready. That was my mistake. That's why I appeared confused.

The last article that I would read was in the *L.A. Times*. It was one that Aubrey had supposedly screened before he gave it to me. The article started off defending my record, work ethic, and reputation. Lots of facts and statistics. In an effort to show how much false garbage I had put up with over my last year, the writer mentioned rumors about my wife divorcing me and rumors that I spent time in drug rehab. The only one the writer missed was the one claiming my wife left me because I was secretly gay. When news of my divorce had leaked out and I was presumed to be single and a very eligible bachelor, it seemed remarkable that I wasn't leaving UCLA basketball games with beautiful women on my arm.

There actually was a beautiful woman in my life at the time. I was with Chris, the woman I had noticed at a game years earlier. She had graduated from UCLA and was working toward her master's degree at USC. But we chose to keep our relationship private, which led to speculation that I was gay.

There was no truth to any of the rumors and I tried to ignore all of it.

I was not harassed with this kind of nonsense until my third year as coach when we were going 17–11. The article did stress how much I loved UCLA, and how much the basketball program meant to me. Once I got through that article, I knew I would go back to not reading anything else. That was it for me.

I needed to get off the grid. I went to the most comforting place I could think of. I bought a one-way ticket to Denver to visit my mom and dad. The only people who knew I was heading to Colorado were Sam, Aubrey, and Chris. It was the best decision I could have made at that time.

There had been articles about my resignation in the *Rocky Mountain News* and the *Denver Post* but it was now old news in my hometown. I think I stayed in Denver for about a week and had

plenty of time to reflect on not only the events of the previous couple of weeks, but really the previous couple of years.

I had plenty of regrets, none of which had to do with quitting my
job. At one point during the last season, I had promised the team
that if I was going to leave the program, I would let them know. But
with the way I resigned, I did not talk with the team and I really
regret that most of all. After I handed Dalis my resignation letter,
I wouldn't step back on the UCLA campus for eight years. When I
returned from Denver it was Coach Hazzard's program and I didn't
want to appear to be doing anything inappropriate by meeting with
his team.

I also regret not handing that letter of resignation to Chancellor
Young and thanking him for taking the chance on hiring a 30-year-
old rookie head coach and believing in him in the first place. Chancellor Young was a good man, and I thought the world of him. I
should have personally thanked him, but I never did.

I wrestled with those two omissions for many years. In my heart,
I still do. One thing I did manage to handle the right way when I got
back to L.A. was a get-together for some of the UCLA secretaries
and staff. I rented a banquet room at La Barbera's in Santa Monica,
which had been one of my favorite restaurants since I was a student. We all had a great time, eating and drinking and telling stories.
There were some tears shed as we parted that night.

I later had lunch with my old trainer, Elvin "Ducky" Drake. He
said he was proud of me and told me that I made the right decision
not to give in and fire my assistants. Ducky said loyalty was the first
responsibility of a coach and I held up my end of that.

I had breakfast with Coach Wooden at VIP's, his favorite place.
And, of course, he would not let me pay. Other than Coach asking
me if I was all right, we didn't talk about basketball at all. I think he
realized I just needed to be around him for a while, and that was
remedy enough.

I remained in the San Fernando Valley for the next year. I did
some basketball camps that summer, which allowed me to travel
and do some fishing. I didn't want to jump right back into coaching,

so I did not pursue any of the few remaining head coaching positions that were open. I had plenty of time the next season to watch
the Bruins. I wanted to see all the players I recruited do well. There's
a catch to this, though. If the team wins a lot of games, it looks like
not getting to the NCAA tournament was my fault. If they lose a lot
of games, then it looks like the team I left behind wasn't very good.
Not true. I had not left the cupboard bare for Coach Hazzard.

UCLA finished the regular season 16–12 Hazzard's first year
and was, again, left out of the NCAA tournament. But this time
Dalis accepted the invitation to play in the NIT. UCLA won five
games in New York to win the tournament and bump their record
to a respectable 21–12.

In a strange way I felt vindicated. I wasn't given the opportunity
to take my team to the NIT, but the team that won the NIT the next
year was made up of the players I'd recruited. Reggie Miller was
named Most Valuable Player of the NIT in 1985.

There's always been a mystery about the NIT Championship
banner. My understanding was the Bruins hoisted that banner to
start the next season. It hung in the rafters of Pauley Pavilion along
with the 10 NCAA National Championship banners for one year.
Then, the NIT banner disappeared and has never again been seen at
the top of Pauley Pavilion.

UCLA's goal will always be to win the NCAA title every year.
They added an 11th NCAA banner in 1995, with my old friend Jim
Harrick as head coach. But expectations have adjusted to reality.
No team will ever match the string of titles and undefeated seasons
UCLA had when I was a player, and no coach will ever again be ex-
pected to live up to the legend of my coach, John Wooden.

Life After UCLA; Being Inducted Into the UCLA Hall of Fame

Even though it was my decision to resign as coach, I felt sad and frustrated. After being so proud to be a player for UCLA, so happy to be the link from past glory days as an assistant coach and so honored to be the head coach, it seemed I was letting a lot of people down when I left after only three years and with three years remaining on my contract. It felt like I had unfinished business.

All three of my coaching seasons were winning seasons, but it wasn't winning by UCLA standards. And it was not the way I, myself, envisioned my own success.

Leaving this way was not the same as retiring with a party, a cake, and a gold watch. I knew I wasn't a loser, but I was disheartened. This was not a good breakup, and I needed time to recover from the disappointment.

I still had confidence in my knowledge of basketball and my skills as a coach and teacher, and I knew that basketball would continue to be my life and career. Coaching and TV commentary would take me all over the world. UCLA and Coach Wooden had given me the fundamentals and the foundation.

But it was eight years after my resignation before I had the desire to go back into Pauley Pavilion.

While I was the head coach at Weber State, from 1985 to 1988, I had no reason to have any interaction with UCLA. Geography put distance between myself and my alma mater when I accepted a coaching job in Kuwait. The Gulf War brought a stop to that assignment, and I came back to spend some time in the NBA as an assistant with the Golden State Warriors.

In 1992 I was, briefly, between coaching jobs. I had been following the UCLA team on TV all season and thinking about going
to a game. I decided to go to UCLA's game against Duke. I figured
UCLA would have a sellout crowd, making it easier for me to come
and go unnoticed. So I called UCLA Coach Jim Harrick and asked
him to leave a single ticket for me out of his allotment in the upper
level. No problem at all. When I arrived at UCLA I noticed many
changes in the campus. I had to walk quite a distance from where I
parked to get to Pauley Pavilion. I took my time. I had intentionally
already missed the tip-off. I thought if I arrived after the game was
in progress it would be easier to slip in unnoticed. At the Will Call
window, one fellow from the ticket office recognized me. He was
surprised, of course, but happy to see me. When I entered Pauley
Pavilion's upper level, the usher who took my ticket and pointed out
where my seat was gave me a big smile and said, "Welcome home."
He did joke about my seat location being up in the rafters, and I told
him that my seat was just fine, the farther away from the hot seat
the better. I stood for quite a while, pretending to watch the game
while waiting for a break in the action. Actually, I was looking to
see if there might be an empty seat on an aisle in another section.
I found one and sat down. I had never been to a game at Pauley
Pavilion when I had not been sitting at court level. It was really an
odd feeling! A handful of people recognized me but a lot more had
no idea who I was, which was great. At halftime a few people did
come over to say hello and I was happy to shake hands and exchange
a few words. Others just looked over and smiled. As I watched the
second half and started to realize that we were not going to win
this one, it occurred to me that maybe I shouldn't ask for any more
tickets. I had asked for tickets to two games over the many years
since I had left, and the Bruins had lost both of those games. With
a few minutes left on the clock I slipped out, avoiding the crowd. I
had returned to Pauley Pavilion relatively unnoticed and certainly
unscathed. I felt good about being back in Pauley, but I knew I had
basically snuck in and snuck out.

In 1994, I was doing both coaching and broadcasting. The Gulf

War had ended, and I was back in Kuwait coaching their National Team (Olympic Team) during the spring, summer, and fall. That left me free during the NCAA basketball season to work for ESPN, Raycom, Fox Sports, and CBS. The UCLA athletic department had been honoring some of its past basketball alumni by recognizing them before home basketball games. I was living in Arizona when I wasn't in Kuwait, and I was pleased to be on the list to be honored, but I was not sure about traveling to Los Angeles, specifically to be recognized before a game.

I was in my third year of doing commentary on some Pac-10 games when I was assigned a UCLA home game. I had worked one UCLA game the year before on the road. My agent, Martin Mandel, told me the league coaches had to agree on whether I would be impartial as an analyst doing UCLA games, and they had concurred that I wouldn't be biased.

The game I was scheduled to do in Pauley Pavilion was against North Carolina State on December 28, 1994. When Marc Dellins and his assistant, Bill Bennett, saw the broadcasters' schedule for that game, they decided that it would be a great opportunity to recognize me. It all fell into place.

I was working that day with Barry Tompkins, who was a terrific play-by-play man. We pre-recorded our opening segment during warmups. Bill Bennett gave me my instructions for the pregame ceremony.

While I waited on the baseline for my cue I felt like the prodigal son returning. When the PA announcer, Chuck White, started my introduction my heart was beating out of my chest. He said: "Few have contributed as much to what is today the storied tradition of UCLA basketball as this man . . ."

The introduction continued as I waited for the signal. White started with my 89–1 record as a player and went on to highlights of my time at UCLA. I got the signal to start walking, as Mr. White said, "Ladies and gentlemen, it is a great pleasure to welcome back to Pauley Pavilion, one of the great Bruins of all time—Larry Farmer."

I walked to center court to a chorus of cheers and a standing ovation. It was hard not to smile my goofy schoolboy smile. I waved to the crowd, acknowledge the coach at North Carolina State, gave Coach Harrick a hug and slapped each player a high five.

The welcome was more than I ever imagined. I felt like the school I loved had forgiven me for leaving without saying goodbye, and I was finally able to embrace my university again. It was at that moment that I knew leaving the head coaching position when I did was the right thing to do. If I had stayed under the circumstances that I was facing in 1984 I might have left with such bitterness I would never have returned. Now, a decade after I walked away, I was back on the court at Pauley Pavilion, once again feeling at home.

When I wrapped up my time in Kuwait, I joined the coaching staff at the University of Rhode Island. It's all about connections. While I had been away, Jim Harrick had led UCLA to its 11th NCAA championship title and had moved on to Rhode Island. We had a great year there, making it to the Elite Eight in the NCAA Tournament.

In 1998, I became the head coach of Loyola Chicago, and coached there for six years. My kids grew up in Illinois, and went to elementary, middle, and high school in Gurnee.

During three years as a broadcaster for Fox Sports Northwest, ESPN, CBS radio, and three years as an assistant at the University of Hawaii, I was able to occasionally stop by the UCLA campus and poke my head into the Men's Gym to watch the current batch of Bruins and pros play pickup games.

My wife, Chris, visited Southern California for Christmas in 2013 with our son, Larry III, and our daughter, Kendall. I was an assistant coach at the University of North Carolina State and did not make the trip, but Chris took the kids to visit the UCLA campus. They saw Pauley Pavilion and the massive displays of UCLA sports history in the J.D. Morgan Athletic Center. It was the first time they had seen pictures of their father in the context of the national championship trophies and banners and photographs. Kendall had her picture taken standing in front of the display case containing my photo as the head coach. It was really the first time my kids had the opportunity to see their dad alongside all the UCLA greats. They had seen my pictures, heard my stories, watched old film, and knew about the UCLA dynasty. But this was up close and personal. It put my place in UCLA's history in perspective for them. At that time Larry was 24 and Kendall was 18.

On April 17, 2013, I made a very sad return to Pauley Pavilion for Coach Wooden's memorial service. Most of Coach Wooden's boys, as he affectionately called all of us who played for him, had returned for the service. His former players had about an hour together in the J.D. Morgan Center before the service—Bill Walton, Kareem Abdul-Jabbar, Gail Goodrich, Keith Erickson, Andy Hill, Henry Bibby, Marques Johnson, Dave Meyers, and others. It was an amazing gathering. There were players there representing just about every era of UCLA basketball. It was a reunion of sorts, and it was great to see all my teammates and other fellow Bruins, but it just wasn't a happy occasion. It was a glorious going home service for Coach Wooden. It gave me time to reflect on how blessed I was to have him as my coach, my mentor, and my friend.

In 2016 I received a call from the Colorado High School Activities Association (CHSAA) informing me I was going to be inducted into the Colorado High School Hall of Fame. I would be just the fifth individual from Manual High School to be inducted.

On May 26, 2018, after driving from Illinois to Michigan, I stopped by my office at Western Michigan University (where I was an assistant coach) to get a folder containing some recruiting phone numbers. It was a Saturday afternoon and the office was empty. I found a letter on the seat of my chair from UCLA. I got a lot of alumni mail from UCLA, so I assumed it was something routine. When I read the words "On behalf of the UCLA intercollegiate athletic department, it is my great pleasure to let you know that we will be inducting you into the UCLA athletics Hall of Fame this October," my eyes filled with tears.

I sat down, clasped my hands together and thanked the Lord for blessing me with that wonderful news.

I was inducted into the UCLA Hall of Fame on October 5, 2018.

My son came from Boston and my daughter from Illinois. My brother Aubrey and his wife, Ora, came from Iowa. During my speech, I thanked those who were no longer with us who had been important in bringing me to this moment—my mother and father for giving me the courage to believe I could make it to UCLA and, of course, Coach Wooden for taking a chance and giving me a scholarship. I thanked my teammates for inspiring me every day. I never wanted to let them down. I thanked Bill Bennett for nominating me.

I had fallen in love with the Bruins while sitting on an ottoman watching them play on a small, black-and-white TV. Fifty years later, standing at that podium in the UCLA Hall of Fame, my heart still belonged to the Bruins.

Afterword
by Jamaal Wilkes

When you're part of something as incredibly exciting, exhilarating, and historic as the college basketball team at UCLA in the 1970s—practices with Coach Wooden, winning multiple championships, and undefeated seasons—it can sometimes seem dreamlike, like a surrealistic blur.

Needless to say, practices were extremely competitive and you had to bring your "A" game. My class alone (1970) had six high school All-Americans and it seemed like UCLA reloaded every year. Our practices were often better than the games, and the second team would sometimes beat the first team. Every recruit who came to UCLA would not become a starter nor a prime-time player, and most players had to embrace a role for the team to be successful. Clearly, the idea of being a role player was a real notion for most UCLA basketball players. Larry embraced his role on the team with enthusiasm and competitive greatness, and he was both a starter and a prime-time player.

During games, Larry and I had our own "insider" competition going—who could beat the other down court for early offense. We played up-tempo both ways, and our 3-on-2 fast-break offense was often devastating. Larry and I both knew that once UCLA got the defensive rebound, usually courtesy of Bill Walton, the ball would go to the point guard in the middle, Greg Lee or Tommy Curtis, and that the other guard, Henry Bibby and later Larry Hollyfield, would take off like lightning down one side. Only one of us could fill the other side, and the other would have to follow the play. So we would race each other to fill the open lane. Believe it or not, I think our "insider" competition helped our fast break be faster. We had a lot of fun with it, ribbing each other, and would settle up over subs or pizza.

One of Larry's signature moves on offense was a lob play. Calling it a lob play doesn't come close to doing it justice. Part of it was because there was no dunking in college basketball. I played with Michael Cooper on the Showtime Lakers and he would do a lob dunk that became known as the "Coop-a-Loop." Every time Michael Cooper would make the play I'd think of Larry Farmer at UCLA. Larry was not only simply a master at it, but had a knack for making the play when it would demoralize the other team and/or our fans would go nuts! They'd start screaming his nickname, "Moose! Moose!" in a frenzy. He'd set his defender up, then slip behind the defender and sky toward the hoop to receive a perfect pass from Greg, Tommy, or Larry Hollyfield. It wasn't uncommon for Larry to make multiple lobs in a game.

I enjoyed reading *Role of a Lifetime*, by one of my favorite teammates. It allowed me to learn about and enjoy another perspective of what I experienced at UCLA. I was particularly interested to read about Larry's experiences following Coach Wooden to become the head men's basketball coach at UCLA.

My respect for Larry as my teammate, my captain, and my friend was established long ago. After reading *Role of a Lifetime*, my appreciation for Larry has been enhanced immeasurably.

Appendix

UCLA Basketball Coaches by Winning Percentage

RANK/COACH	RECORD	WIN PCT.	NO. OF YEARS
1. Gary Cunningham	58–8	86%	2 years
2. Gene Bartow	52–9	85%	2 years
3. Fred Cozens	20–4	83%	2 years
4. John Wooden	620–147	81%	27 years
5. Jim Harrick	192–62	76%	8 years
6. Larry Farmer	61–23	73%	3 years
7. Larry Brown	42–17	71%	2 years
8. Ben Howland	233–107	69%	10 years
9. Steve Alford	124–63	66%	6 years
10. Steve Lavin	145–78	65%	7 years
11. Walt Hazzard	77–47	62%	4 years
12. Caddy Works	173–161	52%	18 years

UCLA Coaches After Wooden

YEARS	COACH	DEPARTURE
1948–75	Wooden	Retired after 27 years
1975–77	Bartow	Resigned after 2 years
1977–79	Cunningham	Resigned after 2 years
1979–81	Brown	Resigned after 2 years
1981–84	Farmer	Resigned after 3 years
1984–88	Hazzard	Fired after 4 years
1988–96	Harrick	Fired after 8 years
1996–03	Lavin	Fired after 7 years
2003–13	Howland	Fired after 10 years
2013–19	Alford	Fired after 6 years

Acknowledgments

Special thanks to my friends who helped in the research for this book.

Bill Bennett
Gerd Clever
Gary Cunningham
Tommy Curtis
Marc Dellins
Ann Meyers Drysdale
Jack Eberhard
Doug Erickson
Jim Harrick
Larry Hollyfield
Lee Hunt
Craig Impelman
Marques Johnson
Curry Kirkpatrick
Don Liebig
Tony Spino
Alex Timiraos
Marvin Vitatoe
Bill Walton
Bob Webb
Jamaal Wilkes
Greg Wooden

Photo Credits